D1454630

Contents

The Chattering and the Song by Femi Osofisan, **The Rise and Shine of Comrade Fiasco** by Andrew Whaley, **Anowa** by Ama Ata Aidoo, **Woza Albert!** by Percy Mtwa, Mbongeni Ngema and Barney Simon, **The Other War** by Alemseged Tesfai, **Death and the King's Horseman** by Wole Soyinka

Contemporary African Plays assembles some of the most exciting drama from the last thirty-five years of African theatre, and spans the continent's disparate regional and cultural traditions.

The Chattering and the Song
'Osofisan has devised an exceptional, skilfully wrought piece of theatre . . . An exceptionally accomplished – even brilliant – play.' Chris Dunton, *Make Man Talk True: Nigerian Drama in English since 1970*

The Rise and Shine of Comrade Fiasco
'It's a brave and original play that grapples with issues – the crisis of expectations brought by a return to peace, the disappointment of those who sacrificed so much in the fight . . . Nudging at both dramatic and political frontiers.' *Guardian*

Anowa
'*Anowa* must surely be one of the most powerful African plays to have been written so far.' Michael Etherton, *The Development of African Drama*

Woza Albert!
'A satire played with devastating energy in a brilliantly witty staging.' *Guardian*
'The most politically potent show ever staged in South Africa.' *Observer*

The Other War
'. . . gives an extraordinary insight into the suffering and resilience of the Eritrean people in a little known war.' *African Theatre*

Death and the King's Horseman
'A masterpiece of twentieth-century drama . . . Soyinka uses the full resources of theatre – song, dance, emblematic costume, fable, parody, as well as intellectual argument – to put a dramatic bomb under Western perceptions.' *Guardian*
'An explosive marriage between Nigerian folk and ceremonial drama and European theatrical conventions . . . Soyinka's text is richly poetical, full of epithets and elements suggesting a visceral oral tradition.' *Daily Telegraph*

Contemporary African Plays

The Chattering and the Song
Femi Osofisan

The Rise and Shine of Comrade Fiasco
Andrew Whaley

Anowa
Ama Ata Aidoo

Woza Albert!
Percy Mtwa, Mbongeni Ngema and Barney Simon

The Other War
Alemseged Tesfai, translated by Paul Warwick,
Samson Gebregzhier and Alemseged Tesfai

Death and the King's Horseman
Wole Soyinka

Edited and introduced by
Martin Banham and Jane Plastow

Methuen Drama

Methuen Drama
This collection first published in Great Britain 1999
by Methuen Publishing Limited

10 9 8 7 6 5 4 3 2

3607354321

Contents

INTRODUCTION   vii

The Chattering and the Song   1

The Rise and Shine of Comrade Fiasco   71

Anowa   137

Woza Albert!   207

The Other War   261

Death and the King's Horseman   303

Introduction

In Africa theatre matters. African theatre is entertainment, but it can also be aesthetically, politically, socially and spiritually committed, and often it is all these things simultaneously. Moreover, much modern African theatre refuses to be compartmentalised into a particular form of presentation. Instead it draws on indigenous performance traditions including dance, music, storytelling and mime, and combines them with ideas of drama drawn from experiences of Western colonialism, to create theatre forms which are syncretic and inclusive in both form and content. At its best African theatre is a total experience of mind, body and soul which engages with, and feeds off, a highly responsive, involved and vocal audience.

This volume brings together six African playwrights from West, East and southern Africa in an attempt to indicate something of the range of the continent's theatre. The plays cover a period of twenty-five years, from the mid-1960s to 1990, and therefore reflect not only a variety of cultural forms of expression but also developments in concerns and approaches to making theatre during that period. The anthology brings together well-known playwrights and plays such as Wole Soyinka's *Death and the King's Horseman* and the South African collaboration which resulted in *Woza Albert!*, with the work of playwrights either little known outside their home countries or previously unpublished. Six plays cannot hope to be representative of the wealth of African cultures and theatre forms which exist. They do offer a taste of the extraordinarily vibrant range of performance cultures and hopefully will contribute to the growing interest in African theatre.

Modern African theatre coincides with the post-colonial period which began in 1957 when Ghana became independent of British rule. Pre-colonial African theatre forms still require much research. They were usually dance, music and poetry-based and served a wide range of functions, including the teaching of social roles and behaviour, explaining the history of ethnic groups, social criticism, celebration and the fulfilment of religious rituals. Colonialism brought varying degrees of suppression of indigenous performance forms. These were less onerous in areas such as West Africa which were considered unhealthy for Western settlers and were therefore governed under a system of indirect rule; and far more repressive in parts of southern and eastern Africa, where settler states were established and efforts were made to eradicate traditional performance modes, which were often seen as antipathetic to European Christian and cultural values, as well as potentially dangerous foci for the incitement of rebellion. In many cases European forms of drama were introduced by missionaries, initially to transmit biblical messages, and later, in mission schools, in an attempt to teach metropolitan languages and inculcate European cultural values. This theatre was seldom meant for mass consumption: instead it was a means of separating off African élites and Christian converts from the mass of traditional peoples.

During the colonial period Africans were usually only allowed to publish or perform drama under the patronage and censorship of their white rulers. Early plays often have biblical themes, reflecting missionary influence; they also tend to be more or less naturalistic, since this was the form favoured by the colonisers. Above all involvement in political debate was strictly censored in almost all cases under colonial rule, so these plays are largely anodyne and imitative.

All this began to change rapidly during the 1960s as many African nations claimed their independence. West Africa was the first region to come to literary prominence with many novelists and playwrights emerging on the international scene. There are a number of reasons for this regional prominence. Throughout the colonial experience local cultures in British West Africa remained vibrant. This gave a strong sense of identity and confidence to a number of writers, several of whom saw the literary reclamation of their history and culture as an urgent task. Also there were a number of élite schools and colleges established in the region, especially in Nigeria and Ghana, and these nurtured many new writers who had access to and interest in both indigenous and Western cultural forms.

Then, there is the question of language. In British West Africa writers such as Chinua Achebe, Ama Ata Aidoo and Wole Soyinka had all been well educated in English. They came from multi-lingual nations whose indigenous cultures had little or no written literary tradition – albeit very strong oral cultures. Their decision, and indeed that of many subsequent West African writers, has been to take English and remould it to express local rhythms and usages, but still to write in an international language. This choice to write in English has made a number of West African writers far more internationally recognised than their peers who, equally renowned within their own countries, have chosen to write in domestic languages.

As with many aspects of African cultures, while it is important to resist an easy homogenistic view, it does make sense to talk about regional trends. Prominent West African writers may have chosen to write in English, but in East and southern Africa different decisions were made. In southern Africa, in order to promote divide-and-rule policies, many literature bureaux set up by the British encouraged and in some cases forced blacks to write in local languages so that their impact would be marginalised. Moreover, literacy in English and/or Afrikaans was essential if one were to have any chance of participating in modern urban society. Consequently, now in those countries there are thriving literatures in both indigenous and metropolitan languages. More recently many playwrights have chosen to write in hybrid languages which reflect peoples' day-to-day experience and maximise accessibility. In Zimbabwe there are playwrights who claim to write in 'Ndenglish', a deliberate mixing of Ndebele and English, and in both the southern African plays presented here we see a basic English script which utilises many indigenous language terms as well as a street language which draws on multiple tongues.

Finally, in East Africa there are trans-ethnic national languages such as Kiswahili which have been promoted as a regional alternative to the need to write in English; while in countries such as Ethiopia and Eritrea, which have ancient scripts of their own, writing has always been predominantly in local languages. Hence the relative paucity of East African theatre which has become known outside the region, and our considerable pleasure in being able to publish the first Eritrean play script ever to have been translated into English – *The Other War*.

This assessment needs to be placed in context. Published theatre in Africa represents the tip of an iceberg of theatrical productions, the vast majority of which are never scripted and certainly never published. It is also necessary to remember the Francophone and Lusophone areas of the continent where patterns of theatrical writing have been influenced by the different agendas of French and Portuguese colonialism.

Returning to West Africa, in Wole Soyinka and Femi Osofisan we have contributions to this anthology by two of Nigeria's most famous playwrights. These two have long had an interesting dialectical relationship, in which the younger Osofisan challenges Soyinka's use of myth as a validation of Yoruba society. Instead Osofisan chooses to use mythology in a much more critical manner which demands that society constantly questions and re-examines the philosophical premises which underlie traditional stories and beliefs. In both cases, however, we cannot but be aware that we are encountering a society which is steeped in rich and expressive indigenous culture which reaches back – not uninterrupted, but still vibrant – into the past as it also looks to the future.

Ama Ata Aidoo comes from Ghana. She is unique in this anthology, both by virtue of being the only female contributor and because her play, *Anowa*, was written earlier than any of the other contributions. Female playwrights are still a relative rarity in Africa for a number of reasons. In many places it is considered disreputable for women to become involved in commercial performances and it is often difficult for women to combine domestic life with the demands of the theatre. These have been factors restricting women's development as playwrights in many societies across the world. Perhaps one of the most potent forces holding back African women playwrights has been the relative lack of educational opportunities for women, particularly during the colonial era.

Aidoo is a triumphant example of a writer who overcame a plethora of social handicaps to produce plays. She is a leading light amongst the small band of African women playwrights which includes her compatriot Efua Sutherland, the Nigerians, Zulu Sofola and Tess Onwueme, Gcina Mhlope from South Africa and Penina Mlama and Amadina Lihamba from Tanzania. She is also recognisably West African in her world view. The pantheon of gods, spirits, the unborn and the ancestors who are constantly encountered in much West African writing give the cultural productions of this region a density, richness, and indeed difficulty for the uninitiated, which is unparalleled in other parts of the continent.

When we move to southern Africa we see the results of a very different historical experience. Here for a hundred years – and for parts of South Africa for three hundred years – white settlers seized African land, forced Africans into ignominious wage slavery, derided and sought to repress African cultures and belief systems, and finally imposed the horrors of apartheid on the people. Protest against this process has never been absent but, as in many other parts of the colonised world, momentum grew after the second world war – which exposed many blacks to differing patterns of race relations – and increased as other parts of Africa gained their independence. In Zimbabwe and South Africa, both represented in this anthology, protest theatre became a force in the 1970s. In Zimbabwe theatre was utilised by the guerilla fighters as a tool for politicisation, while in South Africa plays were mounted predominantly in the black urban townships.

Working against a background of poverty and struggle, this theatre developed its own style of presentation which relies heavily on the plasticity of the performer. Sophisticated staging, costume and props were not available and actors often had to be prepared to decamp quickly if security forces moved in to stop performances. Therefore the primary tool is the actor himself who must create his whole world through mime, sound and a bare minimum of symbolic properties. Reflecting the urgency of the actors' messages and the energy of urban life, many such plays are composed in epic mode, with short scenes building up a collage picture of society.

Tradition is seldom invoked in these deculturised societies, which are rather fighting for a better tomorrow. Instead it is urban black life whose music, dance and speech patterns are invoked in a very physical form of theatre. Because both plays presented here owe a significant amount to actor improvisation, something which is again quite common in recent plays from the region, these are actors' rather than writers' texts and ideas are expressed quite as much through action as through the word. This is also a very macho theatre. Much African theatre has been criticised for giving women a role only as objects and sterotypes. The world of southern African men in particular seems to centre round aggressive assertions of masculinity which influence styles of performance.

An interesting correlation in the two plays from the region here is that both are obviously interested in interpretations of Christianity which draw on the ideas of liberation theology. Saving the world in these plays is a mission not for a figure like Soyinka's Horseman, but for the dispossessed, the ordinary black man, who the new messiahs urge forward to take control of their own destiny. This change of emphasis reflects, perhaps, a change of direction in African writing from the sixties and seventies. So many of the early leaders turned out to have feet of clay and to lead profoundly corrupt regimes, that more recent writing has turned to requiring ordinary people to play their part in forging the future, and to resist the urge to look for and follow apparently heroic leaders who time and again fall victim to the lure of power.

The Eritrean play in this collection reflects yet another cultural heritage. Surrounded by sea and desert and for thirty years involved in a desperate liberation struggle with Ethiopia, modern Eritrean theatre developed in isolation from any knowledge of other theatrical movements in Africa. The playwrights who emerged during the struggle saw drama as utterly divorced from indigenous performance forms. With minimal material at their disposal, the nineteenth-century naturalists (Shaw, Ibsen and Chekhov) were their exemplars, as they had been in other parts of Africa forty years before. This theatre was then adapted to the Eritrean context to provide a strange but powerful hybrid: Eritrean naturalist liberation theatre.

There are many other plays worthy of inclusion in this collection. There are whole regions and many cultures unrepresented by the anthology. It is just a start. However, each of these plays is a superb example of some of the best of African English language theatre and we hope you will enjoy them as much as we have.

The Chattering and the Song

Femi Osofisan is the leading and most prolific member of the 'second generation' of Nigerian playwrights, who are building on the dynamic tradition established by Wole Soyinka, John Pepper Clark-Bekederemo and Ola Rotimi. From the late 1970s to the present day Osofisan has written over twenty-five plays, and his work, widely staged in Nigeria, has been produced in the United States and Britain.

There is a considerable range of style and approach in Osofisan's work and, intriguingly, he often enters into theatrical 'debates' with the older generation of playwrights whose work he respects even when he expresses frustration about it. *No More the Wasted Breed* (1982) is an answer to Soyinka's *The Strong Breed* (1963), and *Another Raft* (1988) similarly responds to Clark's *The Raft* (1964). Osofisan has also ingeniously adapted classic European plays to a Nigerian context: *Who's Afraid of Solarin* (1978) from Gogol's *The Government Inspector*; *Midnight Hotel* (1986) from Feydeau's *Hotel Paradiso*; and the as yet unpublished *Tegonni*, an African *Antigone*. He has also employed and adapted the mythological Yoruba world for the purposes of political and ideological debate.

His work is self-consciously and deliberately theatrical, and fully employs the various languages of Nigerian theatre, including music, song and dance. Osofisan has a very clear sense of the function of his plays. They are crafted to encourage not only political debate but also radical rethinking. They are designed to challenge preconceptions, to subvert inertia and complacency and to offer the possibility of positive

action. That they do so whilst being constantly entertaining
adds to their impact. A consistent feature of Osofisan's
dramaturgy is the 'open-ended' play, which asks the audience
to choose its preferred ending or to determine appropriate
action.

But the plays rarely resort to two-dimensional agit-prop,
they are full of surprises. Heroes turn out to be flawed, easy
slogans are wittily analysed, received opinions are ruthlessly
scrutinised, but a play's audience is finally left to decide for
itself. Osofisan says: 'I'm not there to force people to take a
specific point of view. My major aim in writing is to bring
people to reflect, to question accepted views as they begin to
think. My aim is not to present a view and say "This is what
you must do!" I don't believe you can achieve anything like
that. But you can present the situation and say these are the
options, make up your mind.' (Interview with Akin Adesokan
in *Excursions in Drama and Literature: Interviews with Femi Osofisan*,
ed. Muyiwa P. Awodiya.)

The Chattering and the Song is a relatively early play of
Osofisan's (first produced 1976) but it has enjoyed great
success and points to many of Osofisan's themes and methods.
The version printed here is a new edition, revised by the
playwright in 1996 – in his preface (p. 3) the author outlines
the original political motivations behind the play and suggests
that its themes and conclusions remain pertinent.

In the play General Gowon – leader of Nigeria's federal
forces during the civil war – is implicitly compared with the
historical Abiodun, Alafin of Oyo in western Nigeria in the
eighteenth century – a ruler whose early reputation as a
peacemaker became tarnished by corruption. The Farmers'
Movement Leje reveals he belongs to is also vividly described
in Osofisan's *Morountodun* (produced 1979), and is based on a
real-life rebellion by Yoruba peasant farmers in 1968/9,
protesting at the poverty of their condition.

The Rise and Shine of Comrade Fiasco

The dynamic Zimbabwean theatrical scene of which Andrew
Whaley is a part is a relatively recent phenomenon, dating
back only to national independence in 1980. Prior to that
time the country, then Southern Rhodesia, was under British
rule from 1890 until 1965, followed by a period of racist
government after unilateral independence was declared by the
white settler state. Throughout this time only white arts,
intensely derivative of British bourgeois culture, were
significantly promoted, and all politically challenging material
was severely censored.

However, during the liberation struggle of the late 1960s
and 1970s theatre was invoked by the guerilla fighters as a
means of combating white propaganda, as a means for
politicising rural black Zimbabweans, and as a tool of
discussion in the guerilla camps. This liberation theatre has
been recognised by many as the basis out of which an exciting
national theatre culture has grown, a culture which ranges
from a national community-based theatre movement, to more
professional groups working mainly out of the major towns of
Harare and Bulawayo.

The Rise and Shine of Comrade Fiasco has many elements in
common with other products of the new Zimbabwean theatre.
Much of this theatre is syncretic – drawing on both
indigenous performance forms, which are often music and
dance based, and progressive theatrical influences from the
West. Like much southern African theatre it is also very
physically oriented, with minimal props and set and a heavy
reliance on the plasticity of the actor's body, incorporating
mime and the taking on by actors of many roles within a
single piece of theatre. The question of language, as in so
many African countries, is important in much Zimbabwean
theatre. To a greater or lesser degree many experiments have
been carried out in making theatre which combines two or
more of the major languages of the country – Shona, Ndebele
and English – in order to make the work as accessible as
possible.

Moreover, as in Whaley's plays, much of this theatre is
politically questioning. It has addressed issues ranging from

women's rights, attitudes to AIDS and workers' conditions, to
the more overtly polical: government corruption and
oppression, and, as in this play, the question of disillusionment
with the post-colonial Zimbabwean state in many who fought
for independence. Increasingly the government has felt uneasy
about such theatre, urging people to produce work only about
community issues and not to criticise the wider workings of
government. In recent years much state support has been
withdrawn from what is seen as a challenging theatre
movement. In extreme cases playwrights have been personally
warned to watch what they write and plays have been refused
permission to be taken outside the country.

As a white radical playwright Andrew Whaley is unusual
though not unique in Zimbabwe, where a number of white
liberals now work in collaboration with black theatre workers.
Whaley is based in Zimbabwe's second city of Bulawayo and
is one of the country's best known playwrights. His previous
plays, *Platform 5*, *The Nyoka Tree* and *Chef's Breakfast*, have
looked at the continuing problems of racism and racial tension
in Zimbabwe, at the oppression of women, at corruption and
the disinherited poor who have been given no place in the
new nation. Several plays have won national awards, and both
The Nyoka Tree and *The Rise and Shine of Comrade Fiasco* have
been toured to Britain, where the latter won a Fringe First at
the 1990 Edinburgh Festival. Like almost all those involved in
the arts in Zimbabwe, Whaley is unable to make a living from
working in just one creative medium; he is also an actor,
journalist and filmworker.

The Rise and Shine of Comrade Fiasco was first performed by
the company with which Andrew Whaley is closely associated,
Meridian, in 1990. It arose from a newspaper story dealing
with a supposed combatant who, like Fiasco, appeared in
1987 claiming to have been in hiding, not knowing that
liberation had been achieved seven years previously. This story
intrigued Whaley, particularly as, again like Fiasco, it was
unclear whether the man was a fraud, a madman or a
genuine ex-combatant.

Set in 1986, this play places four of Zimbabwe's
dispossessed in a prison cell, where Jungle, Febi and

particularly Chidhina are forced by the arrival of Fiasco to
confront the reality of what has happened to them since
independence. The examination of personal and national
history and identity is undertaken unwillingly by these
characters as they try to find out who Fiasco is. His
appearance from the heroic past forces the others to look at
how they have failed to live up to the hopes of the liberation
struggle. This is particularly painful for Chidhina, the ex-
combatant, whose antagonistic relationship with Fiasco Whaley
sees as central to the play.

The play moves swiftly, with Jungle, Febi and Chidhina
taking on a number of roles in scenes which tread a thin line
between farce and intensely serious drama as they endeavour
to disentangle and analyse Fiasco's claims. The audience are
frequently addressed quite openly, bringing them into the
world and dilemmas of the play; just as the walls of the cell,
which may well be a metaphor for the state of Zimbabwe's
poor, are frequently breached through fantasy and a refusal to
be limited by conventions of naturalism.

Comrade Fiasco himself remains ambiguous to the end. Is
he a fraud? Is he mad? Is he teacher, leader or saviour? And
is he really reborn to offer a new way forward after the failure
of the midwife of liberation? Fiasco's teaching, if such it is, is
in Christ-like mode, addressed to the poor of the prison cell.
Like so much recent African writing the message appears to
be to resist the urge to become followers of leaders who will
always prove massively flawed, and for the dispossessed to
realise their own potential to create change and freedom, to
accept the challenge and responsibility for their own and the
nation's life. There are distinct echoes here of *Woza Albert!*, but
in Whaley's case we are not allowed to see Fiasco
straightforwardly as a saviour. Instead questions as to a way
forward are always thrown back on his fellow inmates, and by
extension to the audience or reader of the play.

Anowa

Women playwrights are relatively rare in the African theatre.
The late Zulu Sofola from Nigeria, and her compatriot Tess

Onwueme are to be noted, together with Ugandan playwright
Rose Mbowa, Penina Mlama and Amandina Lihamba from
Tanzania, Geina Mhlope from South Africa and Nicole
Werewere-Liking from Cameroon. It is interesting, therefore,
that perhaps the two most significant Ghanaian playwrights
since the 1960s have been women: the late Efua Sutherland
with *Foriwa* (1962), *Edufa* (1967), *The Marriage of Anansewa*
(1975); and Ama Ata Aidoo, whose two plays, *The Dilemma of
a Ghost* (1965) and *Anowa* (1970) are, by any consideration, two
of the finest plays from the contemporary African theatre.

The Dilemma of a Ghost is, superficially, a 'clash of cultures'
play, exploring a common concern amongst West African
writers in the 1960s and 70s, that of the tensions created in
society by the introduction of new and predominantly Western
manners and values into traditional societies. In this particular
play a Ghanaian man returns from his studies in America
with a black American wife. His subsequent treatment of her,
her difficulties in settling into her new home, and echoes of
the corruption of slavery, form the concerns of the play.
Strongly represented here is the attitude and role of women in
both the new and the 'old' world.

But it is with *Anowa* that Ama Ata Aidoo has made
particular impact. This many-layered play stems from a
familiar Ghanaian folk-tale – indeed one common in a variety
of guises throughout West Africa. It deals with the handsome
stranger who enters a community and carries off with him the
most beautiful girl, later to destroy her. But Aidoo's play
builds onto this theme a complex, but theatrically vigorous,
allegory concerning slavery and man's exploitation of man.

The period of the play is deliberately imprecise: it is
simultaneously contemporary and nineteenth century, with
references to Queen Victoria and the slave trade. Its evocation
of the horrors of slavery are amongst the most powerful to be
found in African literature. But arguably its parallel theme is
the way in which the rulers of independent African nations
have been subject to the same mercenary corruption as the
slavers. Anowa's barrenness symbolises not *her* failure to be
productive, but her husband's destructive infertility – the
failure of men to create the future. The chorus figures who

frame the play ensure us of the power of the story-telling circle.

Woza Albert!

First performed in 1980 at the Market Theatre in Johannesburg, *Woza Albert!* is one of the most famous of South African protest plays. Thankfully, the play, like its fellows, is now something of an historical document since the horrors of apartheid, which are *Woza Albert!*'s focus, ceased with the coming of majority rule to South Africa in 1994.

Black South Africa used theatre as a forum for protest against white oppression from the 1930s when H.I.E. Dhlomo started to write historical dramas which displayed a militant nationalism. As in so many other white settler states, missionaries had endeavoured to suppress many indigenous performance forms and to promote their ideal of neo-naturalist drama which propagated Bible messages and European cultural values. Beyond this black theatre experienced little support, whilst imposing theatres were constructed to serve the white population in many towns across the country.

Prior to the mid-1960s many black theatre initiatives were dependent on white support and patronage, but after that time the Black Consciousness movement was increasingly influential and more and more radical black plays were produced. Most of this theatre was for performance in black townships where conventional theatres did not exist and where groups survived on shoestring budgets. These considerations help explain the evolution of a specifically southern African form of black theatre which uses minimal technical support and relies primarily on the physical tool of the actor's body.

From the early 1970s there is a dominant theme to the major township plays: the evils of oppression under the apartheid system and the struggle for freedom. Since apartheid affected all aspects of political, domestic and social life many of the plays chose to work in epic mode with short scenes illustrating evils such as labour conditions, the fragmentation of the family, and humiliation of blacks by whites, with performances often culminating in a call for political liberation. Political analysis was generally minimal since the audience were assumed all to be searching, as a matter of all-important priority, for the same goal of majority rule, and emphasis was put on black consciousness and solidarity. Because the plays come out of the melting pot of urban black South Africa, language is often eclectic, drawing on a number of indigenous tongues as well as urban slang and the *lingua franca* of English. Urban and indigenous dance and music forms are also often integrated into these high-energy, intensely physical performances.

Many commentators have raised the question of why such overtly inflammatory theatre was permitted during the latter days of apartheid. In 1980 an amended government Publications Act recognised that 'the expression of grievances often acts as a safety valve for pent-up feelings' (Van Rooyen, *Censorship in South Africa*, p. 11). It seems highly likely that this was the reason that plays such as Matsemela Manaka's *Egoli*, Mbongeni Ngema's *Asinamali!*, *Sarafina* and *Woza Albert!* were allowed to be performed not only in the townships, but even in such prestigious venues as Johannesburg's Market Theatre and on tour abroard.

Despite these political considerations and the fact that South Africa has now abolished apartheid, *Woza Albert!* remains a powerful and important play in both theatrical and political terms. The idea for the work came from Percy Mtwa and Mbongeni Ngema in 1979 when they were both on tour, as lead performers, in a major Gibson Kente production, *Mama and the Load*. The actors became intrigued by the idea of what would happen if there was a 'second coming' and Jesus Christ appeared in South Africa. In order to develop their idea both actors abandoned the security of work with Kente and spent a year researching and developing their play in conditions of considerable hardship. At this point a number of directors were invited to see the work-in-progress and Barney Simon of the Market Theatre agreed to work on developing the piece to the point of performance.

Many scenes in *Woza Albert!* originate from direct observation and discussion with a diverse group of the inhabitants of Soweto, so that in spite of the fantastic premise of the play it is firmly rooted in black South African experience. The play's most innovative contribution to the protest theatre movement lies in how it unites political and messianic themes. In South Africa Christianity became as political as all other aspects of life. The highly reactionary Dutch Reformed Church for many years justified apartheid by claiming that black people were descendants of Ham and were therefore inherently inferior to whites. In opposition, liberation theology became increasingly influential in black communities, identifying Christ with the oppressed and endorsing political struggle for freedom. The positioning of Christ – here called Morena – as a political activist who experiences all the oppressions visited on blacks, is therefore particularly potent in the South African context.

Woza Albert! was an enormously successful play both in South Africa and abroad. However, because it was conceived in performance and not literary terms it requires of the reader considerable imaginative input. The ambience of the scenes is created almost exclusively through mime, aided only by symbolic costume items such as the red clown noses which are donned to signify the representation of whites. As with many African plays it is also helpful if the reader envisages the very different audience conventions from those which apply in Europe. A township audience would be vocal and involved, and, in spite of being premiered at the Market Theatre, this play is a product of township life. The final resurrection scene in particular would be guaranteed to invoke enormous sympathetic response which transforms it into something approaching a mass rally – an ironic juxtaposition to the many mass rallies which arose out of the funerals of liberation militants.

The Other War

The Other War is the first Eritrean play to be published, and the first to be translated into English. It is very much a product of the thirty-year struggle of the Eritrean people (from 1961 to 1991) to win their freedom from Ethiopian rule. The emergence of Alemseged Tesfai as Eritrea's premier playwright is also a consequence of the liberation war.

Born in 1944 in the southern Eritrean town of Adi Quala, Alemseged took his law degree at the then Haile Selassie I University in Addis Ababa, Ethiopia, and later began a PhD at the University of Wisconsin, USA, before abandoning study to join the liberation struggle with the Eritrean People's Liberation Front (EPLF). As one of a tiny minority of highly educated cadres Alemseged was asked to undertake a number of jobs for which he had no specialist training, and in 1981 this need to utilise scarce intellectual resources led to his being assigned to head the EPLF literature and drama sections.

Cultural work was seen as vital to the guerilla struggle. The Ethiopian state was seeking to eradicate Eritrean identity by a variety of means including allowing education only in the Ethiopian language of Amharic, and discouraging or suppressing indigenous cultural forms of expression. The EPLF's Division of Culture set about promoting art, literature and music which reflected ethnic identities and bonded Eritreans together in their search for social reform and political freedom in order to truly liberate Eritrea – not only from a hundred-year colonial history, but also from a feudal background which stretched back over millennia.

During this period propaganda dramas were already being staged by guerilla cultural troupes in variety programmes which also featured music, song and dance: either composed for the purpose of promoting Eritrean war aims or to celebrate the traditional performance arts of Eritrea's nine ethnic groups. Alemseged's own interest was in developing drama beyond crude agit-prop. He therefore set about reading whatever plays and books about theatre he could obtain. These were in short supply on the war front and comprised only a few texts on basic theatre techniques, some Ibsen and Chekhov, and the like.

As with all Eritrean theatre until very recently, ideas of what constituted the proper form for drama were heavily influenced by neo-naturalistic styles, first brought into the country by the Italians who colonised Eritrea in 1890, and subsequently built on during the years of the British mandate (1941–52). What Alemseged sought to do was to write plays within a naturalist framework which would truly represent Eritrean society and deal with the issues affecting contemporary Eritrean life.

The Other War (1984) is the last of a series of three plays Alemseged wrote during the early 1980s. The playwright says that the seed for the play was sown by an incident he witnessed in 1970 when he was working for the Ethiopian government as a legal assistant to the Ministry of Finance. He was taken by a Minister on a trip to the Ogaden, in southern Ethiopia, where ethnic Somalis were in conflict with the Ethiopian state. In the regional capital, Jijiga, the local military commander and the minister discussed the impossibility of military containment of this strong irridentist movement. The commander then described his alternative strategy of 'sexual mixing', whereby Amharas, the dominant group in Ethiopia, would be encouraged to procreate with local women either on a voluntary or enforced basis in order to dilute the dissident race. Such calculated genocide through the manipulation of sex and love deeply horrified Alemseged.

A decade later Alemseged realised that similar techniques were being promoted in Eritrea to undermine the liberation struggle. Further, he records that the plot of *The Other War* was directly prompted by his hearing of the experience of an Eritrean mother who had fled from Asmara in order to escape from an intolerable home situation with a daughter who had married an Ethiopian cadre.

The Other War, like nearly all other Eritrean playscripts, was written in Alemseged's own language of Tigrinya. It has been enormously popular within Eritrea, both as a play performed by guerilla cultural troupes for fighters and Eritreans living in liberated areas of the country, and later as a video which has been distributed widely amongst the Eritrean diaspora. The idea of translating the play came originally from Paul Warwick, who was working in 1995 as a research assistant on the Eritrea Community-Based Theatre Project – a project set up, post-war, at the invitation of Alemseged Tesfai, to train Eritreans in development theatre techniques and to carry out research into Eritrean performance forms and performance history. Warwick and an Eritrean assistant, Samson

Gebregzhier, worked together to produce a first draft of the play. Alemseged has subsequently developed that original draft to come up with the text as given here.

Alemseged Tesfai emphasises that *The Other War* is not a criticism of cross-ethnic love. He says that, 'Mutual love between individuals, whatever their origin is, is not a concern of this play. The problem arises when love and sex are made to be instruments of social domination and repression.' This play explores the face of war away from the military front, where domestic life becomes another kind of front line, hence 'the other war'.

Death and the King's Horseman

The award of the Nobel Prize for Literature in 1986 celebrated Wole Soyinka's extraordinary talents as a playwright, poet, novelist and essayist. His playwriting commenced when he was an undergraduate at the University of Leeds in the 1950s (with the idyllic satire *The Lion and the Jewel* and the darker comment of *The Swamp Dwellers*) and continues to the present day (with the 1996 production of *The Beatification of Area Boy*). In three decades Soyinka has written and staged over twenty-five plays and revues, always commenting vigorously upon the politics of his country, Nigeria, and the nations of Africa.

Soyinka's own experiences during this time have mirrored the troubles of his country. His early plays increasingly warned of the dangers of political greed and ambition, employing a satirical skill that became fiercer and angrier as his predictions became reality. His epic play *A Dance of the Forests* (1960) set both the tone and the context of much of Soyinka's subsequent writing, challenging the blithely optimistic expectations generated by freedom from colonial rule and invoking the gods of the Yoruba world as witnesses of human folly. This spiritual world is a matter of great fascination for Soyinka, and *The Strong Breed* (1963) and *The Road* (1965), whilst containing materials rich in political and social allegory, are fascinating explorations of the nature of transition between the spiritual and the mortal world, the world of the living and of the ancestors.

Younger critics have sometimes impatiently criticised Soyinka for being bound up with metaphysical speculations when the immediate need is for his powerful voice to support radical reform, but it is the cosmic context of his vision and his writing which, it may be argued, give it its especial power and relevance. This is never more clearly the case than in *Death and the King's Horseman.*

It is important to put this play (which comes very much in the chronological centre of Soyinka's work) into its historical frame. Between August 1967 and October 1969, during the Nigerian Civil War (the so-called 'Biafran War'), Soyinka was imprisoned without charge in circumstances chronicled in his extraordinary 'prison notes', *The Man Died* (1972). Not long after his release Soyinka left Nigeria, an involuntary exile which was to last for five years. (Ironically, at the time of publication of this volume, Soyinka finds himself in the same situation, banned from his homeland because of his outspoken condemnation of the military rule of General Abacha. *The Beatification of Area Boy*, intended for production in Lagos, was in fact premiered at the West Yorkshire Playhouse in Leeds.)

His first theatrical response to the trauma of his detention and the slaughter of the civil war was the play *Madmen and Specialists* (1971), a passionate allegory of cannibalism and destruction, with Armageddon as its closing image. *Death and the King's Horseman* comes four years later, in 1975, composed while Soyinka was living in Cambridge, and when he was also working on the critical and philosophical essays contained in his important collection *Myth, Literature and the African World* (1976). *Death and the King's Horseman* steps back from the anger of *Madmen and Specialists*, and – perhaps as a deliberate 'distancing' device – takes an actual historical incident as its subject.

In December 1944 the Alafin ('king') of Oyo in western Nigeria died. By custom his leading minister (the Elesin, the 'Master of his Horse') would be expected to follow his king into the world of the ancestors, and in January 1945 he prepared to commit what may best be described as ritual suicide. At this point the British District Officer intervened

(suicide being illegal) and detained the Elesin. His son, shamed
by the failure of his father to fulfil his spiritual and
community duty, committed suicide. Interestingly the theme of
the play had previously been treated by a Yoruba language
playwright Duro Ladipo (*Oba Waja* – The King is Dead –
c. 1964). Soyinka takes certain liberties with the historical facts:
the deliberate emphasis of the setting in the context of the
second world war, the presence of the Prince of Wales, the
Fancy Dress Ball at the Residency, and the placing of the
Elesin's son, Olunde, as a medical student in Britain are all
Soyinka's invention. But the play brings together those two
concerns of Soyinka's: the spiritual and the political.

On the one hand it has to be seen as an Ogundian
tragedy. In the Yoruba pantheon, Ogun is the god who –
through the application of great willpower – travelled through
the abyss, the void, between the spiritual and the mortal
world that had been set up at the time of creation. His was
the great act and example of transition. By his amazing
courage the world of the living and the world of the ancestors
were reunited. The Elesin's passage through that same abyss,
following his king to live with the ancestors, marked a spiritual
ritual which – through the example of Ogun – would ensure
the continuing well-being of the people of Oyo. His failure of
will, as the play interprets it, destroys the great deed of Ogun,
threatens the maintenance of the passage between the two
worlds, and imperils the spirit of the dead king and the future
of his people left on earth. Only his son's action in taking his
place averts disaster.

But, as well as being a play in celebration of the god with
whom Soyinka feels especial affinity, *Death and the King's
Horseman* may also be seen to have a contemporary political
message: that the political leadership of the nation, through a
lack of willpower and – like the Elesin – a fatal attraction for
the privileges and flatteries of this world, had acted in a
manner that imperilled the welfare of the people. Here, it can
be argued, Soyinka comments upon the failure of post-
independence Nigeria. In his note to the play Soyinka urges
us to heed its threnodic essence – that is, to see it as a
lament. His message of course, relates equally to a wider
world.

His later plays – *Opera Wonyosi* (1981), *The Play of Giants* (1984), *From Zia with Love* (1991) – continue to identify and scarify rogues and murderers. But of all the treasures of his playwriting, *Death and the King's Horseman* must be regarded as his masterpiece.

Further Reading

General

Martin Banham, ed., *Cambridge Guide to Theatre* (CUP, 1995)
Martin Banham, Errol Hill, George Woodyard, eds., *Cambridge Guide to African and Caribbean Theatre* (CUP, 1994)
David Kerr, *African Popular Theatre* (James Currey, London, 1995)
Jane Plastow, *African Theatre and Politics: the Evolution of Theatre in Ethiopia, Tanzania and Zimbabwe* (Rodopi, 1996)
Don Rubin, ed., *The World Encyclopedia of Contemporary Theatre*, Vol. 3 – Africa (Routledge, London and New York 1997)

Femi Osofisan

Muyiwa P. Awodiya, ed., *Excursions in Drama and Literature: Interviews with Femi Osofisan* (Ibadan, 1993)
Chris Dunton, *Make Man Talk True: Nigerian Drama in English Since 1970* (London, 1992)
Gareth Griffiths, 'Femi Osofisan' in C. Brian Cox, ed., *African Writers* (New York, 1997)
Sandra Richards, *Ancient Songs Set Ablaze: the Theatre of Femi Osofisan* (Washington DC, 1996)

Andrew Whaley

Stephen Chifunyise, 'Trends in Zimbabwean Theatre Since 1980', and Preben Kaarsholm, 'Mental Colonisation or Catharsis', in Liz Gunner, ed., *Politics and Performance: Theatre,*

Poetry and Song in Southern Africa (Witwatersrand Press, 1994)
Jane Plastow, *African Theatre and Politics: the Evolution of Theatre in Ethiopia, Tanzania and Zimbabwe* (Rodopi, 1996)

Ama Ata Aidoo

Dapo Adelugba, 'Language and Drama: Ama Ata Aidoo' in *African Literature Today*, 8, 1976
James Adeola, 'Ama Ata Aidoo' in James Adeola, ed., *In Their Own Voices: African Women Writers Talk* (London, 1990)
Shirley Chew, 'Ama Ata Aidoo' in C. Brian Cox, ed., *African Writers* (New York, 1997)

Mtwa, Ngema and Simon

Eckhard Breitinger, ' "Satirising those aspects of our life we don't approve of . . ." A view of the "Dark Comedies" from the Townships' in Eckhard Breitinger, ed., *Theatre and Performance in Africa* (Bayreuth African Studies No. 31, 1994)
Michael Chapman, *Southern African Literatures* (Longman, 1996)
D. Ndlovu, ed., *Woza Afrika!* (New York, 1986)
Femi Ojo-Ade, 'Contemporary South African Theatre and the Complexities of Commitment' in *African Literature Today*, No. 20 (James Currey, 1996)
Martin Orkin, *Drama and the South African State* (Manchester University Press, 1994)
Bhekizizwe Peterson, 'Apartheid and the Political Imagination in Black South African Theatre' in *Politics and Performance: Theatre, Poetry and Song in Southern Africa* (Witwatersrand Press, 1994)

Wole Soyinka

Dapo Adelugba, *Before Our Very Eyes: Tribute to Wole Soyinka* (Ibadan, 1987)
Martin Banham (with Clive Wake), *African Theatre Today* (1976)
Martin Banham, *A Critical View on Wole Soyinka's 'The Lion and the Jewel'* (London, 1981)
James Gibbs, ed., *Critical Perspectives on Wole Soyinka* (Washington DC, 1980)
James Gibbs, *Wole Soyinka* (London, 1986)

Eldred D. Jones, *The Writing of Wole Soyinka* (London, 1973; revised 1983, 1988)

Ketu Katrak, *Wole Soyinka and Modern Tragedy: A Study of Dramatic Theory and Practice* (Westport CT, 1986)

Bernth Lindfors and James Gibbs, eds., *Research on Wole Soyinka* (Trenton NJ, 1993)

Obi Maduakor, *Wole Soyinka: An Introduction to His Writing* (New York, 1986)

Adewale Maja-Pearce, *Wole Soyinka: An Appraisal* (London, 1994)

Gerald Moore, *Wole Soyinka* (London, 1971; revised 1978)

Oyin Ogunba, *The Movement of Transition: A Study of the Plays of Wole Soyinka* (Ibadan, 1975)

Derek Wright, *Wole Soyinka Revisited* (New York, 1993)

The Chattering and the Song

Femi Osofisan

For you both –
You who departed, leaving your songs as
Your only address –
*   You CHRISTOPHER OKIGBO –*
And for you, whose hands
Have nursed a fountain at my soul's rootings –
*   You WOLE SOYINKA –*
I am offering this work in dedication –
that the fountain may never despair of water, or
your songs lack a throat to sing them.

Author's Note

This play was written some twenty years ago, at the very beginning of my theatrical career, during the regime of the second military dictatorship in Nigeria. The soldiers had come rudely into our political life a few years before, through a bloody coup d'état, ostensibly to save the nation from a civilian leadership that had grown corrupt and cynical. But the euphoria which greeted that action did not last. The soldiers themselves soon broke into fighting factions, and dragged the country into a violent and costly civil war. General Gowon, at the head of the federal forces, fought gallantly to keep the nation together and defeat the secessionist Biafra. And afterwards, he sought to assuage all the hurt by a commendable policy of national reconciliation, based on the generous formula of 'No victor, no vanquished'.

It seemed therefore that the nation was set at last for promising times, for the fulfilment of all those hopes nurtured at Independence in 1960 and celebrated in the writings of our fiery nationalists and founding fathers. Particularly as petroleum, the 'black gold', had been discovered, to add to the numerous resources the country was blessed with.

But these aspirations were not to be. Somehow Gowon squandered those opportunities. Alarmingly, mediocrity and kleptomania became the order of the day. Soon criticism grew loud. But, instead of listening and mending its ways, the Gowon regime became increasingly impatient, and harsh, with its critics.

And so, the fight had to begin, on as many fronts as possible, to rid our country of this dictatorship, and restore freedom and the lofty founding ideals. *The Chattering and the Song* was my own little contribution to this struggle, on the cultural front. And looking back now, across these many years, I feel proud that I wrote such a play. Not only that: it is my hope that, in whatever part of the world and at whatever period of history tyranny raises its head, the play will remain useful to give eloquence to the forces which rise to confront it.

F. O.
1996

Characters

Sontri
Yajin
Funlola
Yetunde
Bisi
Mokan
Leje
Musicians

Alafin Abiodun's court:

Abiodun (Sontri)
Olori (Funlola)
Ayaba (Yetunde, Yajin, Bisi)
Aresa (Mokan)
Latoye (Leje)
Guards (Musicians)

The **Play Director** is Yajin

An obviously worried **Play Director**, *accompanied by the* **Stage Manager** *and a few actors, comes into the playing area and addresses the audience.*

Play Director   Ladies and Gentleman, we are going to start now. Or we may not. A disaster has just occurred, something we could not foresee. A few minutes ago, some members of the security forces arrived here, and took away some of our actors. We don't know when they will be released, and some of them are in the lead roles.

We are in a dilemma therefore what to do. Here you are, all seated and eager. Some of you have come long distances, and perhaps may not have another space in your schedule to come back another day. I don't have to say how much it will pain us therefore to simply ask you to go now and collect your money back, and return to your homes with such a disappointment.

Well, our Stage Manager has come up with a brilliant idea. And perhaps we can still have a show. According to him, some of you here have watched the play quite a number of times. Some have even been heard reciting the lines outside here, and singing some of the songs.

Well, what we propose is this. We are going to challenge such people to please come forward now, and see if they can join us tonight, to fill our missing roles. And if there are enough of you, we shall have a performance. Something to offer the rest of our guests, instead of just sending them away.

It is a most unusual procedure, I know, but let's try it and see. And of course, if we don't succeed, if there are people not satisfied with the experiment, just get up at the intermission, and ask for your money back. We'll be most ready to oblige.

So that's it, let's go now. All those there familiar with our play, and bold enough to attempt a part tonight, let me see your hands! All right, please come forward.

The rest of the cast rise eagerly, and come forward.

Oh good! See what I mean! So many of you! Excellent. And to begin with, let me try you first, with some preliminary instructions. A room! We'll need a room here, with a door! Go on, show me!

The actors rush forward, and erect the framework of a door. With a piece of chalk, they write 'DOOR' on the top frame. All is done with great laughter.

Thanks! Thanks! We'll improvise, yes! It's a room in Mokan's house! And so, Mokan, who'll play Mokan? Okay, you! And Funlola? An artistic type, you know. Ah, you then! Fortunately we still have our Sontri, and the actress playing Yajin. We can start. The rest of you will follow me now, and we'll see what roles to give you. Okay?

So let's begin now, as we always do, by formally welcoming our audience. You know the song we use for that, don't you? Right, let's go! . . .

The actors line up behind him, and they dance out, singing:

We the members
Of Kakaun Sela
Bid you welcome
To a thrilling show tonight:
'The Chattering and the Song'!

When you leave us
We hope you would have learnt
Of the need
To change society:
Just hear Osofisan!

We bid you welcome
To 'Chattering and the Song'
We bid you welcome
So does Osofisan . . .

Lights change, for the Prologue . . .

Prologue

Iwori Otura: The bigger riddle begins . . .

Many years ago. Lights should suggest this. Dawn breaking.

Garden, back of the house. Near disaster area: signs of the aftermath of a wild party.

Yajin, *standing to one corner, barely visible. Enter* **Sontri**, *drunk.*

Sontri (*to* **Yajin**) Jonathan! Are you deaf? Clear this place. What are you waiting for? You can't answer? Drunk, eh? It was a wild party, wasn't it? Listen, I am talking to you!

He lunges forward angrily, trips, tumbles. Tries to pick himself up, fails. Crawls, swearing, towards a bottle. **Yajin** *laughs.* **Sontri** *starts at the voice.*

Sontri Who . . . who is it?

Yajin (*coming forward*) Remember me?

Sontri You!

Yajin So you do get drunk too!

Sontri I thought everybody had gone.

Yajin You asked me to stay behind, remember?

Sontri Yes, yes, I did. I . . . (*Tries to get up, falls again.*)

Yajin (*laughing*) What do you think you are? A frog?

Sontri A frog!

Yajin Look!

She gets down and imitates **Sontri** *trying to rise. Falls.*

Sontri Oh, not as bad as that, Yajin!

Yajin It only remains the croaking.

Sontri (*imitating a frog*) Buuuuh!

Yajin (*the same*) Buu-ooooh!

Sontri   Buuuuh!

Yajin   Buuu-oooh!

Sontri   Great idea! We'll play a game.
Iwori Otura*
Say I am a frog . . .

Yajin   And I?

Sontri   A fish: Iwori Otura!

Yajin   Say I am a fish: Iwori Otura!

Sontri   Then swim for your life:
I leap, leap,
I'm coming after you . . .   .

Yajin   Buuuh buuu-oooh, buuuh, buuu-ooh!
Please Mister Frog, spare me yet:
Iwori Otura:
My life I'll buy with a riddle . . .

Sontri   Hm, Iwori Otura:
Answer if you can . . .
A flaming ember takes his bath
And still maintains his fiery look . . .

Yajin   Iwori Otura!
The ripe palmfruit does wear a flame
It wears a flame: Iwori Otura
Which, even in rain, still burns and glows . . .

Sontri   All right, you win.
Goodbye to the frog. Iwori Otura.
Now I am a hawk . . .

Yajin   And I?

Sontri   A hen!

Yajin   Say I am a hen: Iwori Otura!

Sontri   Then flee for your life:
I drop, I swoop,

* See Glossary on p. 68 for translations of Yoruba phrases and songs.

I'm coming after you . . .
Iwori Otura:

Yajin   Iwori Otura: ack-ack-ack.
An amnesty . . .

Sontri   I'm swooping down, with my beak of steel . . .

Yajin   Oh kind Mister Hawk, don't take my life.
Iwori Otura:
Your grace I'll win with a riddle . . .

Sontri   Then answer me:
Iwori Otura:
What horse is corralled
Yet flies his mane
So high on the roof?

Yajin   Ah, let me think . . .
Iwori Otura:
A bad conscience . . .!

Sontri   Iwori Otura!

Yajin   A bad conscience does wear a mane:
Iwori Otura:
Above the roof of dark pretence,
It wags its mane so restlessly . . .

Sontri   Iwori Otura:
I'll get you yet . . .

Yajin   Iwori Otura: goodbye to the hawk.

Sontri   Goodbye to the hawk: Iwori Otura,
Say I am a stag . . .

Yajin   And I?

Sontri   A doe!

Yajin   Say I am a doe and . . . no!

Sontri (*catches her*)   Yes! Yes! Say you are asleep and I in rut . . .

Yajin (*struggles, with lessening resistance*)   No, please, Sontri!

Sontri (*as the dance slows down*)   Yes! Yes, Yajin.
We buy our life with a little riddle, and then afterwards . . .

Yajin   Yes?

Sontri   Afterwards we have to live it.

Yajin   Yes, I know.

Sontri   And it's another riddle that begins.

Yajin   Always?

Sontri   So it seems. A bigger riddle begins.

Yajin   What shall we do?

Sontri   Mokan is my friend.

Yajin   He loves me.

Sontri   And you?

Yajin   The bigger riddle is starting. Hold me!

Sontri   Don't be afraid.

Yajin   How shall I tell him? I love you, Sontri!

Sontri   Sh! Softly . . .

Yajin   I'm afraid.

Sontri   Hold my hand: dance with me.

Yajin   I'm trembling.

Sontri   Listen! Green banks are the pride of the stream.

Subtly, the game changes to a dance of courtship.

Yajin   Rich harvests are the pride of the banks . . .

Sontri   The rainbow is the pride of heaven:

Yajin   Many colours are the pride of the rainbow . . .

Enter **Mokan**, *unnoticed. He stands watching, smoking.*

Sontri   A straight oak is the pride of the forest:

Yajin   Young leaves are the pride of the oak

Sontri   A brave hunter is the pride of the tribe.

Yajin   A good woman is the pride of the – no, no!
You go too fast, hunter!
First you must say your magic name.

Sontri *releases her, a new dance begins, that is, the theme of the engagement
in marital ritual.*

Sontri   Ah, maiden, didun nile oloyin:
I am the promise left in the trap!
In the forest

Yajin   Didun nile oloyin!

Sontri   I am the berry, I aid the thirsty . . .

Yajin *(remonstrating)*   But your eyes? Their colour of blood? ·

Sontri   Is the strangled scream of the people:
Is the shout suppressed by power . . .

Yajin *(persistent)*   In your eyes, the lust of war

Sontri   Only the echo of a call within
Didun nile oloyin:
I am the carrier: I'll steal your pains
And put good luck in their place . . .

Yajin *(baiting)*   You were the frog, hungry for my skin . . .

Sontri   You were the fish, didun nile oloyin . . .

Yajin   You were the swooping hawk,
With a beak of steel . . .

Sontri   You were the hen: didun nile oloyin . . .

Yajin   You were the stag.
You tried to take me asleep . . .

Sontri   You are my doe, didun nile oloyin . . .

Yajin *(thrilled, but trying other tactics)*   I am poor, hunter, and my
father is old.

Sontri   You'll be a princess, didun nile oloyin . . .

Yajin   These are my finest robes,
These wretched rags . . .

Sontri   I'll take you nude,
And drape you in skins!

Yajin   Your arm is bronze, your muscles strong . . .

Mokan (*breaking in*)   Didun nile Alaya!

The dancers spring apart – the dance ends abruptly.

Yajin   Mokan!

Mokan   If you have finished, I'll take you home.

Sontri   Mokan, I . . .

Mokan (*violently*)   No! (*Calms down, ironic.*) I'm sorry to spoil your show but I'm tired and sleepy, and it didn't seem to be ending. Ready, Yajin? Collect your things.

Yajin (*with determination*)   I am not coming, Mokan.

Mokan   What?

Yajin   It's finished between us.

Mokan (*trying to drag her along*)   When we get home you'll recover your senses.

Yajin (*resisting*)   I am in my senses. And I say it's finished.

Mokan   Since when . . . ?

Sontri   Yajin . . .

Yajin   It finished long ago.

Mokan   You must be drunk. (*To* **Sontri**.) You filled her with booze, ehn!

Yajin   You can't understand, can you?

Mokan   Let's go home.

Yajin   Goodbye, Mokan. I am home.

Mokan (*after a pause*)   And . . . and our engagement?

Yajin   I'm sorry, Mokan.

Mokan   Listen . . .

Yajin   Here's your ring.

Mokan *stands speechless, unmoving. Then he walks away quickly.* **Sontri** *walks after him, stops. He turns round slowly to face* **Yajin**. *She is crying silently.*

Sontri   Tears! The bigger riddle begins.

Yajin   Yes, I'm crying. But I'm not unhappy.

Sontri   I'm glad then.

Yajin   It's you I fear, hunter. Your eyes, their shade of red.

Sontri   Listen, this moment is us. Us only.
Say you are the rain . . .

Yajin   And you?

Sontri   The sun . . .

Yajin   Say I am the rain, and you the sun –

Sontri   Didun nile oloyin . . .

Yajin   You'll tear my garment . . . just for fun . . .

Sontri   Ah never! Didun nile oloyin.
I shall hold your waist
With an arm of gold:
And they will call us both a rainbow!

Yajin   Hold me: I'm no longer afraid.

Sontri   You're at home now.

Blackout. And immediately, coming from outside the stage, the song of musicians, which transfers us back to the present. The time is yesterday evening and the musicians sing on their way to a wedding eve party.

    Tun mi gbe
    Oko mi tun mi gbe o
    Tun mi gbe
    Oko mi tun mi gbe o

Iyawo dun losingin
Iyawo dun losingin
Oko, tun mi gbe!

They come into view, singing and talking, and a spotlight follows them on their route. As soon as they arrive at the house, the spotlight fades, full lights come on, and we are in . . .

Part One

But . . . behind our grins,
Behind our wide, embroidered gowns,
Is coming the piercing knife of Truth.

Late morning. Same situation, years after.

Day before the wedding.

On one side, **Funlola**, *plaiting* **Yajin***'s hair. Two girls,* **Bisi** *and* **Yetunde** *sit beside them, measuring out the thread, holding a mirror, etc. All are casually dressed, except for* **Yajin***, wrapped in hand-woven cloth, with beads decorating her neck and arms and feet.*

On the other side, upstage, the musicians are getting ready, arranging chairs and instruments, practising, testing drums and cords.

As soon as the full lights come on, the musicians begin to sing in praise of the bride.

> Yajin o to nrele oko
> Yajin o to nrele oko
> Se lo ndan gbinrin bi goolu
> Egba owo ko je ka mo tese
> Yajin ko wa bi e ti nsoge . . .

Funlola That's how you and Mokan parted?

Yajin Yes.

Funlola And you met Sontri?

Yajin We danced. Our love started.

Funlola Poor Mokan.

Yajin He got over it after some time. We became friends again, the three of us.

Funlola You mean Mokan reconciled himself to it? He bears no grudge?

Yajin None at all. You should hear me tease him and see the way he takes it. In fact, he's coming here tonight for the bachelor's eve.

Funlola   Ehn! Mokan? Gallantry, generosity or just plain stupidity?

Yajin   You don't know Mokan. All generosity. He can't wear the cloak of misfortune for too long. Something in him just converts it to laughter.

Funlola   You mean there are still people like that?

Yajin   You'll soon see for . . .

The musicians are singing:

> Eee aya won lode o
> Eee aya won lode o
> Eee aya won lode o
> O ba tete so tire mole!

The music swells in praise of **Yajin**. *She turns her head as much as she can in acknowledgement, and the others sway to the music, all laughing.*

Yajin   Save it for tonight, ehn? I don't want you to exhaust yourself yet.
The sekere answers her, and then fades with the music.

Funlola   If they go on so sweetly, I'll soon be looking for a husband myself.

Bisi   Don't you think it's time you did that, sista? I'm sure there'll be enough candidates at the party tonight.

Yajin   Oh, Funlola is only joking. All she is interested in are those canvases in her studio.

Yetunde   But one can paint and still lead a normal life?

Yajin   Not this woman here. She works too hard.

Funlola (*amused*)   You're like members of my family. They say nothing else nowadays. They'd rather see me locked up in the kitchen than in my studio . . .

Yajin   Naturally . . .

Funlola   Okay, so there's music in the chattering of pots and pans, but I don't dig it. I still prefer painting to marriage.

Bisi   Wait till you find the right man, sista.

Yajin   That's what I tell her.

Funlola   You mean like Sontri?

Yajin   Why not? He's an artist too, you know, like you.

Funlola   He paints?

Yetunde   Only with anger. I've . . .

Yajin   With words, silly. All the songs of the Farmers' Movement, their anthem . . .

Funlola   Oh it's beautiful! You mean he wrote it?

Bisi   But everybody knows!

Yajin   Except my friend. Don't forget that she's been away eating leaves in Oyinbo country all these years. Ouch! She's grown vindictive too! (*For* **Funlola** *pulled her hair hard.*)

The drummer, who has been following the conversation, joins with 'J.J.C! E kabo! J.J.C. Welcome!' which the girls pick up till **Funlola** *silences them with threatening gestures.*

Funlola   If you girls are so naughty, then I can guess what your brother'll be like.

Bisi   We're not like him-o! What!

Yetunde   God forbid! To be like Sontri!

Yajin   Traitors! You can't even stand by your own blood.

Yetunde   Why should we? He's not our husband.

Funlola   Tell me more about him. Yajin, I'd like to get a clear picture of him before we meet.

Yajin   What's the bother now? He'll soon be home.

Funlola   But tell me, what's he like?

Yajin   I . . . I really can't describe him . . .

Funlola   The bride is shy now!

Bisi   Give her time. She's still a bride on the road. By this time tomorrow . . .

Yajin   It's not that! It's just that . . . that . . .

Funlola   That what, iyawo! You're marrying a man tomorrow but you don't know what he looks like.

Yajin   But you got my letter.

Funlola   Oh that. I am not talking now of his physical appearance. From your letter I know Sontri's the incarnation of Orunmila himself . . .

The girls burst out laughing again.

Yajin   Funlola!

Funlola   You should read it yourself. Every line spoke of nothing but his handsome looks. But of the man himself, of his personality, zero. Nothing at all.

Yajin   I love him.

The drummers sing: Oko won l'ode o!

Funlola   A-wu! Stop dodging. Tell us something concrete.

Yajin   What do you want? Look it's hard to talk of someone so intimate.

Funlola   Affection intrudes, abi?

Yajin   Words are inadequate, I mean, for such a complex personality . . . None of the usual words seems to fit. Sometimes he's like a . . . mountain, with a volcano inside . . .

A whistle, off. **Yajin** *raises her head and whistles back.*

Funlola (*expectantly*)   Is that him?

Yajin   No it's Mokan. He's come early too! You see?

Whistle again, close.

Will you show yourself, you little bastard?

Enter **Mokan**, *followed by* **Leje**. **Bisi** *and* **Yetunde** *greet them and take their luggage inside. The musicians are resting or relaxing in various postures.* **Mokan** *alone greets them.*

Mokan   Did you say bastard?

Yajin   Of course, I did.

Mokan (*indicating* **Leje**)   That's his name. When he was born they couldn't decide who his father was. Whether it was the parish priest or the carpenter next door. So they named him Bastard.

Leje   Don't listen to him, lady. Believe it or not, my name is Leje. This idiot here often confuses me with his father.

Mokan (*crouching and doing a comic 'walk'*)   Watch me. I am a little brown bastard.

Yajin   Welcome, Leje. Your friend has a broken heart. You'll forgive his errors.

Mokan (*doing another 'walk'*)   I have a broken heart, huh! huh (*To* **Funlola**.) One kobo for the broken heart, ma'am!

Funlola (*playing up*)   Not until I see it. I like to see what I am paying for.

Mokan   But you *are* seeing it! I am the broken heart.

Funlola   You don't look broken to me.

Mokan   Appearances, lady. They're always deceptive.

Funlola   Are they? By merely looking at you, I can guess your name is Mokan.

Mokan   On the head, lady! You hit the nail on the head. So, since you're so good at guessing, I assume you know already that I am in love with you and I am just dying to know your name.

Yajin   If you promise not to flirt with her I might just condescend to introduce you.

Mokan   Condescend! That's jealousy for you. She's afraid of competition.

Yajin   Oh, what makes you so sure she'll have an ugly dog like you?

Mokan   My ugliness, of course. It's my greatest sex appeal.

Funlola   Not with me. I hate ugliness.

Mokan   That was before you met me. Since then, your life history has turned an unsuspected corner!

Funlola   Has it? My name is Funlola. And I hate you.

Mokan   Some day you'll learn of my good qualities. Maybe when I become the Head of State. Then you'll regret not having fallen for me.

Funlola   I'd rather fall for your friend here. He seems a much better proposition.

Mokan   Leje? Ha! You're too late, Funlola. He's already married . . . to booze.

Funlola (*laughing*)   No!

Mokan   Till death do them part. That's why he smells like a mobile stink factory. Too much beer in him.

Yajin   Just say the word, Leje, and we'll hand him over to my father for libel.

Mokan   The old man will only have to smell him from five kilometres off, and he'll be sentenced for contempt of court – trying to pressurise the judge with foul gas.

Yajin   Why don't you shove off, you little bastard? Your mouth is in the way of my preparations.

Funlola   Leje is very silent. You're not shy, are you?

Mokan   He talks. But you have to open his mouth with a beer first.

Funlola (*laughing*)   What do you say, Leje?

Leje   Don't take in anything he says about me, Funlola. We are mortal enemies.

Mokan (*pulling* **Leje**)   Let's go, you booze factory. They say we are in the way. Come on.

Mokan *and* **Leje** *go towards the house. They are stopped by the musicians who step forward to sing a satirical eulogy in honour of drunkards.* **Leje** *escapes into the house, and the musicians pursue, urged on by* **Mokan**.

Funlola   He's . . . they're so pleasant!

Yajin (*after a pause*)   Yes, I know what you're thinking. And to tell you the truth, pleasant isn't a word you can apply to Sontri. But . . . Well, in a way, it's very strange, even to me. We'd all been through College together, the three of us. And I never really looked at Sontri. It was always Mokan, and Sontri was the wild, untamed one, running with street brats, garage touts, and the like, and only just managing to scale through exams. He did not excel like Mokan, but he passed, and when we came out the political crises were beginning . . .

Funlola   That was when you met? I mean . . .

Yajin   When our relationship started, yes. It wasn't easy: he's always been so restless . . .

Funlola   Like all men.

Yajin   Far more restless. He could not settle anywhere. He joined the Army and left. He tried politics and was imprisoned. Then the first coup came, and his old officers brought him out of prison. When the civil war started, Sontri kissed me one evening – and disappeared!

Funlola   Disappeared?

Yajin   For over a year no one knew where he was. And then suddenly he was back and we were reunited.

Funlola   But . . . where did he go?

Yajin   He wouldn't tell. But I know it left a mark on him.

Funlola   How?

Yajin   I mean, a positive mark. He grew . . . harder, angrier, but also more concerned. That was when he joined the Farmers' Movement.

Funlola   But wasn't that subversive!

Yajin   Only in official circles. It's never been a sin to help the poor.

Funlola   And you? You are not afraid?

Yajin (*rising*)   That's what I wanted to tell you, Funlola. You'll be giving me away tomorrow.

Funlola   Me!

Yajin   My parents aren't coming for the wedding.

Funlola   But . . . why?

Yajin   They don't like Sontri. And he hates their guts.

The girls, **Bisi** *and* **Yetunde**, *appear with long brooms and begin to sweep the yard. The musicians also reappear.*

Funlola   It's . . . it's all so . . .

She is cut off by **Yajin** *who screams and leaps upon the stool. Everyone starts, including musicians who run forward.*

Yajin   There! There!

Funlola   But it's only a lizard!

Yajin   Drive it off!

The others collapse in laughter and banter. **Bisi** *and* **Yetunde** *chase off the lizard with their brooms.*

Funlola   Well, come down. The huge crocodile is gone. I mean, at your age! And to think you're marrying tomorrow!

Yajin (*down*)   I can't stand crawling things. My skin . . .

The girls burst out laughing. **Yajin** *stops, then joins the laughter.*

Funlola   What's the joke?

Yajin   Don't mind them, Funlola. I just accidentally mentioned one of Sontri's songs. A funny one called 'Crawling Things'.

Funlola   I'd like to hear it! Please. Sing it for me.

Yajin   Come, finish my hair first. Time's flying.

Bisi   Go on. We'll sing it for you, sista. O ya, Yetunde!

They begin to sing the 'Dance of the Crawling Things', miming the actions, punctuating them with the brooms. The musicians accompany them. The dance is irresistible, and at last **Yajin** *herself stands and joins.*

Chorus: Jijo iya ka wo'ran
            Panla sigi sai sai sai
            Panla!

One haughty thing, he walks the street
He walks the street on myriad feet
And struts as if he owns the sun –

Chorus.

He has no bite he has no fist
He has no tongue to voice protest
This haughty thing is – a millipede!

Chorus.

This millipede, a curious thing
A curious thing of middling mien
It signifies our nation now:

Chorus.

On shaky feet we stumble on
We change our skins like chameleon
Prostrate and mute like crawling things . . .

Chorus.

And on the streets, these crawling things,
These cringing worms seem worthy beings:
We clothe ourselves in carapace . . .

Chorus.

But in our shells, behind our grins,
Behind our wide embroidered gowns
Is coming the piercing knife of Truth:

Chorus.

The knife of Truth, the blade of Life . . .

Suddenly, above the laughter and singing, a yell of anger, from offstage. The dance freezes. The shout of 'SOPONNO-O!' *is repeated, clearly now. Apprehensive,* **Yajin** *motions the girls and drummers into the house.*

Yajin   Go quickly and continue your dance inside. Come, Funlola.

Funlola   Who is . . . ?

Yajin   It's Sontri. I don't know what has annoyed him. But let's . . .

Enter **Sontri**, *very angry.*

Sontri (*shouting*)   Who is it? I swear I'll have his head off for this!

Yajin   What's the matter?

Sontri   Who did it?

Yajin   Did what?

Sontri   My weaverbirds. Who drove them off?

Yajin (*in confusion*)   Your weaverbirds?

Sontri   Yes, my weaverbirds. And stop looking so ignorant! What has happened to those birds on the tree beside my window?

Yajin   Has . . . has something happened to them?

Sontri   Ooooh damn it! Has something happened indeed.

Funlola (*genuinely distressed*)   I am sorry, I . . .

Sontri (*cutting her off*)   Will you shut your trap, too! Who's addressing you? (*To* **Yajin**.) Now where are my birds? You haven't sold them, have you?

Yajin   Don't be silly! Why should I want to . . . ?

Sontri   Motives, damn it! Who has a mother who's on the verge of bankruptcy, with a father struggling in the ruins of

half a century of sin! Motives! You'd sell the birds to start a
Save My Parents From Damnation Fund!

Yajin (*quietly, controlling her anger*) I don't know anything about
those birds, Sontri. They probably flew away.

Sontri Flew away! Of course, emigration is very much in
the air, now. The birds have flown across the border to
become political refugees!

Yajin Sontri, please don't start again. Not today.

Sontri Didn't you listen to the radio? (*Mimicking a news
reader.*) 'Scores of weaverbirds were this morning seen crossing
the border. When questioned, a spokesman for the birds
disclosed that they would be asking the host government for
political asylum. Tons of relief material are already on the
way from the International Red Cross.'

Yajin (*still trying to pacify him*) Believe me, Sontri, I don't
know what happened to your birds.

Sontri Of course, you wouldn't know! And isn't that the
point! (*Seizes the mirror she is holding.*) Look, my dear, that's you!
Those two soft eyes, soft . . . and blind! And those painted
eyelids, those gentle curtains nicely cordoned around your
sweet romantic dreams, while the world groans around you on
wounded wings! Close your windows with curfews of
indifference, there'll be white-robed maidens tomorrow to
dance up the church steps by your side to the blasted altar
and the fat maggot who will be waiting behind it! Shake
yourself, my dear! Shake off this heritage of smugness you've
acquired from your parents and look around you! The
weaverbirds flew away! Of course, of course! As your sister
flew away with that Permanent Secretary until your father
cooked up a charge against him and got him retired! What do
you know about anything!

Funlola (*infuriated*) I am sorry, but I can't keep silent any
longer. You're being unfair. It was my fault! I didn't know the
birds were not to be touched. I pulled down the nests . . .

Even before she has finished, **Sontri** *has leapt at her and gripped her* *with brutal force.*

Sontri   You did what!

Funlola   *(frightened by his savagery)*   I . . . I thought they were causing too much commotion . . .

Sontri   Commotion!   *(He is almost hoarse with anger.)*   Who is this . . . this virgin?

Yajin   *(on the verge of tears)*   Sontri! She's . . . she's my fr . . .

Sontri   *(not listening)*   Commotion indeed!

Funlola   *(in pain)*   You're hurting me!

Sontri   Repeat after me: A commotion is . . .

Funlola   Please let me go!

Yajin   Sontri, will you . . .

Sontri   *(unrelenting)*   A commotion is . . .

Funlola   Ouch!

Yajin   *(desperate)*   You'd better do as he says.

Sontri   Or I'll break your arm off, you goddamn ignoramus! Say after me: A commotion is . . .

Funlola   A commotion is . . .

Sontri   A violent disturbance . . .

Funlola   A violent disturbance . . .

Sontri   Like a riot . . .

Funlola   Like a riot . . .

Sontri   Or a bad government . . .

Funlola   Or a bad government . . .

Sontri   But the chirrupping of birds . . .

Funlola   But the chir . . . chir . . .

Sontri   Chirrupping!

Funlola   Chirrupping . . .

Sontri   Of birds . . .

Funlola   Of birds, ouch!

Sontri   Is called a song . . .

Funlola   Is called a song . . .

Sontri   And the weaverbirds chatter . . .

Funlola   And the weaverbirds chatter . . .

Sontri   In chorus . . .

Funlola   In chorus . . .

Sontri   And their chattering is song . . .

Funlola   And their chattering is song . . .

Sontri   Now, smile.

Funlola   Now, smi— (*stops herself quickly, in confusion.*)

Sontri (*releasing her*)   Keep it up, lady. You'll make an excellent parrot.

Yajin (*her courage flaring up temporarily, through anger*)   Why do you release her? Why don't you carry on your torture till she falls dead at your feet? Because of birds! And she said she didn't know, but . . .

Sontri (*interrupting*)   Ignorance! Ignorance again! No wonder you are good friends: you'll both end well. Tell me, suppose I take your pretty virgin here before your father, what do you think will be the verdict? Ehn? (*To* **Funlola**, *who cringes from him.*) Her father is a judge, you know, if you haven't heard of him then you haven't been breathing. An eminent judge, known and respected from Lagos to Laura Namoda! Esungboro! The Fearful Spirit who deals out death penalties with the same ease as a wealthy man deals out fart into the air! Forty-six years on the bench! Dear father did so well, killing off the nation's bad children that, to reward him, they're going to put him on the Armed Robbery Tribunal! Ha ha ha.

Yajin   Yes, Sontri, why do you stop? You know, it doesn't hurt any more. Or are you out of words?

Sontri (*ignoring her*)   I went to watch him in action once. I swear that, although I was only a spectator, I trembled so much where I sat that I pissed in my pants! (*Laughs.*) I can bear him pronouncing sentence in that full-blown self-righteous tone that he must have borrowed from his barber: (*Mimicking a judge.*) Order! Order! Clerk, record! 'Lady Purity, this court has looked deeply and with understanding into this case before us. Your strongest defence appears to be your unproven claim of ignorance. Unfortunately such a plea is not, in the laws of this country, admissible. Therefore the Tribunal has no alternative but to find you guilty of armed virginity, and to sentence you to death by a lecher squad. You will be executed in a public brothel. So help me, Lord! Whoop, Whoop, Whoop.'

Yajin (*advancing at him, beside herself with rage*)   Enough! Isn't that enough! I swear that if you don't stop I shall . . .

His sudden sharp look sends her back.

Funlola   Why must he be so beastly, so . . .

Yajin (*breaking in, kindly*)   Funlola, please. For my sake!

Funlola   I can't stand it, you hear? I can't!

Sontri (*enjoying their confusion*)   She can't stand it! Her tender little hands are calloused with malignity, and she can't stand it! She's so proud of herself, so proud that, at a nod, she will take her name out and wear it like a badge. She has given out fine, ladylike gestures and, gentlemen, honour demands . . . commands . . . that we reciprocate! (*Mimicking a judge, as before.*) 'Therefore the decision of the lower court hereby stands reversed. Ahem, revoked! The weaverbirds have been proved guilty, beyond all equivocation, of criminal apathy to human affairs; worse, of initiating precedents inherently noxious to the healthy timber of our cherished traditions, ha ha. There can be no doubt that the accused are responsible, as the prosecution has alleged, for the festering of this social epidemic known as freedom. They have been unable to produce evidence of any progressive machinery of legitimate

oppression: no traditions of licit internment, no *de jure* precepts
of censorship, possibly no torture chambers for the use of the
gendarmerie. Even such simple customs as taxation are
unknown: we need only cite one instance: the accused admit
to constructing their nests without having to buy licences,
without procuring cement at inflated tariffs from authorised
profiteers, without *a priori* development plans being forwarded
for intellectual distortion in the Press, and finally, without
waiting for these plans to mature in the patient womb of time
... a preliminary wisely assured elsewhere through the
ingenious invention of red tape ... ahem ahem ... we can
only wonder how their government functionaries manage to
eat, deprived thus of their legitimate ten per cents ...
ahem ... That's just by the way ahem ... Such retrogressive
practices, we repeat, must not be allowed to proliferate!
Therefore, guilty! guilty! guilty! The accused must be pursued,
hunted and massacred without mercy. And for a start, let all
the atrocious nests in question be pulled down with immediate
effect! For which job we recommend the lady Purity
Contractors, Deflowering and Demolishing Agents! (*Jumping
about on all fours and barking.*) Whoop! Whoop! Whoop! Whaah!
(*Rising, in a different voice.*) Lady Purity will now come forward
and receive her medal! (*Runs to the drums, beats and sings.*)

> Obangiji se o ngbohun mi o
> Obangiji se o ngbohun mi o
> Akara aiye je nri temi bu
> Ki njale kan fi mi joye
> Ki ngbaya alaya koko tun wewon
> Kinbimo ko di Gomina
> Obangiji o ... eeeh ...
> Obangiji dakun gbohun mi!

Ladies and gentlemen, will you give the lady a hand! Whoop!
Whoop! Whoop! (*For a second he looks at the ladies, then he breaks
into a wild laugh.*) Of course, they have no sense of humour!
They can only rave when others pull their nests together!
Commotion!

Laughs again. This helps **Yajin** *out of her frozen alarm. She gives him
what is meant to be a withering look, and goes to* **Funlola**.

Yajin   I am sorry I brought you into this. If you wish, you can leave now. I shall understand.

Sontri   That's right. She's the artist, isn't she? I remember. Tell her to run. Running is always easy for these creatures. (*But he pulls* **Funlola** *close and speaks in her face.*) What do you paint, you! Human or animal disintegration, wings rending wrreeetch, straws limp in wind, screams young and rich like lights on gravestones: oh tell me, when you wield your brush of power, do your feathers wind shrouds of broken lives? No? No? Stay here, pretty thing: there will be time to get sick and rush for the nearest toilet. (*Leaves her. and turns his back to them.*)

My heart is full: I am going out again. Handle the guests as you think best till I come. (*Then, his sense of humour surfacing again, he bows to* **Funlola**, *and addresses her in his mocking voice.*) Lady Purity, permit me to remove this odious personality from her lady's chaste sight. Temporarily. (*He goes out, humming the song 'Obangiji'.*)

Funlola   Yajin, are you going to wait till he returns?

Yajin   I . . . I don't know. But it's you I'm thinking of. You don't have to stay any more.

Funlola   You think I'll leave you now?

Yajin   This house is not for people like you. You've no protection, you'll only get hurt.

Funlola   And you?

Yajin (*trying to convince herself*)   It needs a little courage. And then one can get used to it.

Funlola   You still want to go ahead with this marriage?

Yajin   A mountain, with a volcano inside . . . If only he will be still, his mountain holds great promise of fruitful fields . . . If I can tame that fire in his belly . . . don't you see, if only I can calm the tumult of his personality . . .

Funlola   No one can tame a volcano. The anger and the gall are too potent within, and the moment he opens his mouth they gush out in scalding screams of protest. He himself cannot control it . . . nor can you.

Yajin   I can try. I will try!

Funlola   In that case, I don't think I am going to have any hand in preparing your . . .

The rest of her speech is interrupted by **Yajin**'s *scream as she runs back.*

Yajin   Funlola, that lizard again!

Funlola (*throwing something at it*)   You'll never grow up!

Yajin   I just can't stand these cr . . . (*She breaks off laughing.*)

Funlola (*amused too*)   There you go again, 'crawling things'!

Yajin   It's hopeless, Funlola. He's too much a part of me.

Funlola (*laughing, quotes*)
    'One haughty thing
    That walks the street
    That walks the street . . .'

Yajin (*joining*)
    '. . . On myriad feet
    And struts as if he owns the sun . . .'
Will you stay, Funlola?

All of a sudden **Funlola** *is very interested in the personality of* **Sontri**, *in his hold over her friend.*

Funlola (*with surprising enthusiasm, quotes*)   'Behind our masks, behind our grins —'

Yajin (*desperately*)   Funlola, answer me!

Impassioned by their dialogue, they have not noticed **Mokan** *and* **Leje** *come out of the house, bottles in hand, looking at them. The two, at a sign from* **Mokan**, *now break in upon the ladies' attention with a raucous mimic of the song.*

Mokan   Jijo iya ka wo'ran

Leje   Panla sigi sai sai sai!

Yajin (*reprovingly*)   Mokan!

Funlola   And the booze factory! You should be ashamed of yourselves.

Mokan   We are.

Funlola   Well, since you are here, you'd better speak up: this girl is about to ruin her life.

Leje   On what? What is at stake? Tell me the stake first.

Mokan   God, what a question! You heard him bellowing here just now, idiot. You were crouching behind the beer cartons quaking with terror.

Leje (*whistling*)   Phew! Then I declare the gamble worth it. (*To* **Mokan**.) Your card, sir.

Mokan (*reluctantly*)   Well, circles? (*Runs round* **Leje**.) Play.

Leje   Circles? There must be an end to running. How about . . . ? (*Builds a cross with his arms.*)

Mokan   A cross? Good for crucifixion. ('*Crucifies*' *himself on* **Leje***'s extended arms.*) Last card.

Yajin   Good for me too, Mokan?

Mokan   I said, last card. Play, sir.

Funlola   Pay no attention to their babbling, Yajin. You see they've had too much already.

Yajin (*insistent, to* **Mokan**)   What if I held the master card? The power to bang the game down, (*Hits their arms.*) crying: Check!

Leje   Check!

Mokan (*falling, with his neck out like a sacrificial offering*)   Eloi . . . eloi . . .

Leje   . . . lama sabaktani. (*Cuts the offered neck.*)

Mokan (*screaming*)   Yeaah . . . !

Leje (*blessing the sacrifice*)   A-a-amen!

Mokan (*looking up at last*)   But do you have the master-card?

Leje   I suspect foul play.

Yajin   The important thing is . . . to win.

Mokan (*rising, sinister*)   Yajin, you don't have the master-card.

Leje (*singing*)   And the stake is high . . . high . . . high . . .

Yajin   I could try. Help me. Funlola?

Funlola *turns to* **Mokan** *for reply. A little silence. Then* **Mokan** *shrugs.*

Mokan   Well, why not? You aren't her insurance company.

Leje   You have nothing to lose.

Mokan   You can always arrange the 'wake keeping' afterwards.

Yajin   A chance. All I ask is a chance to try. You can at least give your blessing.

Mokan   Gratis, Yajin. I reconciled myself to it long ago. You have my blessing. And to prove it, I am going out right away to bring the dancers I promised for your celebration. (*Pulling* **Leje**.) Let's go, bottle director.

Yajin   Eh, wait. (*Growing excited.*) Dancers . . . dancers . . . Ah, you've given me an idea. Thanks, Mokan. I know what we shall have for entertainment tonight! Will you join me?

Mokan   Gratis. Gratis.

Funlola   Depends on what it is this time.

Yajin (*still excited*)   A play . . . a little scenario . . .

Funlola   A play?

Yajin   Yes, a play. Of Sontri's in fact, one he has probably forgotten. Remember, Funlola, the script I sent you some years back?

Funlola   Er . . . yes! That play! The one I designed a backdrop for, isn't it?

Yajin   Yes. In fact, the design's in the store now. I had it reproduced on a large canvas.

Funlola   You did?

Yajin   I'll bring it out. Please, help me. Let's put up the play tonight.

Funlola   For Sontri?

Yajin   And for all of us. Make it my wedding present.

Mokan   Wait a minute. What's all this about? What play?

Yajin   It's the story of a confrontation. Between Latoye and the famous Alafin Abiodun.

Mokan   Latoye?

Yajin   The son of Basorun Gaha. The only one who survived the palace massacre.

Leje   The rebel, you mean?

Funlola   He was more often called a drunkard.

Mokan   At last, Leje! A chance to play your ancestor on stage!

Yajin (*through the general laughter*)   So will you all stay? Will you join me?

Mokan   Why not? Who would miss seeing the father of drinkers himself!

Funlola   We'll stay, Yajin. Who can leave now, eh, iyawo oju ona? (*Breaks into a song, a deliberate distortion of the musicians' earlier eulogy.*)
   Yajin o to nrele oko
   Se lo mura bi eni nrogun,
   O woleke, o soja bi amure,
   Towo tese lo fi kun pauda o
   E-e-e oko won lode o (*Repeat three times.*)
   O ba tete so tire mole o!

Mokan *and* **Leje** *join in. The song attracts the musicians who come in with* **Bisi** *and* **Yetunde**. *Lights snap off on the dance.*

Part Two

When you put a man in chains,
Kabiyesi,
You free his tongue . . .

Later in the evening. The party is now in full swing in the sitting-room from where the sound of laughter and revelry intrudes occasionally, especially when the wind blows the door open.

*Someone (who will later be identified as **Leje**) comes in and gropes about in the dark. Then, finding the switch, he snaps the light on, revealing a small room, near the sitting-room. Lying about the floor are odd casks, barrels, cartons and various other pieces of bric-a-brac. It is not much used.*

Leje *searches round, till he finds something under a tarpaulin cover: a tin drum, filled to the brim with bottles and ice blocks. His face lights up as he throws off the cover, takes out a bottle which which he opens with his teeth, and drinks. Then he goes to the door and calls.*

Leje   Come in, Mokan. This is the Promised Land.

Mokan *(comes in and whistles as he sees the bottles)*   You found it!

It should be apparent that the two men are already slightly drunk.

Leje   Be my guest.

Mokan *(helping himself)*   I knew you couldn't fail. Enter a house and the first place you discover is where the beer is kept. Even if there were walls of cement round it.

Leje   It's my sixth sense. I can't help it. I've got a very religious sixth sense which keeps me from breaking God's holy commandment.

Mokan   What's that got to do with it?

Leje   The thirteenth commandment given to Moses: Thou shall not thirst!

Mokan   I thought there were only ten in the Bible.

Leje   That was in the past. When Moses was too young to read. Where have you been since?

Mokan   Getting born, I suppose. Anyway your sixth sense seems to be doing overtime: this barrel is full to the brim.

Leje   I told you it's the Promised Land. To reach it you have to be pure in heart. But the road is still long my friend, so drink, drink . . .

Mokan (*whistling again*)   You don't mean . . . ?

Leje   Exactly. To him that is drunk shall more booze be given – it should be a proverb. Let them dance their fill out there. We've got more serious things on our hands.

Mokan   You're right. It's amazing how your brain begins to function when there's booze.

Leje   Yours doesn't work at all, even with booze. (*Deliberate malice.*) It's your girl committing matrimony tomorrow, isn't she? With another man!

Mokan   So what? When a house is fallen . . .

Leje   . . . you don't start painting the bricks. OK, but that's no reason to go mixing with that mob out there, yelling your head off and doing funny dances. You're supposed to be sad.

Mokan (*quietly*)   The monkey sweats, Leje.

Leje   I beg your pardon?

Mokan   It's only the hair on its back. Sometimes you're so blind that you'll miss things even under your nose.

Leje   You're right. The bottle intervenes.

Mokan   I suppose you think it's more dignified for me to sit here and cry myself to sleep.

Leje   Who's talking of sleep! Booze, man! The only way to show your resentment at what they'll be doing to you tomorrow is to drink yourself to death on their account. That way you'll stay forever on their conscience.

Mokan   Well, I don't know. And besides, remember what she said.

Leje   Who?

Mokan   Yajin.

Leje   What did Yajin say?

Mokan   She said not to . . .

Leje   (*interrupting*)   I know what Yajin said!

Mokan   Then why . . .

Leje   Forget it.

Mokan   She said . . .

Leje   I said forget it! It's crazy: how can anybody expect us not to drink! On a bachelor's eve?

Mokan   She was thinking about the play.

Leje   What about it?

Mokan   Her play.

Leje   Well, forget it.

Mokan   She seems to set a lot on it.

Leje   And I say forget it. In the name of the Father and the Holy Booze!

Mokan   Tell me, why do you think Yajin is making us do this? What's behind it? Why's she so intense about the play?

Leje   But she told us! She said . . .

Mokan   Nonsense! Listen, if the monkey's hair hides the sweat, it will not stop us from smelling it. These gestures of atonement can never . . .

Leje   Atonement! But for what?

Mokan   You'll see. Only that you aren't her insurance agent. You can relax. But let me tell you . . .

Leje   Drop it, man. You're making the drink sour. (*Pause.*) And you said you were sad.

Mokan   Of course, I am! (*Looking through the door.*) Or rather,

I think I am. I mean, look at her there on the dance floor. I've never seen her as radiant as that. There must be something in it.

Leje   Go on, sing about it. (*Pulling him back and shutting the door.*) Don't be a fool. Of course, you are sad. (*Pushing the bottle into his mouth.*) Drink. Drink away your sorrow.

Mokan (*drinking*)   It's not fair. You always take me on my weak side. You know the only thing I can't resist is temptation.

Leje   Whom are you quoting? As if you went to school. Sit down.

Mokan (*sitting*)   Well, Jesus fell . . .

Leje (*pulling out a packet of Whot cards*)   And I've got something here to relieve the religious burden of drink. Got a pen?

Mokan (*searching*)   I have a pencil around, somewhere. (*Pulls it out from his hair.*) Han-han, tough luck, it's broken.

Leje   Give me, I've got teeth. Drag that carton here.

Mokan *drags the carton between him and* **Leje**, *who places the cards on it.*

Leje   Deal first. I want to give you every advantage, so you don't start complaining when you lose.

Mokan   And who says I'll lose?

Leje   My sixth sense.

Mokan   Nonsense. I've got a sixth sense too, you know.

Leje   I know. That's why you lost your girl.

They begin to play.

Mokan   I don't see the connection . . .

Leje   Simple. You've got a sixth sense. But it doesn't function. So you lost Yajin.

Mokan   I don't see that it's any of your business.

Leje   Play. Have I said that it's my business?

Mokan   Any time you drink you get talkative. Like a flipping weaverbird.

Leje   Play!

Music from the sitting-room grows and covers their conversation for a moment.

Leje   What did you say?

Mokan   I asked for circles.

Leje   You know I don't know how to lose.

Mokan   Play.

Leje (*stalling*)   I can't concentrate. Too much noise out there.

Mokan   Come on.

Leje   I tell you the noise is . . .

Mokan   Circles! I asked for circles.

Leje   How can I concentrate when they're making such a row?

Mokan   All right. All right. The wind must have blown the door open. I'll shut it.

As he goes, **Leje** *cheats with the cards.*

Mokan (*returning*)   It beats me anyway how any noise could stop someone throwing down a simple card.

Leje (*relishing his certain victory now*)   If it were some other game now, I wouldn't mind. I once played chess at the stadium during a football match. Our club was playing against the Lions and I was on the outside right. Well, in a very short time we reduced the Lions to rabbits. As they scutted about the field, in pitiful disarray, the linesman called me, and we started a chess game on the side. I remember running in to score a goal, and then coming back to win the chess game. That's how good I was.

Mokan (*unimpressed*)   Circles. I asked for circles!

Leje   Well, damn it, I haven't got it!

Mokan   To the market then, instead of telling stories!

Leje   But I've got something better. (*Throws down a master-card.*) Last card. And I want crosses!

Mokan   You cheated!

Leje   Not on a cross. You can't cheat on a cross.

Mokan   Can't you?

Leje   Crosses must always fulfil their purpose. And the only purpose is crucifixion.

Mokan   Someone's definitely going to be crucified tonight. Another game?

Leje   No, thanks. If you're looking for martyrdom, you've chosen the wrong executioner. I always stop at one victory, I don't humiliate my friends.

Mokan   You're afraid I won't get up this time to shut the door, abi?

Leje   It's your honour I'm thinking of. I mean, get up or sit tight – you know I don't know how to lose.

Mokan (*shuffling the cards*)   Leave the risks to me.

Leje   Well, go ahead. Deal. It's your funeral. But it won't be for lack of warning.

Mokan (*dealing*)   Thanks. Except that those who cheat don't really know anything about the game.

Leje   Who cheated? What do you mean?

Mokan   I mean that they always forget that there will be a second game. However long it takes.

Leje   So?

Mokan   So nothing. Idiot.

Leje   The heroic streak. Always that stubborn death wish to test your superiors. Why Yajin didn't cast you for Latoye instead of me, I don't know. I haven't got your passion for humiliation.

Mokan   Humiliation?

Leje   Or worse. Latoye paid with his life. Play.

Mokan   Death could be a kind of apotheosis too. Play.

Leje   Is that what you're looking for? To be disgraced?

Mokan   I said apotheosis. Play. Besides, you forget the other party can also lose.

Leje   Oh yes? Bloody arrogance, I call it. Play. Latoye was . . .

Enter **Yajin**, *calling as she flings the door open.*

Yajin   Latoye! Where's my Latoye disappeared to?

Leje   (*brushing himself hastily, with exaggerated guilt*)   Here, here, Mrs Producer!

Yajin   You've been drinking!

Leje   (*playing hurt*)   Drinking! Do you hear that, Mokan?

Mokan   She was thinking of your reputation. But don't worry, Yajin, we were only rehearsing.

Yajin   Rehearsing?

Mokan   Yes, studied the script . . .

Leje   . . . scanned the words . . .

Mokan   . . . the fashion of speech . . .

Leje   . . . the cut of character . . .

Mokan   . . . the appeal of posture . . .

Leje   . . . the gesture of prestige . . .

Mokan   . . . and plague on the producer!

Yajin   I beg your pardon?

Mokan   Nothing, nothing!

Yajin   You promised to stay sober.

Mokan   We kept our word.

Leje   In the name of the Father and the Holy Booze!

Enter **Sontri**, **Funlola**, **Bisi** *and* **Yetunde**.

Sontri   You found them.

Yajin   Yes. They say they were rehearsing.

Sontri   Evidently, the wrong play, from the look of the bottles.

Mokan   Speak up, Leje! Your honour's at stake.

Funlola   What about yours?

Mokan   Leje's my witness. Ask him, he knows I resisted temptation.

Funlola   Hard enough to fall into it?

Yajin   You won't wiggle out of this one, Mokan, you're both caught.

Mokan   We protest. We're being judged by the female sex.

Leje   Almost as bad as racial discrimination.

Sontri   I will judge you then.

Mokan   Leje, we are lost!

Funlola   See them cringing? Yajin, let's have mercy on them.

Yajin   They don't deserve it.

Funlola   Give them a last chance to clear themselves: ask them to repeat their lines.

Yajin   Good idea! Now let's hear the fruit of your laborious rehearsal.

Leje   After you, Mokan.

Mokan   After me nothing! You're Latoye. You're what the play's about.

Leje Well . . . I can't just talk into the air, can I? I've got to come in on cue.

Funlola Isn't he clever! Well, we'll give you the cue. Sontri, let's start.

Sontri Right, we'll indulge him. Let's start.

Yajin Just a moment. I'll bring some of the musicians.

Funlola And the costumes too.

Mokan Costumes?

Yajin Oh Funlola dug them out of the store of Sontri's old company. I'll bring them so we can try them on. Meanwhile, Funlola, why not put up the backdrop.

Funlola Okay. (*Goes to do so as* **Yajin** *exits.*)

Sontri I hope you remembered my crown.

Funlola What for?

Sontri Ever heard of an Alafin of Oyo without a crown?

Mokan No. Nor without a harem . . .

Leje And calabashes. Don't forget the calabashes!

Mokan Rounded forms! So do we send to the nearest brothel?

Sontri (*insisting*) I need a crown.

Funlola I've found an answer! (*Picks up a calabash and brings it to* **Sontri**.) Will this do?

Sontri (*blows out dust from the calabash and dons it*) Why not? (*To* **Mokan** *and* **Leje**.) Go on, enjoy yourselves. We'll see who will be laughing in a moment. (*To* **Funlola**, *with exaggerated protocol.*) Olori, my queen?

Funlola (*laughing*) Excellent, Kabiyesi. I can't think of a crown more becoming.

Sontri (*pompous*) In that case, His Majesty is ready!

Enter **Yajin**, *with musicians. She begins to distribute costumes.*

Yajin   That's a beautiful crown, Your Majesty. It's almost a pity to spoil it with any other adornment. (*Helps him with his robes and then drapes him with the necklace. Gives him a kiss and stands back to look round.*) Funlola, your artist's eye is still sharp, these costumes are so apt.

Murmurs of approval. She claps her hands.

Okay, take your places.

Yajin *draws* **Mokan** *and* **Leje** *to one side, as* **Sontri** *(***Abiodun***) and* **Funlola** *(***Olori***) replace the former before the Whot pack and begin to play.* **Bisi** *and* **Yetunde** *sit nearby, alternately fanning the Alafin. From the guards (the musicians) rise the royal encomiums in the background. The game is a more ancient form of the card game, each round apparently consisting of drawing cards and dropping them. It should be obvious from its solemnity that a transition has taken place in the character of the actors. As the game goes on, it is obvious that the Alafin is more adroit. He wins consistently till, disgusted, he throws the cards down angrily.*

Abiodun   Won again! I often wonder what you women do with your brains. (*He drinks from the bottle and belches loudly.*) That is, of course, assuming you've got brains.

Olori   But I tried, my lord. Only you're a very clever clever.

This is a good beginning, and **Yajin** *nods in approval. During this 'play' we must feel the characters – especially* **Sontri** *at first searching for words and attitudes, until they gradually, if unconsciously, merge with the figures they are trying to impersonate. One possible way of showing this would be in the change of verbal rhythms and intonation. Now, as the reading gathers momentum,* **Funlola** *begins to reposition objects in the room in more appropriate places, even changing lights, till the scene begins to approximate the actual setting of the drama: a room in an ancient Yoruba palace, circa 1785. The transformations should not be done in a manner that would be obtrusive. The other actors remain on stage, but in the shadows, from where they move in at appropriate moments.*

Abiodun   You tried! I'm glad to hear it. Wonder what the game would have been like if you hadn't. That will be enough for today.

Olori (*rising*)   Thank you, my lord.

Abiodun (*restraining*)   No, stay. There's a man being brought for trial. An agitator, it seems. If he's repentant enough, we might not hang him. You will make sure he shows that repentance.

Olori   Pardon me, but how . . . ?

Abiodun   We hear that he is a fire-eater and might make us lose our temper. Your duty is to see that we do not lose that temper, by finding the right words to cool the flames.

Olori   You want to save him then?

Abiodun   Well, why not?

Olori   It's never happened before.

Abiodun   It's happening now.

'**Olori**   Why, if I may ask?

Abiodun   You may not ask.

Olori (*shrugs*)   I shall try my best for him.

Abiodun (*almost in a whisper*)   Perhaps it is not him I want to save. Perhaps it's myself.

Olori   I don't understand.

Abiodun   You were not meant to.

Olori   I am sorry, Kabiyesi.

Abiodun   We are tired of killing people. It's becoming monotonous. (*Drinks, then claps his hands.*) Aresa! Bring the man in! (*To* **Olori**.) Remind us to ask our scientists to invent a new method of getting rid of undesirable elements. That is, without hanging them or giving them poison or shooting their brains out.

Olori   You could feed them to animals.

Abiodun   You're not a scientist. So it's beyond your competence to advise.

Mokan, *dressed up as* **Aresa**, *chief of police guards, comes forward, pushing* **Latoye** *before him. The latter is, of course, none other than* **Leje**, *who has been 'chained'.* **Aresa** *throws him down on his face and salutes.*

Abiodun   What is his offence?

Aresa   He's an agitator, Your Majesty. For months he has been writing subversive articles. Under a false name, of course. But we finally caught up with him yesterday as he was trying to incite the market people to riot over the increased tariff on salt.

Abiodun   Is that all?

Aresa   Yes, Kabiyesi, I mean no! We got a doctor to examine him, but there's nothing wrong with him. He was certified sane.

Abiodun   Right, wait at the door till we decide his punishment.

Aresa *withdraws.*

(*To the prisoner.*) What is your name? (*Silence.*) You will not answer?

Latoye (*raising his head*)   Find out!

The Alafin and his wife are surprised.

Abiodun (*shocked*). You, son of Gaha!

Latoye (*insolently*)   Full marks, you've done your home work. Now, clap for yourself.

Abiodun   Latoye, son of Gaha! We spared your life, wishing to be merciful. But who says the snake's offspring will not have poison in its mouth?

Latoye   You're a king. It's your privilege to ask questions. Even foolish ones.

Abiodun (*furious*)   You ... you ...

Olori (*interceding*)   Kabiyesi, oba alayeluwa!

Abiodun   You have pluck, young man, like a strutting cock. But even he, with all his flaming crest, has never been seen disputing seniority with fire. Don't try our temper.

Latoye   When you put a man in chains, Kabiyesi, you free his tongue!

A brief pause, while the Alafin decides.

Abiodun   Aresa!

Aresa *runs in.*

Abiodun   Free his hands.

Aresa *(alarmed)*   Kabiyesi, the man could be dangerous . . .

Abiodun   An order is not a request for advice.

Aresa   Forgive me, Kabiyesi, I only wanted to . . .

Abiodun *(harshly)*   Don't!

Aresa *quickly frees* **Latoye***'s hands and exits.*

Latoye *(stands)*   Aresa is right, you know. I don't like you and I don't fear you. I spend nights dreaming of how I'll attack you and cut your neck off.

Abiodun   I don't think you would.

Latoye *(aggressively)*   No?

Abiodun   You couldn't anyway. Even a mad dog still remembers that it has a master. And that that master has a whip.

Latoye   The whip is in my hands now, Abiodun.

Abiodun   So? Tell us about it.

Latoye   I have only just started. Soon that throne you sit on will begin to tremble. There will be nowhere for you to hide.

Abiodun   And who will be after us? You?

Latoye   I am going to shout so much that even Sango will lend me his thunder. I shall raise the whole earth against you.

Abiodun   You talk in the future tense. But your future is in my hands.

Latoye   Tomorrow . . .

Abiodun   Tomorrow you will be dead.

Latoye   Yes, you will kill me. But your hands cannot reach the seeds I have already sown, and they are on fertile soil. Soon, sooner than you think, they will burst into flower and their scent alone will choke you.

Abiodun (*amused, confident*)   You are an agitator, as they said. But you are not even a good one. You fight with mere metaphors. A conqueror finds more concrete weapons.

Latoye   Laugh on. Tomorrow you will be on the run.

Abiodun   Tomorrow! Tomorrow! I tell you you have none!

Latoye   Tomorrow is beyond even you, Kabiyesi.

Abiodun   Why are you doing all this? Because of your father?

Latoye   My father has nothing to do with it.

Abiodun   Because if it is, you are only being stupid. Do you think the man who tamed a lion will fear the feeble scratching of its cub? Your father was a lion who . . .

Latoye   Whom you tamed.

Abiodun   Yes, whom I tamed!

Latoye (*mimicking him*)   Whom I tamed! Congratulations!

Abiodun   I believe you really want to die.

Olori   Latoye, why don't you control your tongue?

Latoye   I am controlling it, madam. I am keeping it at the same speed as his.

Abiodun (*angry now*)   Aresa! Guards!

Olori (*intervening again*)   Please, my lord. Spare him yet. Remember he is young.

Abiodun I know he is young. As I also know he has no respect.

Latoye I respect you, as much as you did my father.

Abiodun Your father was a pestilence on this land. He was a rebel and a usurper. With magic, he, mere Bashorun, bent my royal fathers to his will, and seized power for himself. Then he made this land into a theatre of war, of disease, hunger, and death. I, Abiodun, I was the one who changed all that. I put my foot down firmly on disorder, and established order in its place. I brought food to the famished families, replaced fear and uncertainty with the promise of progress and hope. I have spread peace across the land like an umbrella . . . To do all that, I had to kill the plague first. I, Abiodun, I braved your father's magic lantern and put my blade in his ribs. I killed him, and I killed Chaos . . .

Latoye No doubt you're proud of your achievement. But I have already told you my father has nothing to do with my actions.

Abiodun Then why?

Latoye Why? Why? Because! You're a builder. You killed my father because you needed his blood to mix your bricks.

Olori Latoye! Can't you see he's trying to save you?

Abiodun He's insolent, but we will save him yet. Tomorrow the public Crier will carry the words of your repentance and of your apology to the king; and that will be the end of the matter. You'll settle down to a normal life.

Latoye And grow to be like you, isn't it? Thank you.

Abiodun What did you say?

Latoye I said I don't want to grow into a fat maggot like you!

Abiodun Guards!

Olori Kabiyesi! Kabiyesi!

Latoye (*shouting*) My father was a plague, and you killed him. But you, Abiodun, you are the new plague! The new spot to be scraped out!

Abiodun (*incensed*)   I have ordered rain on kings, and it has poured down in whole floods to drown them! On men with coral beads and necklaces of ivory I have commanded fire, and they have been burnt out of history by the harvest of sheer lightning! And yet you, you mere inconsequential ant, you dare to defy me!

Latoye   Boast away, man! It's another of your royal rights.

Abiodun   If that Aresa doesn't—

Olori   Kabiyesi, wait, wait, please! (*Waves the tormented guards back into the wings.*) Give him another chance! He is only a boy . . .

Abiodun   Shall the scorpion sting, and claim youth as an excuse? He wants to die, let him!

Olori   Are you mad, Latoye? Whom did you see first on waking, which carrier of bad luck? A king talks to you, and you answer with insults! Have you been cursed, and did your head not reject it. Why do you not listen to reason? Do you want to die?

Latoye   Die madam? Look at my muscles ripple with life. The blood pulses in them like chattering birds. But your time is up. The death that is coming is for you. Yes! Because the earth, fouled with your contagion, cries for cleansing! Your fat buttocks are the rotten weight of plague choking the neck of the nation and your smirking lips are full of the breath of germs and contamination. Soon it will be the last card and the cry will hit you where you hide in your safest corner. Last card! Last card! And you will shudder in all your bones because the storm will mount you and eat you up! Last card! Last . . . !

In his rage he has taken hold of the king, who has been so surprised that he has let him. Now, as the calabash crown falls off, the king throws the young man down brutally. Reaching for a sword, he grabs some piece of plank or iron, and he goes after the young man.

Olori (*intervening*)   Kabiyesi! Kabiyesi! Kabiyesi! Think of
what you are doing! Grip your rage in both hands, don't let
it . . .

Abiodun (*bellowing*)   Out of my way! Shall we tolerate men
in our kingdom who say yes to chaos and push insulting
fingers in our nostrils? Out of my way!

Olori (*desperate*)   Guards! Guards! Come in! Don't let the king
profane himself. If he soils his hands with blood . . . !

The guards rush in.

Olori (*pointing to* **Latoye**)   Seize him! Kill him!

Latoye   Stop! Hold it right there! And listen! The Alafin has
summoned you as he summons his dogs. Bark, he orders you!
Bite! And you all leap forward, your fangs bared! But look at
me, I am one of you, dog never eats dog . . .

Olori   What are you waiting for? Kill him!

Latoye   Olori, *you* also reject me, you who were lifted up
from mud, but whose skin keeps the colour of your ancestry?
Back, guards! I am Latoye, you know my name! In the days
of war, I was a companion in the trenches. Or have you
forgotten? I was there on the long campaigns to Abomey,
from which only the real men returned! Soldiers, have you
forgotten? (*There is no sound except the slow approach of the guards.*)
And in the days of peace, did I cease to be a companion? Am
I not one of you, for whom peace became a betrayal? Friends,
but we are always together . . . !

Abiodun   And must I continue to hear this garbage? Can no
one silence him!

Aresa   Fo-o-or-ward!

The guards raise a war cry.

Latoye   Stop! The Alafin says 'shooo' and you lift your
wings and flap forward. Like weaverbirds! But pause, and
think!

Again the war cry.

I am Latoye! If I feign to the right . . .

Guards   You die!

Latoye   Nonsense! When the wind changes direction, all the branches bend with it! (*He lunges forward suddenly, and the men fall back.*) Ha! Ha! Alafin, you forget, I am the whetstone on which many of your men sharpened their swords of valour. And if I feign to the left . . .

Guards   Kill him!

Latoye   How foolish! The sapling which tries to halt the passage of the elephant will be plucked from its roots!

Again the men retreat.

Whenever the storm starts on a journey, not all the branches in the forest can bar its way! If the hill will not yield to the flow of the river, it will have its bosom furrowed! And now I say wind! And I am wind! I say river! I say elephant! Let all your forces melt before me! Freeze!

The guards freeze.

Abiodun   Ah! The toad puffs its belly, and boasts of growing fatter! Will self-deception hide the festering sore in Edun's arse? Latoye, you bushrat, you have challenged the king of the forests to combat, now watch the lion gobble his prey!

Slowly the Alafin begins to dance, mouthing incantations.

Latoye   Alafin, you brought out a cudgel, I laughed at it. How can you then threaten me with a whip! (*With a sense of urgency.*) Soldiers, listen to me! I am going to release you, but only after you release your minds. No one can do that for you but yourselves. Think! Think! with me! For it is that alone that will free you of your shackles.

As the Alafin's curse takes effect, his body and those of the guards react spasmodically with growing frequency through his speech, as if rebounding from a blow.

Look around you. Look into your past, look into your future. What do you see? Always the same unending tale of

oppression. Of poverty, hunger, squalor and disease! Why?
Ah, you and your people, you are the soil on which the
Alafin's tree is nourished, tended until it is overladen with
fruit! And yet, when you stretch out your hands, there are no
fruits for you! Why? Only *your* limbs are gaunt with work and
want, only *your* faces are wrinkled and hollow with sweating
and not getting! Alafin and his men are fed and flourishing,
but they continue to steal your lands. They are rich, their
salaries swell from the burden of *your* taxes! Their stores are
bursting, *your* children beg on the streets. I am begging you,
please, fly out of your narrow nests. Come follow me, raise a
song to freedom! NOW!

The guards break out of their trance and rush forward.

Guards Freedom!

Latoye Freedom! The king has called you out to eat. Eat
him!

*The soldiers rush forward, but **Yajin**'s rush is faster. She joins hands
with the other women except **Olori**, to protect the Alafin.*

Yajin No! Save the king! Quick, form a tight cordon with
me around his royal presence. Shield him! Soldiers, we are
women, but the spirit of our ancestors shall make us strong!
Yes, their blood within us defies your rebellion!

The soldiers are taken aback.

Aresa Yajin, this is not part of the play. Are you rewriting
it? I warn you, it will make no difference. You will be . . . !

Olori (*coming in front of the women*) Enough! I am the Olori. I
am Kabiyesi's first and foremost wife, mother of the palace
and you are my children. Let me be the first to give account.

Latoye Olori . . .

Olori This world is not of our making. We inherited it. The
world is as it has always been. Will you turn it upside down?

Ayaba (*stepping forward*) Eeewo! The world shall not spoil in
our time! (*Saluting.*) Ka-a-biyesi!

With a slow, regal dance, they begin to sing.

> Aye o ni fo mo wa lori
> Aye nyi lo boronboro
> Aye o ke gbajare e gba mi
> Mo se bi didun lo ndun fun
> Eru Oba ni wo ba – Oba to . . . !

Olori (*translating*)
> The seasons pass:
> We do not hear the groan of the world
> It shall be in our life time!

Ayaba (*singing*)
> Aye o ni fo mo wa lori
> Igba nlo titi ayeraye
> Igba kii lu opa Oranmiyan
> Mo se bi iyi lo mbu kun . . .
> Eru Oba ni mo ba – Oba to!

Olori
> The seasons change:
> They do not crack the plinth of Oranmiyan
> They only add to its respect:
> The world shall not spoil on our head!

Ayaba (*singing*)
> Aye o ni fo mo wa lori
> Okun gbogbo o yeye ntu ye
> Ibi okun o tayun losi
> Mo se bi iyi lo mbu kun . . .
> Eru Oba ni mo ba – Oba to!

Olori
> The sea ages:
> Tides do not corrode the coral:
> They only add to its adornment . . .
> The world shall not spoil in our time!

Ayaba (*singing*)
> Aye o ni fo mo wa lori
> Aye o ni fo mo wa lori
> Eji welewele oju Olorun

Ko ni koju sanmon ojin koto
Mo sebi iyi lo mbu kun
Eru Oba ni mo ba – Oba to!

Olori

The sky weeps:
Rains do not furrow the face of heaven;
Rains only polish its glitter:
The world will not break in our time

Encouraged by their singing, the Alafin steps forward. The **Ayaba** *now breaks into royal encomium, and sing softly throughout his speech.*

Abiodun (*slowly he goes into a dance, reminiscent of the ritual occasions he recalls in his speech*)   Well, what are you waiting for? Animals! Spiteful rodents! You talk of the king's demanding, but will the leopard feed on grass? You complain of toiling, but when the land withers in a season of white spots, and Obaluaye thirsts for blood, whose voice will pronounce the message, whose hand wield the knife that will spill the vital fluid? Answer me! When the season insists that *bata* drums be unleashed like hunting dogs, and Sango roams the land with his double-headed axe, whose body will revive the ancient dance to calm the fiery eyes, stay the menace of thunder? Answer! When the new moon summons into chorus the sixteen voices of Igbin, and the earth lays open for its ritual of cleansing, tell me, who will chant Orisanla's sacred incantation?

As his speech continues, the guards are ordered forward by **Aresa** *into a mute scene. Well choreographed, it depicts them in multiple scenes of slavery and drudgery. The effect is to free the guards of sympathy for the Alafin.*

Ah, when our virgins ripen and embellish themselves with camwood and coral, and the young male suitors dance into the square, their voices rough and hungry, whose flesh will receive the voice of the Orunmila to fertilise the vows of alliance? Or shall our seeds be left to shrivel and die in our bosoms, burn up our lives . . . ?

Latoye   Enough!

*The guards burst into laughter. The Alafin, frightened now, shrinks back into the midst of the **Ayaba**, who, cutting off their song, begin a dance of Refuge. This is a dance in which the quarry attempts to ward off an attacking beast, and the music is created with their arms and feet, tongues and bangles. The guards close in gradually during **Latoye**'s speech, doing the Dance of the Attacking Beast.*

For centuries you have shielded yourselves with the gods. Slowly, you painted them in your colour, dressed them in your own cloak of terror, injustice and bloodlust. But Olori, we know now how Edumare himself arranged his heaven, on which model he moulded the earth. To each of the gods, Edumare gave power, and fragility, so that none of them shall ever be a tyrant over the others, and none a slave. Ogun of the forge, king of Ire and outcast; Sango of the flaming eyes, king and captive; Oya, beautiful, unfaithful like women; the great mother Yemoja, whose weakness is vanity; and oh a thousand other Orisa, all the assurance that power shall not be corrupted by abundant privilege, that neither good nor evil shall be the monopoly of a few. Yes, Abiodun, yes, Olori! Sango eats, Ogun eats, and so do the ebora of the forest! But in your reign Abiodun, the elephant eats, and nothing remains for the antelope! The buffalo drinks, and there is drought in the land! Soldiers, seize him! He is ripe for eating!

*They seize the Alafin and his wives, and begin to spin them round and round with growing frenzy, chanting as in a sacrificial ritual. Leading them is **Aresa**.*

Aresa   We worship Osanyin, god of secrets, but if he stands in the path of justice, we haul him into the stream! For all those who seek to unbalance the world, to rearrange it only according to their own greed, there is only one remedy, Abiodun! Death! (*Shouting as one possessed, he brings down his sword on the head of the Alafin and begins to kick his fallen body savagely.*) Die, pig! Die like an animal! And you, Yajin! Bitch! Here's the the moment of reckoning! Die.

*For some time **Leje**, **Funlola**, **Bisi** and **Yetunde** have stopped acting and now watch **Mokan** with amazement. Finally they throw themselves on him to stop him.*

Funlola/Others   It's only a play! Stop now!

Mokan (*subsiding*)   You're right. It would be too sweet for them to die now. It would only spoil the fun. (*To guards.*) Arrest them!

Handcuffs are clamped on the wrists of **Sontri** *and* **Yajin**.

Yajin   What . . . what is this, Mokan?

Mokan   It means the game's ended, Yajin.

Sontri   Can you explain what all this about? These . . . (*Handcuffs.*)

Mokan   Patience, I'll explain in a minute. See? (*He throws down a badge.*) You recognise it?

General gasp of shock and amazement.

Sontri   The secret police!

Mokan   Yes, the Special Squad. These are my men. I must say they are also accomplished musicians. Our interests are in internal insurrection, actual, nascent, or merely projected. So Sontri, into which category shall I put your Farmers' Movement?

Yajin   Mokan, no! Not you! Not . . . (*Breaks down sobbing.*)

Mokan   You're right. Not me. I once believed that, didn't I? It was an age of great and small betrayals, but I said, no, it couldn't be me. I gave my trust, faith everything. And what happened to the woman who took it all? Ha ha! How I've waited for this moment! How many months of planning and watching! I even took to clowning! And wasn't it worth it, my God, just to see you now! Like drenched weaverbirds!

Leje   Mokan . . .

Mokan   You have always been out of it Leje, let's keep it so. You can't understand. I said to myself again and again, what would be the best moment to hit them, to hurt them as bad as they did me? And I joined the Police. And I watched and listened. So you'll seize power for the farmers! So you'll arm them and proclaim a new republic! Who will be

President? You?

Sontri   Any man of their own choice, Mokan. But . . .

Mokan   You, for whom fidelity is like a fairytale! But how simple-minded you all are! Do you think we are dumb then, those of us in whose hands the power is vested at present?

Sontri   There's nothing you can do to stop the birds from singing. Mokan, the revolution is already on wing, you cannot halt it!

Mokan   That's your illusion. I've acted the play with you to the end, haven't I? But see, who's in chains now? Like all dreamers, you forget, don't you, that dreams always have a resting-place, in flesh, and that flesh is vulnerable . . .

Yajin   I despise you Mokan! I am sorry to have ever loved you.

Mokan   Your love! Speak rather of your treachery. It strengthened me! Those who win a game once and relax are only stupid, for there is always a second game. Enough of this jabbering. In the name of the law and the legitimate government of this country, I arrest you both for felony, conspiracy and sedition. Let's go.

Sontri   And so, for a trite affair of your little vengeance, you betray a whole life of dedication! You throw away our vows to help the poor and the needy, to build a nation . . .

Mokan   You are the traitors, trying to pull the nation down. That was why I waited and bided my time. I said, what's the moment to hit them? And the answer was really simple: on the eve of their wedding! How's that for a laugh! And then, quite fortuitously, came your play, Yajin! No, there will be no wedding tomorrow, nor ever, not as long as I am alive! Men, this is the end of our assignment. I congratulate you. Let us go. But with dancing and singing. In full celebration. Nobody out there must suspect a thing! Let's go.

They begin to sing the song 'Tun Mi Gbe' that opened Part One and move towards the door. Blackout.

Epilogue

Didun nile oloyin . . .
Say I am the thread
And you the shuttle
. . . in the loom of the state

Same situation. About an hour later. **Leje** *is seen seated, drinking alone.*
Enter **Funlola**.

Funlola (*surprised*) You, Leje!

Leje Ah, there you are. I won.

Funlola (*menacing*) Won what?

Leje The bet.

Funlola Which bet?

Leje I made a bet.

Funlola I see.

Leje With myself. Look at the cards. I wagered that you
would come back here.

Funlola And so?

Leje My sixth sense. I don't know how to lose.

Funlola (*going towards him*) There's something else you're
going to win very soon.

Leje What?

Funlola This! (*She slaps him, knocking the bottle out of his mouth.*)

Leje (*exaggerated alarm*) God save the booze!

Funlola (*angry*) Get out of this house, you hear? You're no
longer welcome here, you drunken smelling rat! Go away and
join your clever friend in the barracks!

Leje My friend?

Funlola Yes, your friend, the big Police dog with the

poisonous belly of a rattlesnake. Oh, you think you're triumphant, don't you? But you just wait! Wait till morning when Yajin's father sees the Police boss! The whole world will be too small to contain both of you!

Leje   Yajin's father has heard?

Funlola   Scared already? Bisi and Yetunde have gone to see him now. And when he hears ... If I were you I'd start running.

Leje   Thanks for the advice, but you're not me. (*Takes up cards.*) Care for a game?

Funlola   I am telling you to clear out of ...

Leje   I will, I will.

Funlola   Clear out now!

Leje   Softly, softly ...

Funlola   GET OUT! And may the beer you've swallowed here poison all your veins, give you a slow painful death.

Leje (*after a pause*)   Tell me, Funlola ... how deep are you? How sincere?

Funlola   What are you talking about?

Leje (*stands up. His voice and his walk are suddenly different. Almost frightening, so that* **Funlola** *recoils*)   I'm talking about Sontri. And Yajin. If I put a secret in your palm, like this ... (*Takes her hand, stretched out.*) – are you capable of closing your fist tight on it, hidden, until you need it to buy compassion?

Funlola   What secret? What's all this about?

Leje   Yajin will be free in the morning. Her father will make sure of it. And if she comes out, Sontri will also have to be released: Yajin will force that out of her father. Or do you doubt it?

Funlola (*looking at him*)   No. Not now that you say it. I hadn't thought it that way.

Leje   No doubt. I am hoping Sontri will gain from the

experience. We need anger to start a revolution, even a great anger, but once it has started, it will get rid of us, unless we meet it with cunning and compassion. That's why Sontri needed the arrest, Mokan was helping us without knowing it.

Funlola Helping you? Who are you?

Leje You will know in a moment. But first, you! Who are *you*?

Funlola Me?

Leje I was shown some of your work. On your canvas, suffering ceases to be an abstract thing. It screams. Those gnarled limbs, the hollow eyes, the sunken, furrowed faces of the poor . . .

Funlola You don't . . . approve?

Leje Your brush is relentless. The world you capture is the truth, yes, but only the truth of a bystander.

Funlola I . . . I've often dreamt of remaking the world.

Leje But you don't believe it can happen?

Funlola No, pure illusion. Fantasy.

Leje It can, you know. If we work together, all of us, we can remake the world.

Funlola Like the weaverbirds?

Leje Both the chattering and the song.

Funlola In our fragile nests.

Leje Listen, we always say the world is as we met it. But it isn't true! While we sleep, while we fold our arms, there are always a few greedy men who remould the world in their own particular image. And when we wake, the world is already different: there are new fences around us, new chains on our wrists . . .

Funlola Who are you, Leje? Who are you?

Leje Like the weaverbird! In our crowded nests! Funlola, a

man ought to be able to stand up once, even once only, to say
NO to the universal acceptance, someone with a little anger
and a little courage, to stand up and make a little gesture of
refusal – No!

Funlola   No!

Leje   No! But you see, the weaverbirds accept it all, and
everywhere everyday we all are throwing our arms down,
getting down to crawl on our bellies like lizards. We say yes
to everything, we say yes too soon, too easily, because we long
desperately to settle down and rest even before the fight is
done . . . my card, your card last card, check! And the game
is lost . . . (*His voice trails off.*)

Funlola (*going to him*)   Not me, Leje, not me. I have forsaken
all that!

Leje   Yes, and what have you put in its place? Fantasy, the
farthest corner of the nest. Listen, we can bring you fulfilment
if you join us. We can fill your inner craving with the warm
comradeship of the downtrodden. Join us, we can use your
talent and your energy, your deep sincerity. Join the Farmers'
Movement.

Funlola   The Farmers . . .

Leje   Yes. So you know me now.

Funlola   You're Osongongon, the Farmers' leader!

Leje   A nickname. I have many others.

Funlola   You're the one wanted by the Police!

Leje   The Police are ignorant. What is a single man in
revolution? Once a movement begins, in the search for justice,
it will run its course, with or without those who serve to spark
it off. History will not remember us.

Funlola   So why do you want me?

Leje   The movement needs all capable people. The whole
world, you see, is a farm, and all hands must toil both to
cultivate it and eat of its fruit.

Funlola And Mokan?

Leje (*laughing*) My good friend! He keeps me well informed! As they say, if we knew everything about our friends . . .

Funlola (*laughs*) You know, I had always longed to know you. For a long time you were a dream I cradled in my sleep. And now, suddenly you are a reality . . .

Leje Well?

Funlola I am afraid. See, how I shiver!

Leje (*putting his arms round her*) I shall protect you.

Funlola But suppose . . . suppose I am past belief?

Leje Nonsense. No one ever walks that far. Not even in despair. No one voluntarily walks beyond firm ground. That is, without drowning.

Funlola But if they had something to cling to?

Leje Like your art? A means merely to keep afloat?

Funlola Compassion keeps the artist afloat.

Leje All right then, what I offer you is a chance to get your feet back on firm ground.

Funlola You know, you're so persuasive. But what if I wither? If the creative spirit dies in me?

Leje Impossible. You would already have put out roots. (*Smiles.*) Look, your concern is one I am familiar with. In my drive for recruitment, I call on, say, a carpenter, and he asks me: what if I lose my skill? Or, a blacksmith, who asks: what if the fight takes me on the road of exile? Of alienation? What will happen to the old forge, to the tools abandoned?

Funlola Yes? What will happen?

Leje Renewal, I always answer. No one who commits himself will ever be asked to break with his ancestral roots.

Funlola No?

Leje On the contrary! But seasons change, oppression and injustice resurface in new forms, and new weapons have to be devised to eliminate them.

Funlola   Your faith must run deep . . .

Leje   Listen, together, that's how the tribe renews itself, that's how we all survive, together . . .

Funlola   By giving one's life to the cause?

Leje   By extending that life into myriad seedlings.

Funlola   To get involved.

Leje   Like putting out new roots.

Funlola   To stake everything?

Leje   Like growing fresh leaves! Fresh leaves are the pride of the oak. (*He begins the dance.*)

Funlola   The oak is the pride of the forest. Still I prefer the palmtree.

Leje   All right, green fronds then! Green fronds are the pride of the palm! (*She accepts: they dance together.*)

Funlola   Rich palms are the pride of the farmer.

Leje   Good farmers are the pride of the state.

Funlola   Even if they are dressed in red, red the colour of blood?

Leje   Red is the colour of victory. Red feathers are the pride of the woodcock.

Funlola   Woodcocks are the pride of good hunters.

Leje   You see?

Funlola   Good hunters are the pride of the tribe.

Leje   Good hunters are good farmers.

Funlola   I surrender. You're a real tortoise!

Leje   Tortoise?

She pretends to suspend the dance, then laughing, resumes.

Funlola You've won me with your cunning.

Leje Okay, say I am a tortoise and you are ... er ...

Funlola Yes, Ijapa?

Leje A hare! Say you are a hare! Iwori Otura!

Funlola Say you're a tortoise and I a hare ...

Leje Say there's a famine and drought in the land ...

Funlola Say there's famine: Iwori Otura ...

Leje You're searching for food, you're thirsty and dry ...

Funlola Say there's a drought: Iwori Otura ...

Leje In your searching and thirsting,
I come across you: I am the Tortoise,
The great traveller ...

Funlola Please Mister Tortoise, my life's in your hands:
Iwori Otura: you've travelled the world
Lead me into safety, to fertile lands ...

Leje Iwori Otura: just hold my hand
And climb on my back:
I've travelled the world, I know them all,
Those fertile lands ...

Funlola Iwori Otura: be gentle with me,
I'm famished and weak, I'm just like a thread ...

Leje A thread in a loom? The loom of the state?
Say I am a shuttle ...

Funlola And I the thread?

Leje Iwori Otura: across the loom
If we dance as one,
I the shuttle and you the weft ...

Funlola Dancing together,
In the loom of the state: Iwori Otura ...

Leje We'll weave new patterns out of our world
And make of our dance a journey of hope ...

Funlola   You as the shuttle and I the weft . . .

Leje   Iwori Otura: across the loom . . .

Funlola   Our weave and our shuttle, body and soul . . .

Leje   Shall order the world in new designs . . .

Funlola   Shall order the world in fresh designs . . .

Leje   If we dance as one . . .

Funlola   If we strive together . . .

Leje   Iwori Otura!

Funlola   Iwori Otura, both you and me . . .

Both   Iwori Otura . . .

Both   Iwori Otura . . .

Both   Iwori Otura . . . !

Lights begin to fade out slowly, until finally the two are left in a spotlight. The scene lingers. Then suddenly from everywhere, sounds of drumming and singing. The actors, all in their normal dress now, dance in to a movement of harvesting. They chant the Farmers' Anthem. Finally, the audience joins in.

The play does NOT end.

The Farmers' Anthem:

> When everyone's a farmer
> We'll grow enough food
> In the land
> No insurrection
> When all are fed
> Less exploitation
> You eat all you need

Refrain:
> So clear the forest
> Turn up the soil
> Add fertilisers
> Bring in the seeds

Take out the corn
Bring in the yams
Plant them in earth
Tend them with care
Watch them grow with time
In season
Harvest is coming
In the land.

When everyone's a farmer
We'll wipe out the pests
In the land
No more injustice
Labour's for all
No more oppression
All hands to hoe

Refrain.

When everyone's a farmer
We'll burn out the weeds
In our lives
No alienation
Working on the farm
But brothers and sisters
Sharing everything

Refrain.

Glossary

A. Songs

The songs for the play were composed variously by Demola Onibon-Okuta, Tunji Oyelana, and myself. Wale Ogunyemi and I translated the 'Song of the Ayaba', while Jimmy Solanke composed the music.

The translations of the Yoruba songs which I offer here are not exact translations of course. But they convey the meanings I intend, as well as my suggestions for melodic beats, to help directors who may not be familiar with the Yoruba language.

page 13: '*Tun mi gbe, etc . . .*'

Sing my worth,
Oh husband
Sing my worth
A new bride
Brings new excitement
Oh my husband
Sing my worth!

15: '*Yajin o to nrele oko, etc . . .*'

Yajin is wedding tomorrow
And how like gold she glows
The jewels on her arms and feet
Tease with Beauty's secrets.

16: '*Eee aya won lode o, etc . . .*'

Eee, how rare
To find a wife sincere
Eee what care
You need to give to her!

29: '*Obangiji se o ngbohun mi o, etc . . .*'

Almighty God, can you hear my voice?
Let me have my share of the cake of life

When I steal, let me earn a chieftaincy
And if it's a woman, send the husband to jail
And let my son become a (military) governor!
Oh almighty God . . . eee, please hasten to my pleas . . .

34: '*Yajin to nrele oko, etc . . .*'
(playful variation on the first verse on p. 15)

Yajin is wedding tomorrow
And arms as if for war
Her beads and sash like amulets
Powders on both legs and wrists!

B. Yoruba words and phrases

abi   well! Isn't it?
a-wu!   come on!
didun nile alaya   sweet is the husband's home! (A deliberate
   play by Mokan on the phrase following.)
didun nile oloyin   an idiomatic expression meaning, literally,
   'sweet is the home of the seller of honey'
ebora   spirit; a kind of egungun masquerade
edun   colobus monkey
Esungboro   'Devil in town!'
Ifa   god of divination
igbin   a kind of drum, normally beaten for Obatala
iwori otura   normally, an odu of Ifa which signals the success
   of a love affair; chanted here in form of an incantation to
   herald the love between Sontri and Yajin, and suggest its
   successful outcome
iyawo   wife
iyawo oju ona   betrothed
'*J.J.C., e kabo!*'   'Johnny Just Come, welcome!' The term is of
   course for those who arrive from Europe bringing some
   affected mannerisms, especially in their diction.
jijo iya ka woran, panla, etc . . .   a mocking, abusive song
   basically saying that the subject is a fool
kobo   the smallest monetary piece in Nigeria
Obaluaye   god of small-pox

odu   a verse of Ifa divinatory poetry

orisa   name for a god, or gods

Orisanla   god of creation and purity; same as Obatala

Orunmila   god of divination, same as Ifa, above

oyinbo   a white man

Sango   god of thunder and lightning

sekere   a calabash drum strung with beads or cowries and used for music

Soponna   small-pox; or, like Obaluaye, the god responsible for the disease

The Rise and Shine of Comrade Fiasco

Andrew Whaley

Characters

Chidhina, *ex-combatant, mid–late twenties*
Jungle, *gregarious, 'mudyiwa*, forties*
Febi, *trader, ex-chimbwido, late thirties*
Fiasco, *ageless, lost liberator*

The play takes place over one weekend in a prison cell in the Lowveld of Zimbabwe at the beginning of summer 1986. There is no interval.

* See Glossary on p. 134 for translations of southern African phrases and slang.

Darkness. The long hum of a note in monotone. Repeated three or four times. Finally the note moves into a musical phrase that the actors join in together. This tune, arranged and rearranged throughout the play, comes back as a continuous melodic theme time and again. The music, just voices, rises in crescendo as a single spotlight comes up directly overhead centre stage, backlighting a hump shape – two red blankets covering four actors who are interlocked, shoulder to shoulder, head to head, in a sort of circle.

As the music gets stronger, they rise, from their haunches, like a basic organic form. It moves with the rhythm of the voices. It turns once. Suddenly – with feet snapping the ground – one of the actors dips out from under the blanket, out of the ring and faces audience . . .

Chidhina   Tonight! . . . (*He cartwheels across the stage.*) . . . history takes a tumble!

Chidhina *is a young man, late twenties, an ex-combatant. He is in prison khakis. But even wearing these, he has an air of self-possession, a feeling of danger about to be unleashed. He moves into a narrator's spotlight.*

There was a fight in Musongosongo Bar . . . That night, three of us arrested and thrown into this prison cell. Hot as a hell in the lowveld, where the Save flows. Three of us. Me. Chidhina. Handcuffed for clapping a cop.

Actors (*under blanket*)   COP! COP! COP! (*Like the sound of being hit.*)

Chidhina   A fight, in my mind, friend, means war. And Jungle. (*He pulls **Jungle** out of the blanket ring.*) Aaai! That man drink. He discovers bars like flying ants find streetlights. And Febi. (*He pulls **Febi** out of the blanket.*) So you ask: what is a woman doing in stocks with two drunk men? Shortage of space because the stocks are fully packed? Or because they throw her here like a whore? More like, I've got a caterpillar brain, and you need a woman to give this story wings. (*She elbows him in the ribs.*) Febi adds flesh to the bones. She makes the story feel . . . more rounded.
(*Suddenly serious, he turns pointing slowly at **Fiasco** who is completely draped and hidden by the blanket.*) Then comes the fourth. Fiasco!

Freedom Fighter. Fiction, fake or fact. Comrade Fiasco. The
man who came out of a cave, seven years after the fact of
independence, the memories of war still clinging to his skull
like spoils; (**Fiasco** *under the blanket begins whispering, dislocated and
menacing.*) when the gunfire had long ceased; when Zimbabwe
was already free; already flying through its infancy into
adolescence; when history had been forgotten, he creeps up
from behind, following, following.
Just as you think all that time gone is like a museum and you
turn round to the future and go forward with confident strides
– suddenly! something's following and whispering, Fiasco,
Fiasco, Fiasco (*The hissing and whispering get stronger until here*
Fiasco *turns and goes, arms outstretched under the blanket, melting into
the back wall. We never see his face.*) and the past is no longer
another country.

Fiasco *has gone.* **Febi** *and* **Jungle** *move from their positions, take up
a blanket each and sleep on the floor.* **Jungle** *snores.*

Out of nowhere, Fiasco appeared – that night . . . But I'm
jumping. First we were three. And I was feeling pressed . . .
yes . . . badly pressed. (*He starts pacing up and down as if he needs
to use the bucket in the corner.*)
One two three hold it!
Right now, stand still. Take it easy. Now see if you can keep
it up. No! No good. Got to move. Think! One thousand two
thousand three thousand, good boy, four thousand, think of
something else, think. Think! Save it. Save it for a rainy day.
(*Closes his eyes.*) There. Better. Don't rush. Make the body obey
the mind. Good one, my man, excellent. The brain is a
powerful thing. You can do anything, make the body obey,
you been through worse . . . no . . . no . . . it can't wait,
can't . . . (*He dashes over to the bucket, as if he's about to sit on it . . .*)

Jungle (*rising rapidly from sleep*)   Don't use that.

Chidhina   Emergency!

Jungle   This is not the time.

Chidhina   My body doesn't tell time.

Jungle   Better you find a cork.

Chidhina   Come on, man, sleep. Close your eyes.

Jungle   I can't.

Chidhina   Pretend.

Jungle   How can I sleep with you . . .

Chidhina   Put your face under the blanket (*Tries to throw the blanket over* **Jungle***'s face.*)

Jungle   You think that can hide something you are doing there?

Chidhina   Please. Dream, baba. Just throw your mind into some thoughts of pleasure.

Jungle   I am not tired.

Chidhina   Just for once please. Feel exhausted, baba. Like you were five minutes ago.

Jungle   (*growling*) You young men, where is your discipline? Wait till morning.

Chidhina   It can't wait. There must be action. Now! (*He moves decisively.*)

Jungle   Never. (*Getting up fast.*) Did independence come one time? Mzukuru, we waited.

Chidhina   Oh, voetsek. We could still be waiting. Aaag, I'm going, never mind. (*He heads for the bucket.*)

Jungle *jumps up and sits on the bucket, occupying it.*

Jungle   Nikkis.

Chidhina   Come on, get off.

Jungle   No.

Chidhina   Let me use force then.

Jungle   I am here first.

Chidhina   I declared first, my intention.

Jungle   Who intention? For me, this is real, never mind intention.

Chidhina   Mdala, I will clap you.

Jungle   You try, I shit in your face, you watch.

Chidhina   Only one thing stops me giving you five, because you are standing in my way . . .

Jungle   . . . sitting in your way.

Chidhina   One thing: you are old and I'll mess you up.

Jungle   You mess up your pants first.

Chidhina   I'll teach you. I will shit right there in the corner, no worry. (*He heads for the corner.*)

Jungle *jumps up from the bucket and tries to hold him back.*

Jungle   You don't don't, you hear.

Chidhina   I will.

Jungle   I call sergeant.

In the mini fracas, they wake up **Febi**, *she is mad angry.*

Febi (*screaming*)   What is going on?

Chidhina   Febi, he took the bucket. I was there first.

Febi   Why can't you people sleep?

Chidhina   That's what I am telling him, Febi. All he wants to do is wake up and make noise.

Jungle (*seeing* **Febi**, *smiles lecherously*)   What a luck!
Hello, my darling, very happy to meet you. What are you doing here?

Febi   What do you think?

Jungle   Police are looking up, with equality in prisons!

Febi   I am sleeping.

Jungle   Heavens are smiling tonight – just us. Together.

Chidhina   And me.

Jungle (*to* **Chidhina**) This is private, please. (*To* **Febi**.) Don't worry, lovey. Just give me a blanket.

Febi (*kicking him away*) Piss off. Chidhina, get this man off.

Chidhina Old man, don't even think about it.

Jungle (*to* **Febi**) I was protecting you, lovey, from this one using a bucket.

Febi Bucket? For what?

Jungle Convenience. Is it convenient to use a bucket?

Febi You stink of bar.

Jungle And him? His stink was going to be worse than worst – using a bucket? . . . All right, let him drop his peanuts anywhere there. (*To* **Chidhina**.) Carry on, young man. (*Back to* **Febi**.) We will be kissing here independently.

Febi I don't want!

Jungle Don't be grumbling, dear. This is once in a lifetime, secret between you and me, God is my witness.

Chidhina And me.

Febi I don't want!

Jungle Just once. I have seen you at Musongosongo drinking Black Label.

Febi Lemonade!

Jungle All right, sweetheart, I believe your lemonade. (*Whispering.*) I propose you, quiet as a bicycle.

Chidhina *grunts, amused.*

Jungle Young man, cork your ears.

Febi I am not a bitch! (*Screaming.*) I am not a bitch! Not a bitch!

Jungle (*blocking his ears*) Noise down, noise down, Doris.

Febi I am not Doris.

Jungle   I was thinking you were Doris Day, darling, out of Hollywood.

Chidhina   Her name is Febi. Don't insult her with American rubbish.

Jungle   I am praising her.

Chidhina   You are roughing her like a whore.

Febi (*getting up*)   Never mind, Chidhina. If it is Hollywood it's okay. No harm. (*She brushes herself down, secures her extensions.*) But beware of over-friendship.

Jungle   Not over, dear. Just friends.

Chidhina   So don't forget you got me here also, mdala.

Jungle   Do you know Bill Crosby, Louis Armstrong, Nat King Cole, Oscar Peterson? They never using rough tactics. that is from where I learned: in life, I stay musically cool. I'll sing you, Dori . . . Febi. (*He starts singing 'Hello Dori', based on Louis Armstrong's song.*)

Chidhina (*disgruntled, sits on the bucket*)   Are you trying to punish us? No one is convicted yet . . .

Jungle   You see, Febi? He is trying the bucket again.

Febi   What for?

Chidhina (*getting off*)   Forget it. Lost interest.

Jungle   Teach you. You win some and some you lose.

Febi   Same in football.

Chidhina   You should know – with the legs of a striker.

Febi (*rushing to kick him*)   I'll show you a penalty kick for offsides!

Jungle   Hey, hey, hey. Cool. Musically cool, my darlings.

Chidhina (*pushing* **Jungle**)   Blow the whistle on it. The sweet music finished when you pulled the trumpet from the trumpet player's mouth.

Jungle He was playing shit. (*Scornfully.*) Maswerasei Mumbo Jumbo Jazz Wizards. Since when did a wizard sound like a bullfrog? Talking was better than that . . .

Febi (*interrupting*) And you, Chidhina, smashing a policeman. For what? To put us all in trouble. (*Walks away.*)

Chidhina What was a woman doing there? (*He taunts her, handles her.*) Eh? You! Drinking Black Label. Like a lady!

Febi I'm not a bitch! Lemonade!

Chidhina Could be Malawi Shandy. Facts are stubborn.

Jungle I am going to report to the commissioner, putting a lady in a cell with hooligans. I'm going, true, eh, Doris?

Febi (*angry*) Febi!

Chidhina (*sick of hearing **Jungle**'s confusion with names*) Wrap it up. Hey old man, what is YOUR name?

Febi Chidhina, always for arguing and funny games.

Chidhina No. What's his name?

Jungle What you mean?

Chidhina You got a name.

Jungle (*pause, embarrassed*) George.

Chidhina How George?

Jungle *mumbles and turns away.*

Chidhina You like George?

Febi Of course he likes.

Chidhina What's your NAME, George?

Febi Uncle George!

Chidhina How d'you get an English name, George?

Jungle I was born George.

Chidhina How d'you get the King's name, Uncle George?

Jungle (*angry and sulking*)   Because. Correct! King George! What of it? I am allowed.

Chidhina   I like it. Uncle George, Uncle George, Uncle George. Uncle George! – Jungle George!! I like it (*Savouring the word.*) Jungle.

Febi   It's history, Chidhina.

Chidhina (*teasing*)   Aaai . . . It's very confusing. In Africa? It's very good King George got here because African names are trouble, too long, I tell you. We need short names here. George. Peter. John. Nice names. Because the baas, he likes something quick, something fast. 'George! Come here! George! Fagga table. Checha! Checha!' (*He laughs.*) George, well done. Keep it sweet.

Jungle (*in sulky protest*)   And what of Elizabeth? Is it sweet? How long is the queen's name?

Chidhina   Is George queen?

Jungle   He is King.

Chidhina   So are you queen, Jungle?

Febi   He is King.

Chidhina   Therefore kings have short names. And queens are long.

Febi   They can be long.

Chidhina   Because why? Because you still think 1940s and 50s. He still wants colonial names. Because murungu wants you short and sweet.

Jungle   I am independent than you!

Chidhina   With George!

Febi   What of his zinc?

Chidhina   What does your zinc say, Jungle?

Jungle   I gave it inside.

Chidhina   You gave your name away? (*Shakes his head.*)

Jungle   Of course. Do you think you can keep a zinc when you come to jail?

Febi   Majohni took it.

Chidhina   They did you a favour, Jungle. Now, you can start clean. New name.

Jungle   Yes, African name.

Chidhina   So you have an African name.

Jungle   I do.

Chidhina   Now you give it to Majohni. (*Goes round* **Jungle**.) How are you going to learn, Jungle? Giving away names to Britain, now policemen . . .

Febi   We all gave our names. Jungle, you, me. Constable has got them. My identity, yours, his, one by the other, one on top of the other. (*She begins repeating in an under-chorus 'zinc, zinc, zinc' and moving her hands like metal discs being shuffled.*)

Jungle (*quickly to* **Febi**, *coming close next to her*)   You see? CLINKING side by side. (*He joins the 'zinc' chorus.*)

Chidhina   You right. Maybe they got trays of them. Zinc mountains with your face and mine . . .

Jungle   African names . . .

Chidhina   Piled on top of the other . . .

They build in crescendo – 'zinc, zinc, zinc, zinc' – one on top of the other in a syncopated mime.

Febi   . . . drowning in names . . .

Jungle   . . . one sliding against the other . . .

Febi   . . . never meeting . . .

Chidhina   What if they melted?

They stop, see the glob of metal melted.

All those zincs melting into one soft metal?

Febi   Then you would be nameless. Who is going to identify you?

Jungle   So who wants an ID?

Chidhina   Exactly! Who wants foreign names? We choose. Own name. Own voice.

Jungle   Exactly! Can a zinc speak?

Febi   It does. What of deaf and dumb? He just shows his card. Finish.

Chidhina   I don't need a zinc to talk. I don't need my face pressed. That thing doesn't even look like me.

Jungle   It looks like someone squashed a frog on it.

Febi   With my family extended like that, we could even build a scotchcart with all that zinc.

Jungle   It's a waste, sister. We could be making Zimbabwe-assembled zinc cars instead of squashing our faces.

Febi   Down with zincs!

They come together.

Jungle   Forward with scanias!

Chidhina   (*Picking up the rhythm*)   Down with zincs! Pamberi ne scanias!

They all start chanting together, building confidently. Then suddenly **Chidhina** *runs to one of the walls and shouts.*

Down with walls! Forward with Freedom!

The chant builds, as three actors twist and stomp around the cell. Suddenly a man comes flying onto the stage, dressed in a ragged cotton wrap and a holey red jersey. He bumps **Chidhina** *in mid-flight. The others turn and look at him, amazed. The man looks terrified as he tries to become accustomed to the light. It is* **Fiasco**.

Chidhina   (*charged with excitement*)   King George!

Febi   Where did he come from?

Jungle   England?

Febi   Do they wear dresses there?

Chidhina (*flings himself prostrate*)   Your majesty, I'd like you to meet a subject, in fact your namesake, he thinks so highly of you. Your Georgeliness. Georgo, meet Georgo.

Jungle   Ah, pfutseki. Was King George going outside wearing night dresses? (*He goes to* **Fiasco**.) My name is Jungle, excuse me. And you are?

Febi   His Georginess. (*Clapping in welcome. No response. She stops.*)

After a pause, they look at **Fiasco**.

Chidhina   But this is no chef! A chef would have spoken by now.

Febi   Maybe he can't speak. Your ID!

Jungle   Excuse me, shamwari. Have you got an ID? We like to speak of real names here, held with zinc, zinc, only zinc, chete chete.

Fiasco *does not respond.*

Jungle   I think Majohni took it.

Febi (*to* **Fiasco**)   Sweetness, are you some kind of shebeen queen?

Jungle (*strongly*)   Why you putting on dresses for prison?

Febi   Maybe he's a ghost.

Jungle   A witch travelling by skirts.

Febi   He must speak up – whether he's king, queen, I don't care, he must tell people who he is and what he is doing.

Chidhina (*puts his hand up to quell them and moves to* **Fiasco**)   What is your name?

Jungle (*pulling* **Chidhina** *and* **Febi** *back*)   Leave it. He is dangerous. (*To* **Fiasco**.) You must get out of here. You are disturbing a quiet place.

Febi (*accusing*)   It is a criminal this one.

Chidhina   And what do you think we are, in here?

Febi   We are decent, clean. It is just by accident we are here. But this . . . I don't like.

Chidhina   Wait. (*He goes to* **Fiasco**.) We are three here. Febi, Jungle and Chidhina. There. Do you mind introducing yourself?

Jungle *clears off,* **Febi** *and* **Chidhina** *stand their ground as* **Fiasco** *remains wild and silent.*

Chidhina   Easy. Your name. Just your name and then you can go and sit in a corner in your skirt.

Silence.

Febi   Are you mad? Uri benzi here? Did you hear? (*She goes and shouts in his ear.*) What is your name, Your Georgesty?

Fiasco *runs away.*

Chidhina (*getting irritated*)   You heard what the lady said. (*Peers into his eye.*) This guy hasn't got a full chicken house. (*Advancing on* **Fiasco**.) Bra, did you leave your tongue also in the safety deposity?

Fiasco   No!

Febi   He can speak!

Chidhina   Your name. No one is asking you to join parliament. Just name. Proudly, clearly, tell us who you are.

Fiasco *finally darts away and bursts out.*

Fiasco   I am not a name! Why? Why? Why? Why do you ask me? What did I do? What is your role? You want to interrogate me. You want to kill me. SHUT UP! (*He puts his hands over his ears unable to take any more noise. He points at them threateningly.*) I am one brain, not three. You are trying to confuse me with three types of brain. You can't. You can't. Keep away! Don't touch! I can go back any time. I do not need followers. Who are you? And you? (*He lunges at* **Jungle** *who darts away. Then, quietly, almost to himself:*) I am a man among men, from the mountains. Do you know me? I have in me heaven and earth. I teach myself the world how it is going, and whether it is leaning to one side or the other. (*He leans like the world, from side to side. He goes slowly, almost menacingly towards* **Chidhina**.) I know how the sun goes under a rock. I have seen you in the river when you were hiding like a glass. You cannot teach me because I am my own follower. (*He stops. The others stare as he finds the best red blanket and sits down in a tight ball, so that only his face is visible from the blanket.*) My shadow is in three pieces, like a suit.

There is a long silence as they watch him roll up in a ball, to sleep.

Chidhina Jesus wept. They brought a teacher to jail. (*Lights dim and* **Chidhina** *moves forward to talk to audience, in the narrator's light.*) Prison is a place of shadows stirring, shaping the soul. How would you have me bring him out? No. His story was a wall on which shadows jumped, fell, took fright, leapt. A history laced with shadows and bewildering light. Like those films we used to watch on a single, white wall against the night, in Mozambique. I often wondered: if the wall was suddenly blown away, we would watch the thin streams of light from the projector drift away dimly to the stars. But eternity can make you tired. I wanted to know his story: who, why and where he was from – and then there came a glimmer, a pointer, a small source of light . . . Above a village in Tanganda . . . (*Pause. He steps out of the narrator's light pointing into the 'hills.*) there was fire.

Febi (*moving into narrator's light, points into 'hills'*) The villagers saw it on the mountain. A red glow in the night. The beginning of that summer was hot and dry. The bush was brown. Baobabs, thorn scrub. That air where a sound tears the air like paper. The ground is sharp and hard on your feet. They thought maybe it was a bush fire. But night after night, it never moved. They wondered.

They act like old village people.

Jungle (*into the light*) There must be a man there. (*Pointing.*)

Febi But now it is missing. Look!

Jungle There! Jumping . . .

Febi   . . . like the red eye of a spring hare.

Jungle   It is watching.

Febi   Waiting, for what?

Jungle   Winking.

Febi (*breaking away*)   One day it moved.

Jungle   Rubbish. Has a fire got legs?

Febi (*emphatic*)   The fire moved. One night it was THAT side of the road, the next night it was THIS.

Chidhina   It moved?

Febi   From the other side. It crossed the tarred road.

Jungle   Just moving? Did you see this?

Febi   We saw, it changed and crossed the tar!

Chidhina   Find it! Follow to the fire!

Jungle (*frightened, shielding his face*)   No! You can't go at night. You cannot see.

Febi   Afraid?

Jungle   Go in the day time – you can't see at night.

Chidhina (*steps forward. To audience. His arms move in a great circle to bring up the light*)

So. When the sun was shining
They sent the Young and Brave
Up the mountain
to find the Man
Who made the fires move!
Youth detail! At the ready!

They all suddenly snap to attention, shuffle into position and start singing, **Chidhina** *leading, the Youth Brigade song:*

　Iva Gamba, Iva Gamba,
　Iva Gamba Utarise Mhandu!

They come to the end of the march.

Febi   Have we come to the right place?

Jungle (*breathless*)   It is a long way.

They all stand silent for a while looking around, slightly uneasy.
Chidhina *peels away.*

Chidhina   What's this?

Jungle   A cave.

Chidhina   A camp. A man has been staying here.

Jungle   What?

Febi   Look. (*Pointed, stylised.*)

Jungle (*spins round*)   What?

Febi (*walks round to pick up something*)   Baobab.

Chidhina (*walks round to see what she has found*)   Half-eaten.
(*He mimes picking it up.*)

Jungle (*confused*)   Where?

Febi (*ignoring* **Jungle**)   That means someone was eating it.

Jungle   Who is eating what?

Chidhina   This baobab fruit, Muuyu, Jungle, is half-eaten.
That means one of two things. Either someone has eaten half
of it; or it has eaten itself. (*To audience.*) Naturally.

Jungle   You are too fast. How can something eat itself? (*To
audience.*) 'Naturally.'

Chidhina (*to audience*)   Suicide.

Jungle   Slow down. Isn't it, we saw a light on the mountain
in the night? And now we suspect a man was behind the
light. So we are looking for a man. (*To audience.*) Simple.

Chidhina   We know nothing for sure. Don't jump to the
end, Jungle. All we know is half a muuyu. If the whole thing
was finished, we could establish the muuyu was murdered. But
because a fruit or a living thing needs half of itself to be alive
in order to eat the other half (*To audience.*) this could easily be

suicide.

Jungle Did one side of your brain eat the other half, I wonder?

Febi He's got a point, Jungle. If your body was to eat yourself up, there will be one time right at the end, near to finishing the meal, where you can't eat anymore of yourself because there will be nothing left of yourself to eat yourself. (*To audience.*) That is clear!

Jungle (*exasperated, pointing at* **Fiasco**)   Ask him!

Chidhina Who?

Jungle The man under the blanket! (*Frustrated.*) Get spectinglasses! (**Jungle** *goes to* **Fiasco**, *lifts the blanket and shouts:*) Did you murder the muuyu? Or did it suicide itself?

Chidhina (*philosophically*)   But if the muuyu committed suicide, then the man isn't there.

Jungle (*looking completely and utterly flummoxed, lifts the blanket finally*)   THERE IS THE MAN!

Febi Did you eat the baobabs?

Fiasco *looks frightened and nods sheepishly.*

Jungle He admits! He admits!

Chidhina Confession! Now we are getting somewhere.

Febi You should be a policeman, Chidhina.

Jungle Quite right, Febi. Then he can talk till Kingdom come. (*To* **Chidhina**.) You must join the Force, my boy.

Chidhina All I am trying to say is: you must look at the evidence from all sides. Innocence before guilt. Truth is more than the appearance of facts.

Jungle You can stand all day in Harare talking to parking meters, my son. (*Miming.*) 'Did someone expire you or are you self-expired?' (*Pauses as if waiting for the 'parking meter' to respond.*) 'Bloody bastard! Answer when I ask you. (*Starts beating it.*) All right. Last chance. (*He looks for five cents in his pocket.*) You've got

twelve minutes to answer. Right now, my watch is ticking to
zero. All right. Time up! I see EXPIRED, you come with
me.'

Febi (*who has been looking around, suddenly interjects*)   Found
something. Someone was definitely here.

Chidhina   What?

Febi   Footprint.

Jungle (*like a maniac cop*)   Keep it.

Febi   How?

Jungle   For court exhibit.

Febi   A footprint is not a crime.

Jungle   How many feet?

Febi   One.

Jungle   That means the other was murdered. Or Suicided.

Febi   Chidhina. Now we've got two madmen in here.

Jungle   I am just doing investigations how Chidhina taught
us.

Chidhina   Just shut up, Jungle, and come here.

Jungle   What's that?

Chidhina *holds something up.*

Febi   Tin of condensed milk.

Chidhina   Full cream sweetened.

Febi   This must have been taken from village. Our houses.

Jungle (*go right*)   Right. Let's go through facts. First, murder.
Second, robbery. Which means we are looking for a bloody
murdering thief.

Febi   With one foot.

Chidhina   And a sweet tooth.

Febi   And no fingers! There are no fingerprints.

Jungle   Correct. Well done, gentlemen. (*Pause.*) And lády.

Febi   What happens now?

Jungle   We arrest him. (*Goes to blanket, lifts it and shouts.*) You! Stand up!

A confused **Fiasco** *stands up.*

You are under arr . . . arr . . . a roof!

Febi   This man has got two feet.

Jungle   Maybe he's lying. You know how tsotsis are. (*He checks his feet.*) All right, there are two. Maybe one foot is lying.

Chidhina   Better check the mouth, Jungle.

Jungle   Quite right, constable. (*To* **Fiasco**.) Give me your mouth.

Fiasco *looks confused.*

Jungle   Open.

Fiasco *opens his mouth ridiculously wide.*

Febi   Did you eat a full tin of condensed milk?

Fiasco *nods sheepishly.*

Jungle   You see, Chidhina, you should leave interrogations to me. (*To* **Fiasco**.) It is bad for your teeth. (*Waits.*) Hands!

Fiasco *throws his hands up.*

Febi   His fingers are complete and normal.

Jungle (*to* **Fiasco**)   Are you trying to be funny. Normal fingers without fingerprints!

Chidhina   He looks completely normal, Jungle.

Febi   Is it normal living like an animal in the mountains?

Jungle   Arrest him! (*He starts to manhandle* **Fiasco**, *who screeches.*) You come for questioning. Anything you say will be taken down as trousers.

Fiasco *screams like a wounded animal, as* **Jungle** *and* **Febi** *try to take him by the arms.*

Fiasco Am I not free? Am I not free?

Jungle You are free to keep quiet.

They start marching off, **Fiasco** *captive, singing the Youth Brigade song, 'Iva Gamba!'.*

Chidhina Down the rocky mountain
with this vagabond, the Youth Brigade went.
Down the rocky mountain to the primary school where two
hundred parents were meeting with the committee
under a baobab tree.

They stop their march and hold **Fiasco** *as* **Febi** *does two quick stylised steps to the side and speaks as the school chairman to the audience.*

Febi Our children must grow up healthy and well educated.
As you know, from our contributions by parents we cannot
raise enough to build more classrooms and all the time
numbers are growing. The government cannot support us. We
need your help for making bricks, digging . . .

Fiasco *is thrown down at her feet. Commotion.*

Febi What is this? We are holding a school meeting for
Musani here.

Chidhina *and* **Jungle** *behave like an excited posse of party youth.*

Chidhina (*excited*) We found him on the hills.

Jungle Eating muuyu and sweetened condensed milk.

Febi Please move away. This is a school business here and
we are discussing important issues concerning our children,
our future.

Jungle This is important.

Chidhina We are Youth Brigade sent to find the man.

Febi (*looking down at* **Fiasco**) Who is this man?

Jungle   The one who was terrorising our people.

Chidhina   With strange fires at night in the distance . . .

Jungle   Stealing from the people's houses . . .

Chidhina   Taking precious water from the drying well . . .

Febi   Who is this man?

Jungle   Nobody knows.

Febi (*direct to audience*)   Does anybody recognise this man? (*Longish silence.*) Is he from here?

Jungle (*after a pause*)   He is not. (*Hurls* **Fiasco** *towards* **Chidhina**.)

Chidhina   We do not know him. We have never seen him.

Hurls **Fiasco** *to the ground.* **Chidhina** *and* **Jungle** *behave like village parents, shouting like a crowd, beating and kicking him on the ground.*

Febi (*to* **Fiasco**)   Stand up and show yourself to the people.

Fiasco *stands.*

Febi   Why have you been staying in the mountains?

Fiasco (*terrified as the actors encircle him*)   I am not prepared. Do I know you? Why are you asking me question? (*Spinning.*) Why? Why? Why? Why?

Febi (*advancing first*)   Who are you?

They move around him in a choreographed 'dance' of aggression, anger, suspicion.

Jungle   A thief!

Chidhina   Stealing food and water.

Febi   Living like a hyena in our midst.

Chidhina   Running like a jackal.

Febi   Speak!

Chidhina   Alien!

Jungle Spy!

Febi Watching our homes.

Jungle Creating fear and suspicion.

Febi Breaking our meetings.

Chidhina Our homes and families.

Febi Dissident!

Jungle Wild dog!

Chidhina Caveman!

Fiasco *covers his head in his hands.*

Fiasco I am not not not not not not

Jungle Thief!

Chidhina Madman!

Febi Ubhinya! Seize him!

Fiasco (*darts away, menacing, threatening anyone who dares to lay a finger on him*) I am not. I was brought here by force. Who are you? What is this for? You want to kill me! You want to murder me!

He lets out a screech as he attempts to get away. **Chidhina** *floors him.*

Febi Call the police!

As **Chidhina** *fights and pins* **Fiasco** *to the floor, the others chorus round him excitedly.*

Jungle We do not want strangers destroying our peace.

Febi We must be vigilant against people who want to destroy our nation.

Jungle This area is infested with spies and malcontents.

Febi The rubbish that still want war.

Jungle We must be watchful against Renamos and deserters, sucking the life out of our new nation.

Febi (*spits on the ground where* **Fiasco** *lies*)   Bloodsucker! Take him away!

Jungle *makes the sound of a police siren.* **Jungle** *and* **Febi** *move around* **Fiasco**, *grab him and haul him up.* **Jungle** *then mimes a police van starting up. Cursing the vehicle, they eventually move off, siren blaring and exhaust popping, pulling away on a bumpy road. When they stop,* **Jungle** *tries to slam shut the door, succeeds the third time with his backside, immediately runs to the bucket, moves it down stage and sits on it, like a police inspector at his desk.* **Febi** *and* **Chidhina** *have* **Fiasco** *with both arms twisted up behind his back. They wait for the inspector.*

Jungle   Bring him in. (*He tries to look busy with 'papers', but it is sweatingly hot.*) What's the problem?

Febi (*triumphant*)   We have him.

Jungle (*indicating – almost bored*)   The forms.

Febi   We . . .

Jungle   Where are the forms?

Febi   We . . .

Jungle   Are you people doing your jobs? There is laid down procedures to follow arrests. Do you think because it is 39 degrees Celsius in the shade you can lazy around and ignore regulations? I want forms.

Chidhina (*fumbling for papers, hands them to him*)   Is this all right, sir?

Jungle (*studying them*)   You have not written anything.

Chidhina   He is refusing, so we left it, sir.

Jungle   Refusing what? It is simple. You are supposed to have O Levels. Where is name, address, identity particulars? (*Indicating the paper.*) Why have you left this empty?

Febi   We don't know his name, chef.

Jungle   Ask him.

Chidhina   He doesn't have one.

Jungle   Everyone has a name.

Febi   He has forgotten.

Jungle (*looking slowly at* **Fiasco**)   No name?
Have you tried to make him remember? (*He surreptitiously shows a clenched fist.*)

Chidhina   We have. (*Happy, showing a clenched fist. Then pause.*)
He is not available for comment.

Jungle   Is he absent?

Febi   He is present, chef.

Jungle (*looking accusingly at her*)   And address?

Chidhina   He was living in a cave, sir, hideout there by
Tanganda, of which we were not 100% sure of whether we
could write it down as a proper residence. And further to our
investigations, chef, we were unable to establish if he was
having a post office box number or private bag, sir.

Jungle (*stunned in disbelief*)   What the hell does he need a
private bag or P.O. Box if he is living in a cave somewhere?

Febi   For receiving letters and parcels, chef.

Jungle (*slowly, almost menacingly*)   For receiving parcels . . .

Febi   And letters, chef.

Chidhina   There was no number of his dwelling there.

Febi   And obviously, the postman would refuse taking his
bicycle up there.

Chidhina   It is steep, chef, even for goats.

Febi   Too many rocks, chef.

Jungle (*sickeningly sweet to repress his rage*)   Too many rocks,
aikona?

Febi   It is a mountain, chef.

Jungle   I am surprised. Perhaps I should write a special
letter to the postmaster general complaining about inadequate

rural services? (*Suddenly barking at them.*) Did it ever occur to
you – and I am sure it is obvious to anyone except a straw
brain – that this man does not receive letters and parcels at
his mountain address. In fact, I would risk my neck with my
job and salary to say emphatically that this man has received
his first visit to this so-called residence in quite a few months
and years. (*Filthy angry.*) Perhaps, constables, it would be better,
in view of this man's obvious shaky medical condition and
poor health on account of inadequate shelter, if you
personally, constables, had sent him food parcels and gone,
personally, up the mountain to deliver them!! IS MY
MESSAGE QUITE CLEAR!!

Fiasco *has put his hands over his ears at the deafening roar.*

Chidhina   Yessir!

Jungle   Fall off!

Chidhina *stands still.*

Have you forgotten your commands?

Chidhina   Who, chef?

Jungle (*disgusted*)   Just go to sleep.

Chidhina   Here, sir?

Jungle   Anywhere. Just wake up. And go to sleep.

Chidhina *shuffles away.*

Jungle (*to* **Febi**)   You too.

Febi   I am on duty.

Jungle   Don't worry. Just leave me with him.

Febi *shuffles away also.*

Jungle (*looking down at* **Fiasco**)   Now let's get on with
business. (*Roughly picks him up and puts him on the bucket. Attacking.*)
Now why do you not co-operate? Are you guilty?

Fiasco *just looks amazed.*

If you put on a proper trousers and behaved like a gentleman you could be drinking quietly somewhere.

Chidhina (*reverting from being a constable*)   Get on with questions.

Febi   You are not playing a chef correctly.

Jungle (*goes over to them, slouching in a corner. Offended*)   I am doing my best. Are we not all playing policemen here?

Febi   That is not how a policeman talks.

Jungle   Listen, friends. I was designated member-in-charge. Which means I am above you.

Chidhina   We can change that. Febi has got more authority. We can swap and you become just constable.

Jungle   We are trying to do something very natural and realistic here.

Febi   So cut talk of trousers.

Jungle   I know what I am doing. Just let me finish. (*He goes back to* **Fiasco**.) Sorry for that interruption and delay.

Chidhina   When does a policeman say sorry?

Febi   And trousers.

Jungle (*to* **Fiasco**)   These constables these days lack discipline. No no no no no no. Did I ask to be sent here? I could be in Marondera or Chipinge with an organised station. Instead they send me into the desert like Moses where we sweat and drown in heat – no transport for duties, fridges or beer. And now football.

Febi (*exasperated*)   Why are you talking football?

Jungle   You should know. You got the striker's legs.

Febi (*getting up, furious*)   I'll show you how a striker kicks.

Jungle (*placating*)   All right, Febi, easy, dear. National pastime. We have got the army coming from Birchenough next week and those boys know how to kick. (*Turning to* **Fiasco**.) Those army boys, they will destroy our members, I can assure you. Two of our boys are on leave, one sick and two of the best sharpshooters were called away to the tea estates. I tell you, we have got big problems coming.

Chidhina (*putting his head between his knees*)   I don't believe this, Jungle.

Jungle (*ignoring. To* **Fiasco**)   Do you play football?

Fiasco *stares at him.*

Jungle   We can provide shorts, never mind boots. I can see those feet are used to thorns and rocks.

Febi   Stop pussyfooting around with soccer.

Chidhina   This is a police investigation not a Zifa cup tie.

Jungle (*indignant*)   I am giving a true picture of a police station! (*To* **Fiasco**.) You never know, mukomana, this could be your lucky day. What is your number?

Fiasco *stares at him.*

Jungle   What number do you play?

Fiasco *goes into another world, shaking and mumbling in a trance, repeating the same thing over and over.*

Do you have a special number you like?

Fiasco *suddenly lurches up, mumbling, manically, driving* **Jungle** *back into a corner. Almost inaudible,* **Jungle** *strains to listen, the smile stuck to his face.*

Fiasco   Z555. Z555. Z555.

Jungle (*struggling to hear*)   Number 5? Full back? Because goalkeeper we have already got . . . no place for Maradona . . .

Fiasco (*suddenly breaks into a fierce toyi-toyi around the cell*)   Z555! Z555! Z555! (*He then rolls across the floor into his cave hideout.*)

Chidhina   What the fuck is he on about?

Febi   One thing for sure, he is not meaning football.

Fiasco, *completely and utterly distracted. He is aware of no one else. He stops, goes down on hands and knees, puts his ear to the ground, listens to the air. Then he scurries to the blanket, crawls under it like an animal going into hiding, comes out the other side of the blanket. Constantly alert . . .*

Febi   Look. He's back in his cave.

As **Fiasco** *sits in a tight huddle, he starts to remove a piece of wire from round his neck. It is a bit of telescopic radio aerial. He lengthens the aerial and starts making radio noises.*

Jungle   Ma-aerial.

Chidhina   He's cracked in the fucking head.

Febi   He wants to make contact somewhere.

Chidhina   He'd be better off with a bucket. *(Starts going towards him.)* Hey mister man, what's your problem? Trying to get through to your wife or lawyer? You think you going to get out of this stinking pisshole in a hurry?

Fiasco *is making radio noises, gibberish communications.*

Chidhina   He lost his spacecraft. Hey, sputnik, try howling. *(He howls like a dog.)* They left you behind. I saw them go that way.

Jungle   Leave him, young man. Just watch.

Chidhina   Some bloody spaceman who thinks he's still in orbit.

Febi   That man has been in the mountains.

Chidhina   But what's he been doing up there?

Febi   Travelling to far places.

Jungle   Let me speak to him.

Febi   He's talking to his wireless, Jungle.

Chidhina   Last chance, Uncle George. If you don't make any sense out of him, we try other methods.

Jungle   You are too rough.

Chidhina   And you are useless, giving speeches about bloody football. Get organised, Uncle George.

Jungle   All right, all right, all right. Leave it to me. (*He goes to* **Fiasco**. *He tries the soft approach.*) 'Scuse, sha. What is happening?

Fiasco (*listens to his radio, talks, listens, then looks at* **Jungle**) They are coming.

Jungle   Who is coming?

Fiasco   From the mountains. Like rain. (*He keeps up a continuous radio dialogue.*)

Jungle   Who is coming?

Fiasco (*still on the radio*)   Yes. Yes. Yes.

Jungle   Who?

Fiasco   From Mozambique.

Jungle   Is that where you are from? (*He stops, pauses.*)

Fiasco   I was born in Tokyo. My father was a ploughman in the Far East using only a copper penny as a plough. Mozambique was buried after my uncle.

Febi   Where is your family?

Fiasco   I was carried in a clay pot until my mother cracked. But then the floods came, the floods ... I don't know. But I know news, news is coming, news is coming, news from Mozambique. Like a bird, it is going to land just now. (*He 'sees' the bird flying and landing. He starts making radio noises again.*) Like a rain, like a rain. Because I am a black man. I am a black man. I am a black man. One day I was working and sweating, dripping with work, and the sun was at three o'clock. Then I shook my body like a dog – and rain came! Rain came! I know weather, in my work. A white man cannot tell you about rain because he have got office and paper. He has written a list to try to tell him how the world works. He has taken helicopters to get near to the sky, but as he goes nearer, the sky is jumping like a locust. (*He leaps.*) He can't reach . . .

. . . Soon (*He leans over, in* **Jungle**'*s ear:*) . . . Zimbabwe will be free.

Febi It is already free.

Fiasco No! Forces will be coming.

Febi What forces?

Chidhina He is Renamo!

Fiasco *looks at* **Chidhina**, *then moves away.*

Febi What freedom are you talking about?

Jungle Leave him. I am in charge of investigations.

Febi But no one understands what he is on about. How long has he been up there? For what purpose? Should we not be explained?

Jungle Yes, but slowly, in time.

Chidhina He has had enough time. So far as I can see, Jungle, the only thing you managed to get out of him is that he's got sunstroke.

Jungle He was allowed fresh air in the mountains.

Febi He could as well find fresh air in the valley, in the villages.

Chidhina And the radio?

Jungle I don't know! We are all still trying to find out!

Chidhina (*to* **Fiasco**) What is the radio for?

Fiasco For news. World. (*He moves away and scours the east, waiting.*)

Chidhina (*serious*) You are beginning to upset me, you know that? What news? (*Silence.*) What news? This is your fault, Jungle. Leaving you in charge . . .

Jungle Because you keep interrupting and challenging everything I try. The only person you believe is yourself, nothing else.

Febi   Oh, keep quiet, you two. Between the two of you, nothing ever comes out, nothing of truth.

Chidhina   And how have you helped piece this thing together?

Febi   At least let me speak to him.

Chidhina   We've all been speaking to him and all we get is riddles and ravings. How long do we go on asking nicely?

Jungle   Well, that is your frustration.

Chidhina   Too bad. He came down from the mountain. Into this system. He came down. Whether he's bloody Moses or what. Nobody goes there unless he's MNR or National Parks. Nobody hides there. The last time was during war. (*Goes direct to audience. His voice is urgent, tripped back to another time, vivid.*) The whole of the southeast is littered with caves. Rocks that close like zips. Silent. From Rusitu, through Chimanimani to Chirinda and Chipinge, coming into the baobab country further in from Mozambique where the mountains absorb you like a womb, you reach the granite, with sharp-toothed overhangs, rocks shaped like the blade of an axe. How could he hide there? What other secrets had he left behind? The further you come in, the more the trees thin out, the caves give you as much cover as a banga. You would have to be a thin, invisible sort of person to survive without protection. Unless you could carve yourself up under a cave that covers you like an axe blade. Into fragments. You'd have to be a shadow yourself.
(*To* **Fiasco**.) How did you hide? I know the area. I was there.

Febi   Chidhina knows from the war. He was there, as a freedom fighter.

Chidhina   We'd have to carve you up into smaller pieces to make you fit.

Jungle   Come on, Chidhina.

Chidhina   I want blood.

Fiasco We are together.

Chidhina Bullshit. Nothing is together. Everything is in pieces.

Fiasco I have always been with you.

Chidhina (*hauling him up in one movement*) This is as close as we will ever be. (*He holds his face to his own and continues to push him round.*)

Febi Why can't you just leave it, Chidhina? You can see he is helpless against you.

Chidhina Not as I can see. What the hell is this guy on about? Muttering numbers, declaring unity with me, talking like he knows me . . .

Fiasco . . . from the bush! Yes!

Chidhina (*holding him even closer*) Don't shit with me!

Fiasco I am with you, comrade.

Chidhina Never. You are not with me. You, coming from one fucking prison on your bloody mountain to this. No! You came down, down here, into this system, so you must know WE are government in here, you learn OUR rules – emergency powers declaration. (*He smacks him to the floor.*) We are not just poor people you can piss around with more fucking bullshit, you are not some fucking vakuru putting on puppet masks and preaching socialism with Swiss accounts while they put us victims of capital and international bankers and owners, and we sit here in this shitpit with the stink of our own urine getting up our noses when even now they are shaking hands at dinner parties and farting back lies to us next week in the papers, throwing black freedom at us while they eat butter. And we wait, wait! No. We are suffering and he must suffer too. Is he something special? This? (*He kicks him.*)

Fiasco (*on the ground*) I am a fighter without a bazooka, a chef without a briefcase. I am a minister without a rally, a tycoon without a passport.

Chidhina (*kicks him on the floor*)   I don't give a shit who you are.

Febi *and* **Jungle** *go to the fallen* **Fiasco**.

Fiasco (*still on the ground, hardly audible*)   I found a brother.

Jungle   You have found us. Don't worry.

Fiasco   We are fighting together. Now he wants to fight me.

Febi (*gently*)   What is your name?

Fiasco *just looks up slowly at her, still sprawled on the ground.*

Febi   What is your name?

Fiasco (*very slowly, quietly*)   Fiasco.

Chidhina   What did he say?

Jungle   He was hissing like a snake.

Immensely tired, **Fiasco** *manages to drag himself onto his hands and feet and beckons* **Chidinha** *to come close to him.* **Chidhina** *comes towards him, wary and bends.* **Fiasco** *whispers in his ear.*

Fiasco   Comrade Fiasco. I come to free Zimbabwe. (*With this, he falls asleep in* **Febi***'s arms.*)

Febi   Freedom fighter.

Chidhina (*quiet menace*)   You'll pay for this. (*He is deeply affected by this revelation.*)

Jungle   Maybe it's true.

Chidhina   Crawling out of a cave, out of the past.

Jungle   I don't smell something wrong.

Chidhina   I do. I smell things best left forgotten coming to the surface. I smell musty bones and death rising above the ground. If . . . If . . .

Febi   Forget it.

Chidhina   I thought it was forgotten. But this, is this the proof? Is this rodent crawling out of the cave all that's left?

Jungle Let it rest.

Chidhina How does it rest? All those years. What has he done with them?

Febi He didn't know, Chidhina. Who knows whether he is a lost comrade or not?

Chidhina That's not the point. He has brought it back. Things I had left behind. Memories.
What did you do with your memories, Fiasco? Did they climb around the walls of your prison cave? Did you talk to echoes of the past? Did you smear your own shit on the wall of your cave memories? Or did you wipe away the memories with your finger, Fiasco?

They all look aghast. **Febi** *wraps the blanket around* **Fiasco***.*

Chidhina That's right, Fiasco. Curl up and die. (*He turns round and walks away, then turns back to look at* **Fiasco***.*) Comrade. You should have died.

Febi *starts singing a lullaby: 'Nyarara Mwan' angu, yedu-ye'.*

Jungle *watches as* **Chidhina** *sits down against the bucket and faces away, his energy drained. As* **Febi** *quietly sings, he hesitantly gets up and faces the audience. Behind him,* **Fiasco** *lies curled up in the overhead circle of light, held by* **Febi***.*

Jungle Comrade Fiasco was lost for eight years. In a cave. How can I tell you more than that? I cannot question the invisible. Maybe if there was beer in here I could be eloquent and give reasons and maybe this and maybe that, but there is no evidence to deny, no proof to confirm. Just eight years. For me, it must be some kind of miracle. A parable. I believe. But one thing was worrying me. If he was silent all that time and unable to find us, did he try? What stopped him trying? His own voices? His own faith maybe? And we, on our side, why could we not find him?

Jungle *starts to pace around the circle of light describing a white hole in the centre.* **Febi***'s singing tails off as she watches him.*

Febi What are you doing, Jungle?

Jungle   Measuring. How big a hole do you think Fiasco
would have to fall into to disappear for eight years?

Febi   Size hole? You could vanish a camel through the eye
of a needle. It doesn't take size to disappear.

Jungle   Do you think it takes courage?
You see, it worries me, Febi. Watch.
(*He walks round the circle, measuring the large hole again.*) That is a
hole. Now inside is history, in there. Now you see, a man
disappears inside there for eight years, counting hours minutes
seconds days months until everything is in darkness, only his
eyes shining out. Now my worry is: if no one can see him,
then what has happened to history?

Febi   Which history?

Jungle   His history. Ours. Zimbabwe history.

Febi *stares at the hole.*

Febi   You mean Zimbabwe inside the cave?

Jungle   The brain. The brain is a cave. So inside your head
where did the history go?

Febi   Mine? (*She looks puzzled.*) I know my history.

Jungle   And him?

Febi   Who knows? What of you?

Jungle   My history? Some I know, some disappeared. (*Pause.*)
Febi, what size of hole could swallow a revolution?

Febi   So that people forgot all about liberation?
(*Takes* **Jungle***'s hand.*) Just try this. Now just say we are
different Zimbabweans, and we have not met each other since
eight years.

They face each other in front of the circle of light, centre stage.

Jungle   We knew each other before eight years?

Febi   Yes. Then we didn't meet for eight years, like political
parties, and now we meet again. (*She takes his hand. She is very
matter of fact. Communicates directly with audience.*)

Jungle (*nervous about this*)   Yes.

Febi   So what happens?

They both shuffle.

Jungle (*to audience*)   I say hello. (*To* **Febi**.) Hello!!

Febi (*a bit shy and awkward*)   Hello.

Full of nervous excitement as they get into the improvisation

Jungle   I haven't seen you for eight years.

Febi   Eight years? Is it that long?

Jungle   It seems short. Did you disappear?

Febi   I was here.

Jungle   It shows how I was missing you all that time.

Febi   Ah come on, did you think about me once?

Jungle   Every day.

Febi   You are fibbing.

Jungle   True. I didn't miss a day without thinking, how is Febi? Where is she, I wonder?

Febi   I was here. Why didn't you try to find me?

Jungle   I didn't know where to look.

Febi   How is that? If you were thinking seriously you would have come to find me. (*Turning away.*)

Jungle   Where were you?

Febi   That was for you to search.

Jungle   But now you are here so everything is all right.

Febi   But times have changed. You took so long.

Jungle   Never mind, we are together.

Febi   But my life changed in the meanwhile. I had babies.

Jungle (*shocked*)   And many boyfriends too?

Febi   I had boyfriends.

Jungle   When you knew I was looking for you?

Febi   You never came.

Jungle   But you should have waited. (*Takes her hand.*) All right, all right, never mind. I'll forget boyfriends and babies, I will pretend you never had them.

Febi   But I did. That is my history.

Jungle   All right, let's start again. Different history.

Febi   No, Jungle. That is me, my history. Either accept or forget it. You said you thought about me every day.

Jungle   I did.

Febi   So?

Jungle   You chose the wrong path.

Febi   For you, maybe.

Jungle   I can't talk to you now. You disappointed me.

Febi   But all that time you hoped for me, thought of me? Was that nothing?

Jungle   You spoiled it now.

Febi   Spoiled? We were just coming together after eight years! That is something wonderful.

Jungle   Don't try to declare unity with me, it doesn't work.

Febi   I am just talking friendship. After eight years, I am not asking you to sleep with me.

Jungle   Pity.

Febi (*to audience*)   Men and politics. Sex and unity. They all want security under one blanket.

Jungle   So let's see. Maybe unity is good.

Febi   And what of free will? You can't force.

Jungle   Women are weak. (*Goes and grabs her as if to fondle her.*)

Febi   Get off, Jungle. What are you doing?

Jungle (*suddenly coming to his senses*)   Sorry, sorry, Febi, I didn't mean. Things are just getting mixed up now between acting and thinking, playing and life. (*Going round the arc of the circle.*)

Febi   But I told you my history. I can't just forget everything. We change, we grow.

Jungle (*darts a look at* **Fiasco**, *then goes up to* **Febi** *and whispers aloud*)   What of his eight years?

The following is done conspiratorially.

Febi   Did he speak during that time?

Jungle   He forgot, even his language.

Febi   It's as if nothing happened.

Jungle (*an idea*)   Can we measure?

Febi   Eight years, in years? (*Goes to* **Fiasco**.)

Jungle   By hands and feet.
Measure. (*Starts pacing it out.*)
We are. November 1986. Going backwards . . .

She goes forward and he steps backwards. Each step has a rhythm.

November '85. November '84. November '83. November '82.

Febi   You are disappearing, Jungle.

Jungle   '81. '80.

Febi   Independence already. Did time go so fast?

Jungle   I've lost it.

Febi   Independence . . . start the other way.

Jungle   From '78? This is the time we think Fiasco disappeared.

Febi   Then come forwards.

Jungle   Too difficult. Too far, Febi.

Febi   Try. It is important, Jungle. Forward with the years of

Fiasco! (*Clenched fist salute.*)

Jungle   Forward! November 1978. Year dot.

The following goes quickly, as he takes one step forward with each year.

Jungle   November 1979. One year.

Febi   People's power. Six fire. Lancaster House.

Jungle   1980.

Febi   People's independence. The land, the land is ours. No more fighting.

Jungle   (*feeling rain on his upturned face*)   And rain, Febi, rain! Such a rain as never . . .

Febi   Where was he?

Jungle   Still dreaming.

Febi   The rest of us finished dreaming and started work. Work!

Jungle   November 1981. (*Pause.*) Three years of Fiasco silence.

Febi   My baby came that year.

Jungle   Don't interrupt. I forget. Where were we?

Febi   November 1981.

Jungle   November 1982. Four years. And he was there all this time. It is hard enough counting, never mind staying one place all that time.
(*To* **Fiasco**.) Are you crazy, talking to air?

Febi   Come on, Jungle, Zimbabwe's still an infant.

Jungle   All right, four years . . . November 1983. Five years . . . (*To* **Fiasco**.) Come on, man, get up. Time is flying and jumping.

Febi   Quick, Jungle. November 1983 . . .

Jungle   It makes me nervous, five years, five years . . .

Febi   Hurry up. The years are fading. Soon you won't be able to remember what year it is.

Jungle (*conscious effort*)   I remember.
(*Takes one step forward.*) November 1984. Six years.

Febi   Only two more years, Jungle. Two more, take it easy.

Jungle   November 1985. Seven years.

Febi   One small step and we are there. Just one, Jungle.

Jungle   I can't. Where is he? Why is Fiasco not here? He must be here for the moment, for the moment he appears after years.

Febi (*urgent*)   I'll get him.

Jungle   Quick, Febi. I can't hold it forever.

Febi (*roughly rousing* **Fiasco**)   Up! Up! Come on! Your time is here.

Fiasco   What's going on? Where am I?

Febi   Prison.

Fiasco   Why was I brought here?

Febi   To come out of hiding.

Fiasco   I don't want. Leave me.

Febi   Too late. Your year is near. You must be there. (*She hauls him to* **Jungle**.)

Jungle   Greetings, Fiasco. One more year.

Fiasco   Of what?

Jungle   Before you enter.

Febi   It is one year, but really it will be over in some few seconds.

Fiasco   No!

Jungle   He doesn't want.

Febi   He must.

Jungle (*suddenly breaks his line*)   It is not working, Febi.

Febi   Get back. You can't break time like that.

Jungle   When it is over what are you going to do?

Febi   At least we have done it then.

Jungle   Done what?

Febi   Moved!

Jungle   For what purpose?

Febi   I don't know. Because we said we were going to measure.

Jungle   But you can't, you can't . . .
(*He is dejected.*) It is just numbers.

Febi   It is a celebration, Jungle.

Fiasco   What celebrating?

Febi   You, Comrade, you.

He looks perplexed, but this brings **Jungle** *in sympathetically.*

Jungle   Today we celebrate eight years . . . eight years of . . . what eight years . . .

Chidhina (*still sitting*)   What is this? What celebration is going on?

Febi   For Comrade Fiasco.

Jungle (*reacting to* **Chidhina**'s *presence*)   Ladies and gentlemen, let us now celebrate and sing about eight years, eight important years, of Comrade Fiasco. And we have the very man here, Comrade Fiasco. Everybody I would like you all to join in celebrating this Comrade Fiasco. Let us give him a pam-pam.

He starts clapping and cheering. **Febi** *ululates,* **Fiasco** *starts dancing, and* **Chidhina** *looks on utterly contemptuous.* **Chidhina**'s *presence silences* **Febi** *and* **Jungle** *but* **Fiasco** *continues stamping his feet into the earth, moving until he stops rebelliously in front of* **Chidhina**.

Chidhina (*pause*)   I suppose you think that is a joke. (*His back is to audience.*)

Jungle   We have been celebrating national birthdays and the like. I thought Fiasco also . . .

Chidhina (*interrupting*)   I suppose this is your idea, Jungle.

Jungle   We were just investigating and it came up.

Chidhina   There is nothing to celebrate, Jungle. Leave you alone for five minutes and you come up with ideas even this idiot wouldn't dream of.

Febi   They were important years, Chidhina. Our birth. Our struggle.

Chidhina   Fiasco? Is that a struggle?

Jungle   You are oppressing us. We were quite fine till you came.

Chidhina (*moves round* **Fiasco**)   Sitting in his cave palace, pinching other people's food and water, running and hiding like a lizard. Shall we celebrate lizards now?

Febi   All right, comrade, be reasonable. (*To* **Jungle**.) He has got a point.

Fiasco (*proudly*)   Take me to my commander.

Chidhina   What commander?

Fiasco   I was told when I crossed I would find him.

Chidhina   What for?

Fiasco   Instructions.

Jungle   Maybe he is telling the truth.

Febi   What commander? (*To* **Fiasco**.) You must say names. All the names we know from round here. This one, for example (Chidhina) was Freeborn. We know him as one of the boys from here. Do we know Comrade Fiasco? That is a new name.

Fiasco   We were many.

Febi   Who were your commanders?

Fiasco   We were tricked out of commanders. Now you are tricking . . .

Chidhina (*snaps*)   State the names.

Febi   How do we know for sure you are right?

Chidhina (*squeezes his testicles*)   We don't. He doesn't know because he lies. (*He pushes him back and down under the overhead light, as in an interrogating room.*)

Fiasco   No.

Chidhina   Names! Names! Names!

Febi (*squeezes*)   Kissinger Tricks. Tambamangwana. Chikwapuro. Our commanders, do you know them?

Jungle   There was also, later in '79, Mujamba Jeche.

Febi   What of Mujamba Jeche?

Fiasco *doesn't remember.*

Febi   Bloodfist. And our boys . . . Hondo. Skorokoro. Sweet Banana.

Jungle   Big Shot. Long March. Micky Jegger.

Chidhina   Pfura Zuva Shoot the Sun. Cyclops. Crazy Fire. Gazilikachaka.

Febi   Hakuna rinda. Moto M'kuru. Blow-out. Force Ten.

Jungle   Mapanga. -Ndebvudzembwa. Bongozozo.

Chidhina   Comrade Giap. Comrade Qagambisa ubagibengomgq'belo. We know them all. You are a stranger. (*Pulling his head back.*)

Fiasco   I hadn't chance to meet them.

Chidhina   You can't fool us. I thought maybe, maybe there is one comrade, one. But you, I can see you are trying to deceive, capitalising on our disappointment . . .

Febi   Our brothers . . .

Jungle   And sisters. Remember Nhema Zisi.

Chidhina   Our brothers and sisters who died for truth, must they hear this lie of yours? I am sick of lies! (*He hurls* **Fiasco** *down on the ground.*) THE TRUTH! (*He waits, watches, then picks him up and heaves him again, his head bashing the floor.*)

Fiasco (*sprawled on the ground*)   Truth.
There was a storm.

Chidhina   What storm?·(*Hurls him again.*)

Fiasco   The day we crossed. From nowhere. There was a heavy storm.

Chidhina (*moving suddenly with great clarity and decision, hauls him up under the overhead spotlight*)   So I ask you: what storm?

The actors look stunned.

Section! Fall in!

The actors get into a line, backlit from overhead. Low lighting.

Today we find out who is a fighter for freedom.
(*He is mad, shouting orders in a frenzy. Passes the actors first before speaking.*) Today you join the thousands of brothers and sisters who have gone before you to reclaim what is ours. Today there are thousands of you, moving through the bush like a sea. The white settlers will get the shock of their lives when they see the Mozambique Channel and the Indian Ocean rising like a tide to the doorsteps of their suburban homes. The bush will be like the streets of Salisbury as you move in with the winds and tides from our bases in Mozambique, through the rain and mist and a hundred kinds of wet, soaking up the tea estates, the Conex Sections, the villages and concentration camps where they think they can keep the masses from us. Today the land will be drenched with a new rain as you move forward into the liberated and semi-liberated zones. Together you are a sea. Alone, a drop. A drop of water is well hidden in an ocean of people. Zimbabwe!

Others   Pamberi!

Chidhina   Vana vevu mukai.

Others   Pamberi!
(*They sing.*) Ndakanzwa izwi richigogodza mukati memoyo
wangu . . . Zarura Zarura musio uregere garira ripinde.
[*Translation: I heard the word knocking inside my heart. Open the door
and let the guerilla in.*]

Chidhina   You have been issued weapons. Look after them.
They are your freedom. (*These words come over the song.*)

Fiasco (*panicking*)   My number, I have it. Z555, Z555, Z555.
(*He goes on mumbling and repeating the number.*)

Chidhina   Look after it. Section! Move!

They get into line.

Tonight we leave the base camp. This night we cross the
border.

Chidhina *leads the way, then* **Febi**, *and* **Jungle** *bringing up the
rear.* **Fiasco** *stays standing behind. They sing as they move. Then
singing becomes bush noises. Sounds of animals, birds, distant dogs
barking and village sounds. They creep on, merely silhouettes.*

Jungle   Freeborn, I'm tired. And hungry.

Chidhina   Move up! No more games, Jungle. We are not
fooling around.

Jungle   I preferred being policeman.

Chidhina   Too late, we are in it.
(*Starts speeding up.*) Come on, Mhengo.

Chidhina *who has gone ahead splits up the section considerably.
Suddenly, he stops and crouches.*

Chidhina   Enemy! (*He breaks to a fighting position. The word goes
down the line . . .*)

Febi   Mhandu! (*She breaks away to a fighting position.*)

Jungle (*horrified*)   Ndoramani Ndolas!

He breaks away to the fighting position. They lie there tense, waiting.

Jungle (*whispering to* **Febi**)   Where is Fiasco?

She looks round. **Fiasco** *is terrified, centre stage. Suddenly all hell breaks loose. Freeborn (***Chidhina***), Mhengo (***Jungle***) and Pepu (***Febi***) let off hellish 'rattatats' using voice and bucket at the enemy!* **Fiasco,** *who has been trying to crawl away on his belly, burrows into the ground. The firing breaks and Freeborn peels away to block* **Fiasco***.*

Chidhina (*menacing*)   Are you brave enough?

Febi (*doing same*)   Where are you going, Fiasco?

Jungle (*doing same*)   Are you crawling home?

Chidhina   They will kill you when they see you.

Febi   Coward!

Jungle   Let Kalashnikov help you now.

Febi   Whose side are you on?

Jungle   Deserter!

Chidhina   Is this how you fight for Freedom, Fiasco?

They all start chanting

Kill Fiasco!

They have covered themselves in a blanket and, using the bucket as a beast-head, chant and echo into it: 'Kill Fiasco!' advancing to a crescendo.

Fiasco (*gives a blood-curdling scream*)   No!! It was not like that! I am not a coward! I came to fight.

Chidhina   You ran away. Like a dog.

Fiasco   No. You can't tell my story. All along it has been you, you and you. Telling my story. All along it has been you inventing. I have my own words. My own memory.

General lighting fades as **Fiasco** *is focused into the overhead spotlight. The actors retreat to the fringes of light quietly.*

(*Quiet.*) Sometime on the journey there was a storm. Yes. There must have been about thirty of us as we moved. Night. And then something I never experienced before in my life. A storm. The skies turned, filled with the roar of buffaloes. And lightning that made me see my own blood running like a

flood through my body . . . but I can hardly remember . . .
everything was turning inside out, as if bombs were going off
inside me, bullets breaking my body. I felt wet like a wound
that covered my whole body. Meat. For vultures. My flesh
naked like a skinned buck.
Then I did not know where I was or where to run or where I
was coming from because every direction was the same . . .
and then, the sun, it was sun and lightning, all in one, the
world exploded in a white light!

Suddenly **Chidhina** *rises up with a whooooooosh, like a flare, and*
Fiasco *dives to hide, to shut out the blinding light.*

It lasted forever . . . forever . . . whichever way, I couldn't
escape that light. It was in my head, a torch, boiling my
brains. I thought: this is what God has done to us. This is
God.
(**Fiasco** *lies there, softly sobbing with the memory.*) It was a long
time I lay there. Still dark, but the rain stopped. Nothing to
see. Just darkness. And I thought: I am not the only one. I
felt grief for my family, brothers and sisters, sons and
daughters of Zimbabwe. Zimbabwe. But also power (*Actors*
make the sound of advancing helicopters.), I was given power. I
heard helicopters and their light swept across the bush. That's
when I felt something cold next to me. Z555. My freedom. I
knew I must hide before the sun broke. So I took it up.
(**Fiasco** *gets up with his weapon. He looks dazed, transformed*) . . .
And I walked, arriving at a river. It was furious, swollen from
the rains, a stream gone mad. I just started through it . . .

Two actors use the blanket as water, as he wades and struggles through
the torrent.

. . . deeper and deeper . . . washing me down

The blanket starts to get tied up in his hands.

. . . and then a force pulling my Kalashnikov, Z555 going
down, pulling down, something stronger than twenty men
ripping it from my hands. (*He struggles demonically to hold on to*
his weapon.) It went! My freedom! I dived, up and down, up
and down.

On his last dive frantically searching for his weapon in the raging river bed, **Chidhina** *pushes him down in the tangle of blanket-water. At last he hauls himself free, crawls and flops down. There is a long silence.*

I crossed the river.

Febi *starts singing the sad theme song of Comrade Fiasco. At the end of the song,* **Jungle** *takes the blanket, holds it over him like a cave, then wraps it round him for warmth.*

Chidhina *(standing over him)*   Until you came to the cave.

Fiasco *(quietly)*   I lost it.

Chidhina   Your passport.

Fiasco   The river took it.

Chidhina   Your ticket to freedom. Mutengesi.

Fiasco   I am not a sellout.

Chidhina   How many cuts shall we give you? Thirty? Seventy?

Jungle   Leave, Chidhina.

Chidhina   He threw it away, he must pay the penalty.

Febi   It was a mistake a long time ago.

Jungle   He saw God.

Chidhina   He lost his tiny head.

Fiasco   I am back now.

Chidhina   IT IS FINISHED!

Fiasco   No.

Chidhina   It is finished. The struggle is finished. Go back to your cave, Fiasco. You are just a memory. No one remembers or cares what you saw, God or the inside of an enemy bullet. Go back. You are lucky. You missed the labour queues, the waiting and disappointment. You missed that. You missed becoming a security guard or a driver. You didn't end up rotting in a district office receiving and writing memorandum.

You sat in a cave thinking about a river, about a gun, about a God that no one remembers! ·

Febi   What about magic, Chidhina?

Chidhina   What magic!!?

Jungle   Yes! Protection somehow?

Chidhina   You think he is an invisible somebody, mudzimu – protected. A witch, George? A mermaid in the river? Do you think they did this, George?

Jungle   Of course, anything can happen. I heard his story. It comes from his heart.

Chidhina (*almost stopping from his previous thought*)   Or is it politics, George? Ordinary day to day politics? Every day, George, we are disappearing. Like this chameleon here who arrived too late to make any difference. We already disappeared, George, into history, like our people hunting for their I.D. numbers – it's no different from our friend Fiasco – losing numbers in the queues – (*He begins an involved parody.*) – 'come back tomorrow, bring a birth certificate, convince me you were born, why are you registered for Save, you must go to Chivhu, that is the area where you were born, ah sorry, no, we are closed, you must come back Thursday, we can't register you, you must bring your school record, why haven't you got a letter from the headmaster, you must go back to Save'! People, people, people marching up and down up and down, to this office and that, waiting while the clerk is finding his pencil or the form or his girlfriend's telephone number and telling you that there are no more forms, they are closing, this is the wrong office – and you, George, you, want to tell me about magic. Those people are becoming invisible, George, trying to find their identity. Six years, eight years, who cares, as long as they are worried . . . Now let's talk of magic, how a system can make people disappear. (*Something snaps in him, and he gives* **Fiasco** *a cracking blow that sends him reeling.*) I WILL NOT WAIT! He can choke on his fucking dreams. (*He gives* **Fiasco** *another shocking blow, then grabs the blanket and puts it over his head, stifling him.*) No more of your stupid faith, comrade.

He snuffs out **Fiasco** *until he is motionless. When the body is still,* **Chidhina** *gets up, stuffing the blanket over his face, stands up and looks down at the body.* **Jungle** *and* **Febi** *look on shocked, immobile, helpless.* **Chidhina** *moves away, tired like a man who has just run a marathon, and sits in a back corner. Silence.*

Jungle (*voice thin*)   What have you done?

Chidhina (*pause*)   There was a heavy storm.

Febi   He is not moving.

Jungle   He could be . . .

Chidhina (*not even looking up*)   What?

Jungle   He looks . . .

Chidhina   What? Say it, Jungle. Say what you mean.

Jungle   He looks . . . dead.

Chidhina   You said it. Well done. You could never say it before. Now you know what death looks like.

Febi   Is he pretending?

Jungle   It was an argument, discussion!

Febi   This is trouble.

Jungle   This is a police station!

Chidhina (*looking up for the first time with a wry smile on his face*)   What policeman looks in his own cell?

Jungle   They will look. They know he is here.

Chidhina   Who is here, Jungle? A madman, without a name. Nobody clapped eyes on him before.

Jungle   There will be questions. How? Who saw him die?

Chidhina   Who saw him?

Febi   Who saw him, Jungle?

Jungle   They will see the blows. They will check four scenic [*forensic*] and see murder. You killed someone inside a police station.

Febi   They did that before. Rhodesians and CID. Even during sixfire, my brother and six others, Chipinge. When I went there to try and release him, I heard. From poison.

Jungle   But Chidhina has done it. Murder.

Chidhina   Don't talk of murder.

Jungle   You trying to tell me he just suicided himself? Like a baobab?

Chidhina   Could be. Facts are strange.

Jungle   I saw. With my own eyes.

Chidhina   You wouldn't say that, Jungle. He just passed away. Better still you did it.

Jungle   I did not touch him.

Chidhina   Then how did it happen? YOU interrogated him. You were playing chief-of-police.

Jungle   I did not kill him.

Chidhina   He was interrogating him, wasn't he, Febi?

Febi   I have to admit.

Jungle   But it was not me. Febi, you can't say . . .

Febi   I know, Jungle. But we must think. It is better to say he just passed away, in the night.

Jungle   He was a comrade. Our brother.

Febi   We don't know, honest, Jungle. We never met him before. A comrade, without boots, or bandolier, no weapon or identification.

Chidhina   He must produce his situpa, George.

Jungle   I don't believe this. You who have been talking of lies and truth.

Chidhina   What truth? Whose truth? I warned him.

Jungle (*letting it all out*)   You are sick. Worse than ever what he was. The things you spoke of, you betrayed! You betray us!

Chidhina (*with the fury of grief*)   I BETRAYED NOTHING. I kept my AK47 until they took it back to the armoury. I fought. I did not run away. I believed. For Zimbabwe. For our people. I believed that God could be with us. I even believed in the power of being invisible, the power to hide from the enemy, amongst the people, in the heart of the masses, in the villages, just as we could disappear without trace, vanish before the enemy could spot us. I did not betray us. Over and over I held my faith, I was not alone, we were one, all of us . . .

Febi   This was a mistake, Chidhina.

Jungle   You should not have done this.

Chidhina (*weeping*)   Why? Why does he come back, just when I was forgetting, just when I thought the memory of my disappointed hopes would not come back? Why did he not stay where he was, forgotten, buried in the past? I remembered revolution and all that time ago, all that time since then, I realised, me, me, me, I had not moved. And I am older.

Febi (*going to* **Chidhina**)   You are still young and handsome.

Jungle (*deliberate interjection*)   You must remove extensions.

Febi   What of extensions?

Jungle   That is for young people, not war veterans.

Febi   I am running my fashion shop.

Jungle   It shows.

Febi   Jungle my life is not just for cooking and looking after others. I was chimbwido once, but now I have still got life, I still go looking for bargains in Botswana and Bulawayo. I am in business, not running three acres of mealies.

Jungle   You should be looking at agricultural extensions not hair extensions.

Febi Do you think that just because women come from Ndima or Tanganda they cannot look smart? You don't know Zimbabwe, my friend.

Jungle I know culture. Now you want to apply on your own head some wire which they make the same factory they make brushes and brooms. Are African women now dusting with their heads?

Febi Obvious you don't know culture.

Chidhina (*quietly interjecting*) Cover him.

Jungle and **Febi** *suddenly look round. They have forgotten he is there, that* **Fiasco** *is dead.*

Chidhina Put the blanket on him properly.

Jungle and **Febi** *both go to the blanket and cover* **Fiasco**. *Long silence.*

Febi (*having neatly arranged the body, she is overwhelmed by emotion of this death, this life, his history*) The sounds from war to peace must have been different. He MUST have seen: that is war, that is peace. I was thinking of how we used to cry away the s'khwehle that would fly into our fields. Wailing women all afternoon to drive the birds away. Maybe he thought someone had died, (*Bitter.*) maybe war and life sound the same.

Jungle Sounds would be different after war. Herding sounds, cattle, people calling, cars and buses. Independence has got a happy sound.

Febi (*the sight of* **Fiasco** *unleashes these memories and images*) Do you know when I was still very young and we were suffering, I worked at the mission. The sisters first put me to laundry, washing with my hands those long grey gowns and the white collars and the dhuku which had to be pressed perfect.

Chidhina Why are you telling us this?

Febi Because I remember a picture of that time that looks like now, with him lying there. I did that washing work two years, because my mind was on improvements and my mother was suffering. I knew work those days, work. I know work. In the evening I carried a sort of wheelbarrow with those neat nuns' dresses, socks, hats, everything piled nice – Sister Georgina, Sister Paula, Sister Janet, each different sizes – every day! They don't like to put on a dirty clothes.

Chidhina   Do nuns wash their own underpants?

Febi   Why?

Chidhina   I am interested.

Febi   Smalls, as they call it. Smalls, they wash themselves.

Jungle   Was that Catholic, Febi?

Febi   It was.

Jungle   I was born Methodist.

Chidhina   You are an Abel man, Jungle.

Jungle (*solemn*)   Methodists don't have nuns.

Febi   Only Catholic.

Jungle (*solemn*)   That is why it was a surprise to me to find out that they wear mabhurukwa.

Febi   Nuns?

Jungle   Methodists.

Febi (*going back*)   I worked hard. For two pounds ten shillings. Then the Superior said, she noticed my efforts: we are short in hospital, you can work there.

Jungle   Is that how you became a nurse? From the laundry?

Febi   Later, I went for training at Mount Selinda, but those days, my orders were just with a thermometer, putting it in the patient's mouth, then the real nurse comes to check and I take the thermometer (*She shakes it with her hand to get the mercury down.*) just that (*Repeats the flicking gesture.*) like so (*Repeats.*) into the next.

Jungle   It was Fahrenheit those days, which is higher degrees than centigrade, not so? There was inflation only concerning temperatures.

Febi   You just had to flick like so (*She repeats the gesture.*) and the mercury went normal. (*She looks over at* **Fiasco**.) That is where I learn about a dead person.

Chidhina   What is the temperature of a dead person?

Febi   You never do that.

Chidhina   You might have learnt something new.

Febi   I did only what is required. I put the eyelids down. (*She does this very solemnly.*)

Chidhina   Do Methodists do that, Jungle?

Jungle (*put out*)   I don't know. I never saw a dead Methodist.

Febi   I had to take them to the mortuary in a sort of cart . . .

Chidhina (*marvelling*)   Jungle, I tell you, these missionaries are amazing. I didn't know Febi was organising scania funeral society for the holy sisters.

Febi   True story. I know dying. Dying I know . . . (*She drifts off into deep remembrance.*)

Jungle   Your heart is dark, Chidhina, dark as night.

Chidhina   What do you want me to do? 'I'm sorry, Fiasco. I am truly sorry. This should not have happened.'

For the first time since he choked **Fiasco**, **Chidhina** *has got up.* **Febi** *meanwhile prepares the body and* **Jungle** *acts like a priest, launching into a song that rises into a tumultuous thing. When* **Jungle** *is in full flight,* **Febi** *is kneeling by the body, and* **Chidhina**, *standing, eventually closes his eyes with the force of the prayer. Imperceptibly, the body moves. No one sees it, then suddenly* **Jungle** *notices, carries on praying with one eye observing, until* **Fiasco** *gives a convulsive twitch . . .*

Jungle   It moved! Fiasco. (*He leaps up, terrified.*) It moved. (*He pulls* **Febi** *up onto her feet and clings to her.*) Fiasco is alive.

They all stare at the body, which lies still. Then **Chidhina** *stoops and stares for signs of movement.*

Chidhina (*long pause, as they watch him looking*)   Where?

Jungle   Under the blanket.

Chidhina *is about to lift the blanket off*

No don't! (*He pulls* **Chidhina** *away.*)

Febi   What did you see?

Jungle   Fiasco is living.

Febi   Can't be.

Chidhina   Tell us, Febi. From your experience, is he dead?

Febi   I don't know. The blanket . . . (*As she goes forward to lift the blanket . . .*)

Jungle (*pulling her away*)   No! Nobody touch him! (*He defends* **Fiasco** *like a shrine, as if he would die protecting it.*)

Chidhina   Maybe we should call the police to sort this out. I don't like it.

Jungle   No. Nobody! Until this is finished and settled. (*Ordering them away.*) Stand there!

They move. **Jungle** *turns round to the body, piously. He launches hysterically again into the same song prayer when* **Fiasco** *twitches.*

Jungle (*jumping*)   Again!

Febi   You are joking, Jungle.

Chidhina   Making me agitated, George.

Jungle   I saw. With my own eyes.

As they all look, **Fiasco**'s *left foot kicks.* **Jungle** *points. Then the right arm twitches.* **Jungle** *points.* **Fiasco**'s *knees jerk.* **Jungle** *points. There is pause. They watch avidly. Then* **Fiasco**'s *right arm travels down to his groin which it gives a very thorough scratch.* **Jungle** *points.*

Chidhina   Nerves.

Febi   It can happen. The nervous system, when energy is released.

Jungle   That is not nerves. That is kicking, and scratching.

Fiasco *convulses violently.*

Chidhina   That is maniac nerves.

Jungle   Nerves nerves. That is kicking.

Febi   Like a baby, inside.

Fiasco *kicks even more.*

Jungle   You see? You see?

Febi   In all my years nursing, I never saw such a thing.

Jungle   He is fighting ancestors.

Fiasco *goes mad.*

Chidhina   Punch-up! Enemy contact!

He flies away. **Febi** *starts backwards.*

Jungle   No. Look!

Fiasco'*s head begins to emerge from the blanket, like a man emerging from sleep. The longest sleep on earth. He has a gigantic yawn, brushes his face, his head, ruffles and scratches. Yawns, stretches. Still half asleep.*

Chidhina   Unbelievable!

Jungle   You see? You see?

Febi   This is truly a miracle! He's just coming out, I can almost feel it, like a baby.

Jungle   Bring him out.

Febi (*yanking his head*)   Forceps delivery! Was liberation not enough of a midwife, my lovely! Aaaiiiyi! But he's heavy, Zimbabwe's biggest.

Jungle   With hairs on his head!

Chidhina   And beards.

Jungle   Born to a strange mother, this.

Chidhina   A jail of a mother! Prison womb.

Febi   Come on, baby, struggle and push, struggle! Push!

Chidhina (*hands on* **Fiasco***'s head*)   PULL!

Febi   Out with it, OUT!

They all pull with one almighty heave and **Fiasco** *comes up onto his feet in a great upward rush. He is naked . . .*

Jungle (*barely able to contain his excitement and leaping up and down with glee*)   He is up! He is out! No more suicide – this is self-birth! No more murder – he has born himself! You see! You see! Investigations have brought a new man.

Fiasco *looks stunned and weak.*

Febi   It's a boy, no question.

Chidhina (*gives him a slap across the face and another across the back which knocks* **Fiasco** *over*)   Fiasco!

Jungle   What was that for? You want to kill him all over again?

Chidhina   Just helping him with his breathing.

Fiasco *is crouched on the floor trying to get his breath.* **Chidhina** *whacks him again.*

Chidhina   Wakey, wakey, rise and shine!

Fiasco *gets up on his feet.*

Jungle (*quickly fetching a blanket to put around him*)   We are with the ladies here.

Fiasco (*holding the blanket round himself. He is elated and speaks in a big masculine voice*)   I was born alive!

Jungle (*singing*)   Happy Birthday to you, Happy Birthday to you! Happy Birthday, Comrade Fiasco, happy birthday to you.

Chidhina   Don't overdo it, Jungle.

Jungle (*starting up again*)   How old are you now? How old are you now?

Febi *joins in.*

How old are you, Fiasco? How old are you now?

Chidhina   All right, enough celebrations, enough . . .

Jungle (*carried away*)   Speech! Speech!

Chidhina   We don't need speeches, always forever speeches.

Jungle   He didn't have his tongue before.

Febi (*agreeing*)   So he must use the power of speech.

Chidhina   I was just enjoying silence.

Jungle   Speak!

Fiasco (*confidently*)   When you see a bird sleeping in a tree, you must not believe it cannot fly. Its time will come. And so me also.

Jungle (*hugging* **Febi**)   This is a teacher, I tell you.

Febi   He doesn't need degrees.

Jungle   He is a leader.

Fiasco (*for the first time he seems truly angry*)   I am not a leader! I have got nothing to tell you. What can I say? I disappeared. I had visions. I spoke to old people there in the cave who covered the darkness of the cave with light as if it was daytime? I can tell you all that and you still won't believe.

Jungle   We believe.

Fiasco   Therefore we are together. (*He embraces them.*) There is nothing to say.

Febi   You can teach us.

Fiasco   I give you a rally.

He fetches the bucket and ceremoniously gets up onto it, coughs, clears his throat, etc. **Febi** *and* **Jungle** *sit, back to audience, facing the raised* **Fiasco**.

Fiasco Down with slogans!

Febi/Jungle Down!

Fiasco Down with slogans!

Jungle Dow . . . (*Looks sheepish.*)

Fiasco Why are you looking for leaders? Are you afraid of yourself? Is that why you come after me looking for something? Is that why you pull me into this prison? Are you afraid that I was too free? I am sorry, my history does not fit yours.

Chidhina You mean, after all this you have nothing to say.

Fiasco (*looks at* **Chidhina**) One thing: I am not free. All my life I had visions and dreams.

Chidhina We don't want visions – we want results.

Fiasco I can never fight visions, never. Life comes to me and lands on my shoulder like an eagle. I am not free because I am slave to freedom. Sorry for that.

Chidhina (*claps his hands slowly, sarcastic*) Well done, comrade. So we have the body of Fiasco, we have the man, but not the dreams. Let ME tell YOU something. I don't deny you your chance for freedom. Tomorrow you walk out of here, so-called free man, with all your sanity in one piece. Your name, your number, your body. They will welcome you, bath you, scrub you and clean you. They will sterilise you with four thousand dollars demobilisation. A warrior's pension. You'll walk out into the land of the living, back to your family and friends, maybe even a job.
And then?

Fiasco I will not be so hungry as I was.

Chidhina What have you brought back for us? Us!

Jungle We understand how he suffered.

Febi And we accept.

Chidhina What have you brought back for us? Don't get

me wrong, I salute your sort of courage, your endurance to survive. Even, I salute your sort of truth. It is yours, yours alone. We all got our caves, Fiasco. Even mine, back then, in the mountains, was pink and warm and safe. But every time I thought it was beautiful, I knew I had to leave it, fight, rejoin the comrades. I was ground force! I love fighting. Up there you just had the best eight years of your life, comrade. So rise up. (*Indicates to* **Febi** *and* **Jungle** *to raise him up on the bucket.*) Raise him up!

They do this with an almost blind obedience.

Higher!
Higher!

Jungle   That's as high as he can go.

Febi   Unless you want us to put him on our backs like bloody slaves.

They leave **Fiasco** *on the bucket and withdraw.*

Chidhina   Comrade Fiasco, even you are risen, I remember one fact, Z555. I am from that school, comrade. As you were talking, I dreamed I found your Z555 in the mud, rusted and clogged, still with its old magazine in it, well primed. I pick it up. Your freedom. (*He mimes picking it up.*) And pass it up to you. And maybe in a small corner of it, Z555 still shines.

Fiasco *holds the weapon.*

You clear the sights, cock the weapon and aim.

Fiasco *stares at* **Chidhina**.

Chidhina Aim, Fiasco!!

Fiasco   Aim at what? It doesn't fire.

Chidhina   Your freedom is fucked, Fiasco. (*He pulls him off the bucket and puts the bucket on* **Fiasco**'s *head, raising his arm in a clenched fist salute.*) Forward with silence!

Fiasco   No! (*He removes the bucket from his head.*) I was ever born alive!! I will never die. I shall first ask God to kill me.

Chidhina   Well, when you do ask, make sure whoever
buries you that they tell your story. Because we are fed up
with the insult of a silent burial with half your history rubbed
out. So rise, Fiasco, warts and all. And let your history shine.
That day, the day you do that . . . history . . . (*He cartwheels
across the stage.*) . . . takes a tumble.

Chidhina *starts a powerful, rhythmic, pulsating rendition of 'Rise and
shine, Comrade Fiasco'; the others rejoin into a four-pointed star, stomping
and clapping, the lights come down to blackout.*

Glossary

baba Shona/Ndebele: father
banga A large hacking knife, like a scythe
bra as elsewhere: brother
checha! hurry up!
chef from Portuguese: leader, chief, boss, commander. Used
    during liberation struggle in Mozambique.
chete chete Shona: emphatic, 'only'
chimbwido Shona: cooks and helpers for the guerrillas
Conex Sections in Rhodesia, Conex was the agricultural
    extension department. During the war, many district officers
    received security fencing protection
dhuku Shona: head scarf
Fagga table checha from Fanakalo or chilapalapa or 'kitchen
    kaffir', a colonial concoction of a language, only spoken in
    the imperative: 'Make the table quick quick'
hayikhona Ndebele: a negative interrogative
'Iva gamba utarise mhendu' Shona Freedom song about
    vigilance: 'Be like a hero and look out for the enemy'
Lancaster House ceasefire agreement signed in 1979 which
    brought the war to an end, set a time for democratic
    elections, independence and a constitution, with
    controversial white minority provisions for ten years
mabhurukwa Shona: panties, pants, trousers; from the
    Afrikaans 'broeke'
majoni colloquial name for policemen (plural), especially white
    policemen during colonial days
mdala Ndebele: old man
mhandu Shona: enemy
mudiwa beloved
mudzimu Shona: ancestral spirit
mukomana Shona: boy
murungu Shona: white man
mutengesi Shona: sellout
muuyu Shona: baobab fruit
muzukuru Shona: term of familiarity for a younger man;
    nephew
ndolas equivalent of 'ndoramanis'. Used mainly in the

southeast of Zimbabwe

ndoramani   Shona: guerilla word for the enemy

nikkis   from Afrikaans: 'nothing', 'never'

Nyarara Mwan'angu   Shona lullaby: 'Hush, my child'

Nzuzu   water spirit who sometimes claims victims, transforms them into humans with healing powers

pfutseki   Shona: variation on 'voetsek'

Renamos   Mozambique National Resistance (MNR), a rebel force supported by right-wing groupings in Portugal, South Africa and the United States, against the Frelimo government. In destabilising Mozambique, MNR bandits also brought the war to the contiguous eastern border of Zimbabwe

scania   nickname for scotchcarts used by city vendors, particularly in Bulawayo. The Bulawayo municipality appears to have sanctioned the word by putting up a 'Scania Parking' sign at Makokoba market

sex and unity   the 'unity' refers to the historic unity agreement between the two major political parties (formerly 'liberation movements'), ZAPU and ZANU-PF in 1987, in which the two merged

sha   shortened version of shamwari

shamwari   Shona: friend

situpa   colloquial term for identity card or pass, used in Rhodesian days, but still heard now

sixfire   ceasefire

s'khwehle   Ndebele: small quails

toyi-toyi   used for all the liberation armies: a vigorous military training march whereby a formation of soldiers jog, holding AK's above their heads singing in unison

tsotsi   widely used in southern Africa: thief

ubhinya   a bandit, living in the bush, who resorts to using force to direct person(s) towards a particular action

Uri benzi here?   Shona: Are you mad/round the bend?

vakuru   Shona: elders. Colloquially, 'big shots'

Vana vevhu mukai   Shona: Children of the soil, arise!

voetsek   orig. Afrikaans: roughly, 'get lost' or 'piss off'

Zifa   Zimbabwe Football Association

zincs   colloquial term for metal identity discs, post-independence

.

.

Anowa

Ama Ata Aidoo

For my mother
'Aunt Abasema'
who told a story and sang a song

Characters

Old Man   *being 'The-Mouth-That-Eats-*
Old Woman   *Salt-And-Pepper'*
A **Man** *and a* **Woman**, *who don't say a word*
Anowa, *a young woman*
Kofi Ako, *her man who expands*
Osam, *her father who smokes his pipe*
Badua, *her mother who complains at the beginning and cries at the end*
Boy, *a young slave, about twenty years old*
Girl, *a young slave girl*
Panyin-na-Kakra, *a pair of boy twins whose duty it is to fan an empty chair*
Hornblower
Slaves, carriers, hailing women, drummers, messengers, townspeople

Author's Note

Stage
Unless the producer has much ingenuity and can rely on speed, it is necessary for the stage to have parts to it, either at adjacent angles (right stage, left stage) or perpendicularly (upper stage, lower stage). The latter is what is maintained throughout the script and the doors are therefore upper left, upper right, lower left, lower right. The second stage could be narrower (smaller) than the first and, in fact, any space between the audience and the real stage can serve for this purpose.

Cast
The list is quite long but the scenes are such that one person can play two or more parts if necessary.

Costume
Anything African will do as long as a certain consistency is followed. Otherwise, a set of Ghanaian costumes might be made up of the following:

Anowa: At the opening of Phase One she has a single piece of material about 2 yards long and 45 inches wide wrapped round her body. Later in Phase One she adds a similar piece to the original, having one tied round the lower half of her body and the other wrapped over her chest. In later scenes she may change the style of the second cloth and wear it like a shawl, or drape it round her shoulders and arms to express what she is feeling – cold, lonely or sad: but it should be the same pair of cloths throughout the play.

Badua and **Old Woman**: Same as **Anowa** in Phase One. The anonymous **Woman** of Phase One: An old cloth wrapped round her for a skirt, and an old-looking, old-fashioned cotton blouse, probably with pleated and fussy sleeves.

Kofi: In Phase One and first part of Phase Two he wears men's work clothes. These consist of a pair of long knickers and a jumper-shirt, both of them old-looking and possibly patched. From the middle of Phase Two he is always in men's leisure clothes, for example a large piece of printed cotton (4 to 6 yards wide) worn around the whole body and the top edges gathered on the left shoulder. In the last part of Phase Two and throughout Phase Three, the Ghanaian *kente* (or any rich-looking fabric like velvet or silk) should be substituted; in these scenes, he should wear open sandals, a gold head band, rings and other gold jewelry (stage gold!).

Anonymous **Man** of Phase One, **Boy** and other male slaves: Men's work clothes.

Old Man and **Osam**: Men's leisure clothes.

Lighting

A skilled and extensive use of lighting could be very effective, especially to indicate the beginning and ending of scenes, since this helps to simplify the set and speeds up the movement of the play. Of course, the curtain of a conventional stage can always be used.

Libation

A realistic one may be poured only if it can be managed without clumsiness.

Music

As long as it would help to create the right atmosphere and comment on the action, the Ghanaian forms may be replaced by other African or any other folk music. The Atenteben which is here intended as a symbol for Anowa, is a single, delicate but wild wind instrument. The Horn (Bull's) is usually old and turned dark brown by sacrificial blood. It is an appendage of the stool and symbol of state, village or group power. An individual acquired a horn (but never a stool) if he felt he was rich and powerful enough. In fact, the acquisition of such a horn was a declaration of power. The horn sang the praises of its owner(s), its language codes being very similar to those of drums. A Fontonfrom is an essentially dignified, low-rumbling drum in a big man's ensemble.

The Procession

It is not necessary to follow closely the instructions set down. The important thing is to create an impression of opulence and crowds; and the degree of the sumptuousness of the set and for the whole of Phase Three should be managed to suit the facilities available for any particular production.

Ending

It is quite possible to end the play with the final exit of Anowa. Or one could follow the script and permit The-Mouth-That-Eats-Salt-And-Pepper to appear for the last scene. The choice is open.

Prologue

Enter 'The-Mouth-That-Eats-Salt-And-Pepper'.

Old Man *always enters first from the left side of the auditorium.* **Old Woman** *from the right. Each leaves in the same direction. She is wizened, leans on a stick and her voice is raspy with asthma and a lifetime of putting her mouth into other people's affairs. She begins her speeches when she is half-way in and ends them half-way out. Her entries are announced by the thumping of her stick, and whenever she is the last of the two to leave the stage, her exit is marked by a prolonged coughing. She is never still and very often speaks with agitation, waving her stick and walking up and down the lower stage. He is serene and everything about him is more orderly. He enters quietly and leaves after his last statements have been made. The two should never appear or move onto the upper stage. There is a block of wood lying around on which the* **Old Woman** *sometimes sits.*

Old Man   Here in the state of Abura,
Which must surely be one of the best pieces of land
Odomankoma, our creator, has given to man,
Everything happens in moderation:
The sun comes out each day,
But its heat seldom burns our crops;
Rains are good when they fall
And Asaase Efua the earth-goddess gives of herself
To them that know the seasons;
Streams abound, which like all gods
Must have their angry moments and swell,
But floods are hardly known to living memory.
Behind us to the north, Aburabura
Our beautiful lonely mountain sits with her neck to the skies,
Reminding us that all of the earth is not flat.
In the south, Nana Bosompo, the ocean roars on. Lord of
    Tuesdays,
His day must be sacred. We know him well and even
The most unadventurous can reap his fish, just sitting on his
    pretty sands,
While for the brave who read the constellations,

His billows are easier to ride than the currents of a ditch.
And you, Mighty God, and your hosts our forefathers,
We do not say this in boastfulness . . . (*He bends in the fingers of his right hand as though he were holding a cup, raises it up and acts out the motions of pouring a libation.*) but only in true thankfulness,
Praying to you all that things may continue to be good
And even get better.
But bring your ears nearer, my friends, so I can whisper you a secret.
Our armies, well-organised though they be,
Are more skilled in quenching fires than in the art of war!
So please,
Let not posterity judge it too bitterly
That in a dangerous moment, the lords of our Houses
Sought the protection of those that-came-from-beyond-the-horizon
Against our more active kinsmen from the north;
We only wanted a little peace
For which our fathers had broken away
From the larger homestead and come to these parts,
Led by the embalmed bodies of the Three Elders.
And yet, there is a bigger crime
We have inherited from the clans incorporate
Of which, lest we forget when the time does come,
Those forts standing at the door
Of the great ocean shall remind our children
And the sea bear witness.
And now, listen o . . . o listen, listen,
If there be some among us that have found a common sauce-bowl
In which they play a game of dipping with the stranger,
Who shall complain?
Out of one womb can always come a disparate breed;
And men will always go
Where the rumbling hunger in their bowels shall be stilled,
And that is where they will stay.
O my beloveds, let it not surprise us then
That This-One and That-One

Depend for their well-being on the presence of
The pale stranger in our midst:
Kofi was, is, and shall always be
One of us.

First sign of **Old Woman**.

But what shall we say of our child,
The unfortunate Anowa? Let us just say that
Anowa is not a girl to meet every day.

Old Woman   That Anowa is something else! Like all the
beautiful maidens in the tales, she has refused to marry any of
the sturdy men who have asked for her hand in marriage. No
one knows what is wrong with her!

Old Man   A child of several incarnations,
She listens to her own tales,
Laughs at her own jokes and
Follows her own advice.

Old Woman   Some of us think she has just allowed her
unusual beauty to cloud her vision of the world.

Old Man   Beautiful as Korado Ahima,
Someone's-Thin-Thread.
A dainty little pot
Well-baked,
And polished smooth
To set in a nobleman's corner.

Badua *enters from a door at upper right and moves down but stops a
few steps before the lower stage and stands looking at* **Old Man** *and*
Old Woman.

Old Woman   Others think that her mother Badua has spoilt
her shamefully. But let us ask: Why should Anowa carry
herself so stiffly? Where is she taking her 'I won't, I won't' to?
Badua should tell her daughter that the sapling breaks with
bending that will not grow straight.

Badua *(bursting out suddenly and pointing her fingers clearly at* **Old
Man** *and* **Old Woman** *but speaking to herself)*   Perhaps it was
my fault too, but how could she come to any good when her

name was always on the lips of every mouth that ate pepper
and salt?

She turns round angrily and exits where she had come from. **Old Man**
and **Old Woman** *do not show they had been aware of her.*

Old Man   But here is Anowa,
And also Kofi Ako.
It is now a little less than thirty years
When the lords of our Houses
Signed that piece of paper –
The Bond of 1844 they call it –
Binding us to the white men
Who came from beyond the horizon.

Exit **Old Man**.

Old Woman   And the gods will surely punish Abena Badua
for refusing to let a born priestess dance!

Phase One

In Yebi.

*Lower stage. Early evening village noises, for example, the pounding of
fufu or millet, a goat bleats loudly, a woman calls her child, etc.*
Anowa *enters from lower right, carrying an empty water-pot. She walks
to the centre of the lower stage, stops and looks behind her. Then she
overturns the water-pot and sits on it facing the audience. She is wearing
her cloth wrapped around her. The upper part of her breasts are visible,
and also all of her legs. She is slim and slight of build. She turns her
face momentarily towards lower left. During a moment when she is
looking at her feet,* **Kofi Ako** *enters from the lower right. He is a tall,
broad, young man, and very good-looking. The village noises die down.*

*He is in work clothes and carrying a fish trap and a bundle of baits.
He steals quietly up to her and cries, 'Hei!' She is startled but regains
her composure immediately. They smile at each other. Just then, a*
Woman *comes in from the lower left, carrying a wooden tray which is
filled with farm produce – cassava, yam, plantain, pepper, tomatoes, etc.
Close behind her is a* **Man**, *presumably her husband, also in
work clothes, with a gun on his shoulder and a machet under his arm.
They pass by* **Anowa** *and* **Kofi** *and walk on towards lower right. The
woman turns round at every step to stare at the boy and girl who
continue looking shyly at each other. Finally, the* **Woman** *misses a step
or kicks against the block of wood. She falls, her tray crashing down.*

Anowa *and* **Kofi** *burst into loud uncontrollable laughter. Assisted by
her* **Man**, *the* **Woman** *begins to collect her things together. Having got
her load back on her head, she disappears, followed by her* **Man**.
Meanwhile, **Anowa** *and* **Kofi** *continue laughing and go on doing so a
little while after the lights have been removed from them.*

Upper stage. The courtyard of Maami **Badua** *and Papa* **Osam**'s
*cottage. Village noises as in previous scene. Standing in the centre is an
earthen hearth with tripod cooking pot. There are a couple of small
household stools standing around. By the right wall is a lie-in chair
which belongs exclusively to Papa* **Osam**. *Whenever he sits down, he
sits in this. By the chair is a small table. The lower stage here represents
a section of a village side street from which there is an open entrance into
the courtyard. In the background, upper left and upper right are doors
connecting the courtyard to the inner rooms of the house.*

In the pot something is cooking which throughout the scene Maami
Badua *will go and stir. By the hearth is a small vessel into which she*
puts the ladle after each stirring.

    Badua *enters from upper right, goes to the hearth, picks up the ladle*
and stirs the soup. She is talking loudly to herself.

Badua   Any mother would be concerned if her daughter
refused to get married six years after her puberty. If I do not
worry about this, what shall I worry about?

Osam *enters from upper left smoking his pipe.*

Badua   Besides, a woman is not a stone but a human being;
she grows.

Osam   Woman, (**Badua** *turns to look at him.*) that does not
mean you should break my ears with your complaints. (*He
looks very composed.*)

Badua   What did you say, Osam?

Osam   I say you complain too much. (*He goes to occupy the lie-
in chair, and exclaims, 'Ah!' with satisfaction.*)

Badua (*seriously*)   Are you trying to send me insane?

Osam   Will that shut you up?

Badua   Kofi Sam! (*Now she really is angry.*)

Osam   Yes, my wife.

Badua *breathes audibly with exasperation. She begins pacing up and
down the courtyard, with the ladle in her hand.*

Badua (*moving quickly up to* **Osam**)   So it is nothing at
a–a–l–l (*Stretching the utterance of the last word.*) to you that your
child is not married and goes round wild, making everyone
talk about her?

Osam   Which is your headache, that she is not yet married,
or that she is wild?

Badua   Hmm!

Osam   You know that I am a man and getting daughters
married is not one of my duties. Getting them born, aha! But

not finding them husbands.

Badua   Hmm! (*Paces up and down.*)

Osam   And may the ancestral spirits help me, but what man would I order from the heavens to please the difficult eye of my daughter Anowa?

Badua   Hmm! (*She goes and stirs the soup and this time remembers to put the ladle down. She stands musing by the hearth.*)

Osam   As for her wildness, what do you want me to say again about that? I have always asked you to apprentice her to a priestess to quieten her down. But . . .

Roused again, **Badua** *moves quickly back to where he is and meanwhile, corks both her ears with two fingers and shakes her head to make sure he notices what she is doing.*

Osam (*chuckles*)   Hmm, play children's games with me, my wife. One day you will click your fingers with regret that you did not listen to me.

Badua (*removes her fingers from her ears*)   I have said it and I will say it again and again and again! I am not going to turn my only daughter into a dancer priestess.

Osam   What is wrong with priestesses?

Badua   I don't say there is anything wrong with them.

Osam   Did you not consult them over and over again when you could not get a single child from your womb to live beyond one day?

Badua (*reflectively*)   O yes. I respect them, I honour them . . . I fear them. Yes, my husband, I fear them. But my only daughter shall not be a priestess.

Osam   They have so much glory and dignity . . .

Badua   But in the end, they are not people. They become too much like the gods they interpret.

As she enumerates the attributes of priesthood, her voice grows hysterical and her face terror-stricken. **Osam** *removes his pipe, and stares at her,* *his mouth open with amazement.*

They counsel with spirits;
They read into other men's souls;
They swallow dogs' eyes
Jump fires
Drink goats' blood
Sheep milk
Without flinching
Or vomiting
They do not feel
As you or I,
They have no shame.

She relaxes, and **Osam** *does too, the latter sighing audibly.* **Badua** *continues, her face slightly turned away from both her husband and the audience.*

I want my child
To be a human woman
Marry a man,
Tend a farm
And be happy to see her
Peppers and her onions grow.
A woman like her
Should bear children
Many children,
So she can afford to have
One or two die.
Should she not take
Her place at meetings
Among the men and women of the clan?
And sit on my chair when
I am gone? And a captainship in the army,
Should not be beyond her
When the time is ripe!

Osam *nods his head and exclaims, 'Oh . . . oh!'*

Badua   But a priestess lives too much in her own and other people's minds, my husband.

Osam (*sighing again*)   My wife, people with better vision than yours or mine have seen that Anowa is not like you or me. And a prophet with a locked mouth is neither a prophet nor a man. Besides, the yam that will burn, shall burn, boiled or roasted.

Badua (*picks up the ladle but does not stir the pot. Throws her arms about*)   Since you want to see Nkomfo and Nsofo, seers and dancers . . .

Anowa (*from the distance*)   Mother!

Badua   That is her coming.

Anowa   Father!

Osam   O yes: Well let us keep quiet about her affairs then. You know what heart lies in her chest.

Anowa   Mother, Father . . . Father, Mother . . . Mother . . .

Osam *jumps up and confused, he and* **Badua** *keep bumping into each other as each moves without knowing why or where he or she is moving.* **Badua** *still has the ladle in her hands.*

Badua   Why do you keep hitting at me?

Anowa   Mother!

Osam   Sorry, I did not mean to. But you watch your step too.

Anowa   Father!

Osam   And where is she?

Anowa *runs in, lower right, with her empty water-pot.*

Badua   *Hei*. Why do you frighten me so? And where is the water?

Anowa   O Mother. (*She stops running and stays on the lower stage.*)

Osam   What is it?

Anowa (*her eyes swerving from the face of one to the other*)   O Father!

Osam Say whatever you have got to say and stop behaving like a child.

Badua Calling us from the street!

Osam What have you got to tell us that couldn't wait until you reached here?

Anowa O Father.

Badua And look at her. See here, it is time you realised you have grown up.

Anowa Mother . . . (*Moving a step or two forward.*)

Badua And now what is it? Besides, where is the water? I am sure this household will go to bed to count the beams tonight since there is no water to cook with.

Anowa Mother, Father, I have met the man I want to marry.

Badua What is she saying?

Anowa I say I have found the man I would like to marry.

Osam
Badua } Eh?

*Long pause during which **Badua** stares at **Anowa** with her head tilted to one side.*

Anowa Kofi Ako asked me to marry him and I said I will, too.

Badua Eh?

Osam Eh?

Badua Eh?

Osam Eh?

Badua Eh?

Osam
Badua } Eh – eh!

Light dies on all three and comes on again almost immediately. **Osam** *is sitting in his chair.* **Anowa** *hovers around and she has a chewing-stick in her mouth with which she scrapes her teeth when she is not speaking.* **Badua** *is sitting by the hearth doing nothing.*

Anowa Mother, you have been at me for a long time to get married. And now that I have found someone I like very much ...

Badua Anowa, shut up. Shut up! Push your tongue into your mouth and close it. Shut up because I never counted Kofi Ako among my sons-in-law. Anowa, why Kofi Ako? Of all the mothers that are here in Yebi, should I be the one whose daughter would want to marry this fool, this good-for-nothing cassava-man, this watery male of all watery males? This-I-am-the-handsome-one-with-a-stick-between-my-teeth-in-the-market-place ... This ... this ...

Anowa O Mother ...

Badua (*quietly*) I say Anowa, why did you not wait for a day when I was cooking banku and your father was drinking palm-wine in the market place with his friends? When you could have snatched the ladle from my hands and hit me with it and taken your father's wine from his hands and thrown it into his face? Anowa, why did you not wait for a day like that, since you want to behave like the girl in the folk-tale?

Anowa But what are you talking about, Mother?

Badua And you, Kobina Sam, will you not say anything?

Osam Abena Badua, leave me out of this. You know that if I so much as whisper anything to do with Anowa, you and your brothers and your uncles will tell me to go and straighten out the lives of my nieces. This is your family drum; beat it, my wife.

Badua I did not ask you for riddles.

Osam Mm ... just remember I was smoking my pipe.

Badua If you had been any other father, you would have known what to do and what not to do.

Osam Perhaps; but that does not mean I would have *done*

anything. The way you used to talk, I thought if Anowa came
to tell you she was going to get married to Kweku Ananse, or
indeed the devil himself, you would spread rich cloth before
her to walk on. And probably sacrifice an elephant.

Badua And do you not know what this Kofi Ako is like?

Anowa What is he like?

Badua My lady, I have not asked you a question.

Anowa *retires into sullenness. She scrapes her teeth noisily.*

Osam How would I know what he is like? Does he not
come from Nsona House? And is not that one of the best
Houses that are here in Yebi? Has he an ancestor who
unclothed himself to nakedness, had the Unmentionable, killed
himself or another man?

Badua And if all that there is to a young man is that his
family has an unspoiled name, then what kind of a man is
he? Are he and his wife going to feed on stones when he will
not put a blow into a thicket or at least learn a trade?

Osam Anyway, I said long ago that I was removing my
mouth from my daughter Anowa's marriage. Did I not say
that? She would not allow herself to be married to any man
who came to ask for her hand from us and of whom we
approved. Did you not know then that when she chose a
man, it might be one of whom we would disapprove?

Badua But why should she want to do a thing like that?

Osam My wife, do remember I am a man, the son of a
woman who also has five sisters. It is a long time since I gave
up trying to understand the human female. Besides, if you
think well of it, I am not the one to decide finally whom
Anowa can marry. Her uncle, your brother is there, is he not?
You'd better consult him. Because I know your family: they
will say I deliberately married Anowa to a fool to spite them.

Anowa Father, Kofi Ako is not a fool.

Osam My daughter, please forgive me, I am sure you know
him very well. And it was only by way of speaking. Kwame!

Kwame! I thought the boy was around somewhere. (*Moves towards lower stage and looks around.*)

Badua What are you calling him here for?

Osam To go and call us her uncle and your brother.

Badua Could we not have waited until this evening or dawn tomorrow?

Osam For what shall we wait for the dawn?

Badua To settle the case.

Osam What case? Who says I want to settle cases? If there is any case to settle, that is between you and your people. It is not everything one chooses to forget, Badua. Certainly, I remember what happened in connection with Anowa's dancing. That is, if you don't. Did they not say in the end that it was I who had prevented her from going into apprenticeship with a priestess?

Light dies on them and comes on a little later. **Anowa** *is seen dressed in a two-piece cloth. She darts in and out of upper right, with very quick movements. She is packing her belongings into a little basket. Every now and then, she pauses, looks at her mother and sucks her teeth.* **Badua** *complains as before, but this time tearfully.* **Osam** *is lying in his chair smoking.*

Badua I am in disgrace so suck your teeth at me. (*Silence.*) Other women certainly have happier tales to tell about motherhood. (*Silence.*) I think I am just an unlucky woman.

Anowa Mother, I do not know what is wrong with you.

Badua And how would you know what is wrong with me? Look here Anowa, marriage is like a piece of cloth . . .

Anowa I like mine and it is none of your business.

Badua And like cloth, its beauty passes with wear and tear.

Anowa I do not care, Mother. Have I not told you that this is to be my marriage and not yours?

Badua My marriage! Why should it be my daughter who

would want to marry that good-for-nothing cassava-man?

Anowa He is mine and I like him.

Badua If you like him, do like him. The men of his house do not make good husbands; ask older women who are married to Nsona man.

Osam You know what you are saying is not true. Indeed from the beginning of time Nsona men have been known to make the best of husbands.

Badua *glares at him.*

Anowa That does not even worry me and it should not worry you, Mother.

Badua It's up to you, my mistress who knows everything. But remember, my lady – when I am too old to move, I shall be sitting by these walls waiting for you to come back with your rags and nakedness.

Anowa You do not have to wait because we shall not be coming back here to Yebi. Not for a long long time, Mother, not for a long long time.

Badua Of course, if I were you I wouldn't want to come back with my shame either.

Anowa You will be surprised to know that I am going to help him do something with his life.

Badua A–a–h, I wish I could turn into a bird and come and stand on your roof-top watching you make something of that husband of yours. What was he able to make of the plantation of palm-trees his grandfather gave him? And the virgin land his uncles gave him, what did he do with that?

Anowa Please, Mother, remove your witch's mouth from our marriage.

Osam *jumps up and from now on hovers between the two, trying to make peace.*

Osam *Hei* Anowa, what is wrong with you? Are you mad? How can you speak like that to your mother?

Anowa   But Father, Mother does not treat me like her daughter.

Badua   And so you call me a witch? The thing is, I wish I were a witch so that I could protect you from your folly.

Anowa   I do not need your protection, Mother.

Osam   The spirits of my fathers! Anowa, what daughter talks like this to her mother?

Anowa   But Father, what mother talks to her daughter the way Mother talks to me? And now, Mother, I am going, so take your witchery to eat in the sea.

Osam   *Ei* Anowa?

Badua   Thank you my daughter.

Badua *and* **Anowa** *try to jump on each other.* **Badua** *attempts to hit* **Anowa** *but* **Osam** *quickly intervenes.*

Osam   What has come over this household? Tell me what has come over this household? And you too Badua. What has come over you?

Badua   You leave me alone, Osam. Why don't you speak to Anowa? She is your daughter, I am not.

Osam   Well, she is not mature.

Badua   That one makes me laugh. Who is not mature? Has she not been mature enough to divine me out and discover I am a witch? Did she not choose her husband single-handed? And isn't she leaving home to make a better success of her marriage?

Osam   Anowa, have you made up your mind to leave?

Anowa   But Father, Mother is driving me away.

Badua   Who is driving you away?

Anowa   You! Who does not know here in Yebi that from the day I came to tell you that Kofi and I were getting married you have been drumming into my ears what a disgrace this marriage is going to be for you? Didn't you say that your friends were laughing at you? And they were saying that very soon I shall be sharing your clothes because my husband will never buy me any? Father, I am leaving this place. (*She picks up her basket, puts it on her head and moves down towards lower left.*)

Badua   Yes, go.

Anowa   I am on my way, Mother.

Osam   And where is your husband?

Anowa   I am going to look for him.

Osam   Anowa, stop!

But **Anowa** *behaves as if she has not heard him.*

Anowa, you must not leave in this manner.

Badua   Let her go. And may she walk well.

Anowa   Mother, I shall walk so well that I will not find my feet back here again.

She exits lower left. **Osam** *spits with disdain, then stares at* **Badua** *for a long time. She slowly bows her head in the folds of her cloth and begins to weep quietly as the lights die on them.*

Enter 'The-Mouth-That-Eats-Salt-And-Pepper'.

Old Woman   *Hei, hei, hei!* And what do the children of today want? Eh, what would the children of today have us do? Parenthood was always a very expensive affair. But it seems that now there is no man or woman created in nature who is endowed with enough powers to be a mother or a father.

Old Man *enters and walks up to the middle of the lower stage passing* **Old Woman** *on the way.*

Old Woman   Listen, listen. The days when children obeyed their elders have run out. If you tell a child to go forward, he will surely step backwards. And if you asked him to move back a pace, he would run ten leagues.

Old Man   But what makes your heart race itself in anger so? What disturbs you? Some of us feel that the best way to sharpen a knife is not to whet one side of it only. And neither can you solve a riddle by considering only one end of it. We know too well how difficult children of today are. But who begot them? Is a man a father for sleeping with a woman and making her pregnant? And does bearing the child after nine months make her a mother? Or is she the best potter who knows her clay and how it breathes?

Old Woman Are you saying that the good parent would not tell his child what should and should not be done?

Old Man How can I say a thing like that?

Old Woman And must we lie down and have our children play jumping games on our bellies if this is what they want? (*She spits.*)

Old Man Oh no. No one in his rightful mind would say that babies should be free to do what they please. But Abena Badua should have known that Anowa wanted to be something else which she herself had not been ... They say from a very small age, she had the hot eyes and nimble feet of one born to dance for the gods.

Old Woman Hmm. Our ears are breaking with that one. Who heard the Creator tell Anowa what she was coming to do with her life here? And is that why, after all her 'I don't like this' and 'I don't like that', she has gone and married Kofi Ako?

Old Man Tell me what is wrong in that?

Old Woman Certainly. Some of us thought she had ordered a completely new man from the heavens.

Old Man Are people angry because she chose her own husband; or is there something wrong with the boy?

Old Woman As for that Kofi Ako, they say he combs his hair too often and stays too long at the Nteh games.

Old Man Who judges a man of name by his humble beginnings?

Old Woman   Don't ask me. They say Badua does not want him for a son-in-law.

Old Man   She should thank her god that Anowa has decided to settle down at all. But then, we all talk too much about those two. And yet this is not the first time since the world began that a man and a woman have decided to be together against the advice of grey-haired crows.

Old Woman   What foolish words! Some people babble as though they borrowed their grey hairs and did not grow them on their own heads! Badua should have told her daughter that the infant which tries its milk teeth on every bone and stone, grows up with nothing to eat dried meat with. (*She exits noisily.*)

Old Man   I'm certainly a foolish old man. But I think there is no need to behave as though Kofi Ako and Anowa have brought an evil concoction here. Perhaps it is good for them that they have left Yebi to go and try to make their lives somewhere else.

As lights go out, a blending of the Atentenben with any ordinary drum.

Phase Two

On the highway.

The road is represented by the lower stage. A dark night. Wind, thunder and lightning. **Kofi Ako** *enters from lower left. He is carrying a huge load of monkey skins and other hides. He looks exhausted and he is extremely wet from the rain.*

Kofi Ako (*softly and without turning round*) Anowa. (*Silence.*) Anowa, are you coming? (*There is no response from anywhere. Then, frenziedly.*) Anowa, *ei* Anowa!

Anowa (*also entering from lower left and carrying basket*) O, and what is wrong with you? Why are you so afraid?

Kofi Ako *turns round to look at her.*

Kofi Ako (*breathing loudly with relief*) It is a fearful night.

Anowa But you do not have to fear so much for me. Why Kofi, see how your great chest heaves up and down even through the folds of your cloth! (*Laughs.*)

Kofi You just let it be then. (*She giggles more.*) And I can't see that there is anything to laugh at ... Look at the lightning! Shall we sit here in this thicket?

Anowa Yes.

They move to upper stage, and stay in the central area. **Kofi Ako** *puts his own load down with difficulty. He then helps* **Anowa** *to unload hers and sits down immediately.*

Anowa *Hei,* you should not have sat down in the mud just like that.

Kofi Ako As if it matters. Now sit here and move nearer. (*He pulls* **Anowa**, *shivering, down by him.*) Anowa, see how you shiver! And yet my tongue cannot match yours. (*Mocking her.*) 'I am strong ... O ... O ... It is not heavy. My body is small but I am strong!' *Ei,* Anowa!

Anowa But I am strong.

Kofi   We can see that. You know what? Shivering like this, with all your clothes wet, you look like a chick in a puddle.

Anowa   And how about you? (*Beginning to rummage through her basket as though looking for something.*)

Kofi Ako   Do you compare yourself to me? See how big I am. (*He bares his chest and spreads out his arms.*)

Anowa (*pretending to be shocked*)   Ahhh! And this is why we should fear more of you. You are so tall and so broad. You really look like a huge something. There is too much of you. (*Touching different parts of him.*) Anything can get any part of you . . . a branch from a falling tree . . . a broken splinter, and ow, my mouth is at the dung heap, even lightning . . . But I am so little, I can escape things.

Kofi Ako   I was not born to die in any of these ways you mention.

Anowa   O seasoned Priest, and how was I born to die, that you are so afraid of me?

Kofi Ako   I have no idea about that one. What I know is that if you stay out longer in this weather, you are going to be ill. And I cannot afford to lose you.

Anowa   You will never lose me.

Kofi Ako   I thank your mouth.

Anowa *fishes out a miserable looking packet of food from the basket.*

Anowa   Are you hungry? Here is what is left of the food. Oh, but it is so wet. (*She giggles but gives it to him.*)

Kofi Ako (*clutches hungrily at the bundle*)   They are good. How about you?

Anowa   No, I am not hungry.

Kofi Ako   Perhaps you are ill already. (*Begins to wolf the stuff down.*) Mm . . . This life is not good for a woman. No, not even a woman like you. It is too difficult. It is over two hundred miles to the coast and I wonder how much we have done . . .

Anowa We are near Atandasu, this means we have only about thirty miles or more to do . . .

Kofi Ako Is that it? Do you know how many days we have been walking?

Anowa No, I have not been counting the days. All I know is that we have been on the highway for about two weeks now. (*Fights sleep.*)

Kofi Ako The ghost of my fathers!

Anowa But think of it, if we are not too tired to go a little further, we shall be there tomorrow.

Kofi Ako *Ei*, Anowa. You ought to have been born a man.

Anowa Kofi.

Kofi Ako Hmm . . . hmm?

Anowa Why don't you marry another woman?

Kofi Ako *registers alarm.*

Anowa At least she could help us. I could find a good one too. (*Throws up her head to think.*) Let me see. There is a girl in one of the villages we go to e . . . h . . . what is the name?

Kofi Ako Anowa, please don't go on. You know you are annoying me.

Anowa Ah my master, but I don't understand you. You are the only man in this world who has just one wife and swears to keep only her! (*Silence.*) Perhaps it is your medicine's taboo?

Kofi Ako What medicine are you talking about? What taboo?

Anowa Ah Kofi, why has your voice gone fearfully down and so quickly?

Kofi Ako But you are saying something about medicines and taboos which I don't understand. Were you not the same person who said we didn't need anything of that kind?

Anowa And if I said that, then it means from now on I

must not mention medicines and taboos, not even in jest?
Kofi (*Pause.*) . . . what use do you think they will be to us?
Who is interested in harming you or me? Two lonely people
who are only trying something just because the bowels are not
as wise as the mind; but like baby orphans, will shriek for
food even while their mother's body is cold with death . . .

Kofi Ako   Anowa, the man who hates you does not care if
you wait in the sun for your clothes to dry before you can go
and join the dance.

Anowa   But who hates us?

Kofi Ako   My wife, you speak as if we left Yebi with the
town singing and dancing our praises. Was not everyone
saying something unkind about us? Led by your mother?
Anowa, we did not run away from home to go mushroom-
hunting or fish-trapping.

Anowa   I heard you, my husband. But I do not want us to
be caught up in medicines or any of those things.

Kofi Ako   I too have heard you, my wife. Meanwhile, I am
eating all the food . . .

Anowa   Set your mouth free. Mine feels as though it could
not stand the smell of anything.

Kofi Ako (*putting his hand on her forehead*)   Anowa, please, don't
be ill.

Anowa   My mother has often told me that except for the
normal gripes and fevers, my body has never known real
illness.

Kofi Ako   Ah, but my wife seems to be extraordinary in
more things than one. Anowa . . .

Anowa   Yes?

Kofi Ako   We do need something to protect us. Even
though no one dislikes us enough now to want to destroy us,
how about when we begin to do well? Shall we not get hosts
of enemies then?

Anowa (*trying to keep voice light*) But my husband, why should we begin to take to our sick-beds now with illness that may affect us in our old age? Kofi, I just don't like the idea of using medicines.

Kofi Ako But there are many things we do in life which we do not like – which we even hate ... and we only need a bead or two.

Anowa But a shrine has to be worshipped however small its size. And a kind god angered is a thousand times more evil than a mean god unknown. To have a little something to eat and a rag on our back is not a matter to approach a god about.

Kofi Ako Maybe you feel confident enough to trust yourself in dealing with all the problems of life. I think I am different, my wife.

For some time **Anowa** *quietly looks down while he eats.*

Anowa Kofi, that was unkindly said. Because you know that I am already worried about not seeing signs of a baby yet.

Kofi Ako It is quite clear that neither of us knows too much about these things. (*Pause.*) Perhaps it is too early to worry about such a problem. We can consult a more grown-up person, but I know you would not like us to do anything like that.

Anowa (*very loudly*) Listen to what he is saying! Is it the same thing to ask an older person about a woman's womb as it is to contract medicines in pots and potions which would attract good fortune and ward off evil?

Kofi Ako I swear by everything that it is the same. And Anowa, it is too fearful a night to go screaming into the woods.

Anowa That is true.

More thunder and lightning. **Anowa** *begins to nod sleepily. Having finished eating,* **Kofi** *throws the food wrappers into the woods behind him. Then he notices* **Anowa** *nodding.*

Kofi Ako   Anowa, you are very tired. (*Jumping up.*) Let me prepare somewhere for you to sleep.

Then he goes off-stage by upper right. **Anowa** *goes on nodding. Meanwhile the storm continues convulsively.*

Anowa (*startled awake by a peal of thunder*)   What I am worried about are these things. (*She gropes towards the baskets and begins to feel the skins.*) See how wet they are. Tomorrow, they will be heavier than sheets of rock. And if it continues like this, they will all rot. Creator, (*She looks up.*) do as you like, but please, let your sun shine tomorrow so we can dry out these skins. We must stop in the next village to dry them out. Yes, we must stop if the sun comes out.

Kofi Ako (*entering with a couple of plantain or banana leaves which he spreads out to form some kind of mat in the centre of lower stage*)   To do what?

Anowa   To dry out the skins. They are so wet.

Kofi Ako *concentrates on preparing the mat.* **Anowa** *starts nodding again.*

Kofi Ako   Eh? (*He turns round and sees her.*)

Anowa (*mumbling*)   The storm has ruined the whole corn field. Every stalk is down.

Kofi Ako (*moving with urgency, he picks her up in his arms*)   Come Anowa, you are dreaming. Come to sleep. (*Carries her to the leafy bed.*) Yes, Anowa, sleep well. Sleep well, and let every corn stalk go down. We shall not return to see the ruin. (*Pacing up and down in the length of lower stage.*) Sometimes, I do not understand. Wherever we go, people take you for my sister at first. They say they have never heard of a woman who helped her husband so. 'Your wife is good' they say 'for your sisters are the only women you can force to toil like this for you'. They say that however good for licking the back of your hand is, it would never be like your palms. (*Pause.*) Perhaps if they knew what I am beginning to know, they would not say so much. And proverbs do not always describe the truth of reality. (*His face acquires new determination.*) Anowa truly has a few strong ideas. But I know she will settle down. (*Addressing the sleeping woman.*) Anowa, I shall be the new husband and you the new wife.

Now the storm is raging harder, thunder roars and lightning occurs more frequently. He stares at her for some time and then as lights begin to dim, he spreads out his big figure by her. Lights off. Pause.

When lights come on again, same scene without the leafy bed. The sun is shining and **Anowa** *is spreading out skins from the baskets while* **Kofi** *stands looking on.*

Then **Anowa** *holds her nose elaborately. Both of them burst out laughing. He moves in to help her.*

Kofi Ako   Our noses are certainly suffering.

Anowa   And yet what can we do? Without them, where would we stand?

Kofi Ako   Nowhere indeed.

Anowa (*looking into one of the baskets and picking it up*)   About two of them in here are too rotten to do anything with. (*She makes a movement of wiping sweat off her face, then yawns.*)

Kofi Ako   Come out of the sun. (*He takes the basket from her and places it away from them.*) Come, let's sit down in the shade.

They go and sit near one end of the lower stage.

Anowa (*breathing audibly*)   Did your friend the doctor tell you what is wrong with me?

Kofi Ako   Yes.

Anowa   What did he say?

Kofi Ako   I should have asked him whether I'm to let you know or not.

Anowa   Ho! I think you can tell me, because he would not have forgotten to warn you, if he thought I should not know.

Kofi Ako (*quietly and with a frown*)   He says there is nothing wrong with you.

Anowa   Then why. . . ?

Kofi Ako Let me finish. He says there is nothing wrong with your womb. But your soul is too restless. You always seem to be looking for things; and that prevents your blood from settling.

Anowa Oh!

Kofi Ako Anowa, are you unhappy? Do I make you unhappy?

Anowa (*with surprise*) No.

Kofi Ako Perhaps this work is too much for you.

Anowa No. I think I have always been like that.

Kofi Ako (*alarmed*) Like what?

Anowa I don't know. I can't describe it.

Kofi Ako Maybe you should stop coming on the roads.

Anowa (*alarmed*) No. Why?

Kofi Ako Why not?

Anowa I like this work. I like being on the roads.

Kofi Ako My wife, sometimes you talk strangely. I don't see what is so pleasing on these highways. The storms? The wild animals or bad men that we often meet?

Anowa There are worse things in villages and towns.

Kofi Ako Listen to her! Something tells me (*He stands up.*) it might be better if you stayed at home. Indeed I have been thinking that maybe I should eh . . . eh . . .

Anowa My husband, I am listening to you.

Kofi Ako You remember, you were telling me to marry another woman to help us?

Anowa Yes.

Kofi Ako Hmm, I don't want to marry again. Not yet. But I think . . . I think . . . that perhaps . . .

Anowa *Eheh!*

Kofi Ako I think the time has come for us to think of looking for one or two men to help us.

Anowa What men?

Kofi Ako I hear they are not expensive ... and if ...

Anowa (*getting up so slowly that every movement of her body corresponds to syllables or words in her next speech*) MY hus-band! Am I hear-ing you right? Have we risen so high? (*Corking her ears.*) Kofi Ako, do not let me hear these words again.

Kofi Ako (*mimicking her*) 'Do not let me hear these words again.' Anowa, do you think I am your son?

Anowa I do not care. We shall not buy men.

Kofi Ako Anowa, look here. You are not always going to have it your way. Who are you to tell me what I must do or not do?

Anowa Kofi, I am not telling what you must do or not do ... We were two when we left Yebi. We have been together all this time and at the end of these two years, we may not be able to say yet that we are the richest people in the world but we certainly are not starving.

Kofi Ako And so?

Anowa Ah, is there any need then to go behaving as though we are richer than we are?

Kofi Ako What do you want to say? I am not buying these men to come and carry me. They are coming to help us in our work.

Anowa We do not need them.

Kofi Ako If you don't, I do. Besides you are only talking like a woman.

Anowa And please, how does a woman talk? I had as much a mouth in the idea of beginning this trade as you had. And as much head!

Kofi Ako And I am getting tired now. 'You shall not

consult a priest ... you shall marry again ... we do not need medicines ... ' Anowa, listen. Now here is something I am going to do whether you like it or not. I do not even understand why you want to make so much noise about something like this. What is wrong with buying one or two people to help us? They are cheap ...

Pause. **Anowa** *walks around in great agitation.* **Kofi Ako** *continues in a strangely loud voice.*

Everyone does it ... does not everyone do it? And things would be easier for us. We shall not be alone ... Now you have decided to say nothing, eh? Anowa, who told you that buying men is wrong? You know what? I like you and the way you are different. But Anowa, sometimes, you are too different.

Anowa *walks away from him.*

Kofi Ako I know I could not have started without you, but after all, we all know you are a woman and I am the man.

Anowa And tell me, when did I enter into a discussion with you about that? I shall not feel happy with slaves around ... Kofi, no man made a slave of his friend and came to much himself. It is wrong. It is evil.

Kofi Ako (*showing alarm*) *Hei*, where did you get these ideas from? Who told you all this?

Anowa Are there never things which one can think out for oneself?

Kofi Ako Yes, so now you are saying I am a fool?

Anowa (*collapsing*) O the gods of my fathers!

Kofi Ako What shall the gods of your fathers do for you? I know you think you are the wise one of the two of us.

Anowa Kofi, are you saying all this just so I will take a knife and go cut my throat?

Kofi Ako Am I lying?

Anowa When and where and what did I do to give you this

idea?

Kofi Ako   This is the way you have always behaved.

Anowa (*her voice going falsetto*)   Kofi! Kofi!

He sits down by her.

Hmm! Kofi, we shouldn't quarrel.

Kofi Ako   No, we should not.

The lights die on them and come up in a little while, on the upper stage. It is the courtyard of **Badua**'s *and* **Osam**'s *cottage. It is early evening. Village noises.* **Osam** *and* **Badua** *are having their evening meal.* **Osam** *is sitting in the lie-in chair, his food before him. He swallows a morsel.* **Badua**'s *food is on her lap. She is not eating. Presently she puts it down and gets up noisily. She turns right, she turns left. She begins to move around aimlessly, speaking at the same time.*

Badua   I haven't heard the like of this before. A human being, and a woman too, preferring to remain a stranger in other peoples' lands?

Osam (*looking up from his meal*)   Sit down, sit down. Sit down, and eat your food.

Shamefaced, **Badua** *sits down.*

Osam   Hmmm, I was telling you. This child of yours . . . hm . . . She was never even a child in the way a child must be a child.

Badua (*turning round to face him*)   And how must a child be a child?

Osam   *Ei*, are you now asking me? I thought this is what you too have known all along. Ah, Nana, I beg you. Maybe that was not well said. (*Pause.*) But I must say it has happened before us all. Has it not? Walked out of that door, she did, how long ago is that?

Badua   Hmmm!

Osam   . . . and has never been back since. I have always feared her.

Badua (*shocked*)   You have always feared her? And is that a good thing to say about your own bowel-begotten child? If you fear her, then what do other people do? And if other people fear her then since a crab never fathers a bird, in their eyes, who are you yourself? After all, what has she done? She only went away with her husband and has not been back since.

Osam   And that, you will agree with me, is very strange.

Guessing he might want a helping of the soup, she gets up and goes for his bowl.

Badua   Yes, it is strange, but that does not make me say I fear her. (*She takes the bowl to the hearth, and returns it to him after she has filled it.*)

Osam   But don't other women leave their homes to go and marry? And do they stay away forever? Do they not return with their children to the old homestead to attend funerals, pay death debts, return for the feeding of their family stools? And Badua, listen here, if they did not do that, what would homes-and-homes do? Would not the clans break up for lack of people at home? The children of women like Anowa and their children-after-them never find their ways back. They get lost. For they often do not know the names of the founders of their houses . . . No, they do not know what to tell you if you asked them for just the names of their clans.

Badua   Anowa has not yet had children.

Osam   There you are. And is not that too strange? She has not had children. And barrenness is not such a common affliction in your family, is it?

Badua   No, they have been saying it for a long time around here that she and her husband sold her birth-seeds to acquire their wealth.

Osam   Of course, women have mouths to talk with. And indeed they open them anyhow and much of the time what comes out is nothing any real man can take seriously. Still, something tells me that this time she has given them cause.

Badua O Kofi Sam! (*She returns to her seat and places her bowl on her knee again.*)

Osam What have I done? I am not saying that they are right. But it certainly looks as if she and her husband are too busy making money and have no time to find out and cure what is wrong with her womb.

Badua Perhaps I should go and look for her.

Osam Go and look for her? How? Where? And anyway, who told you she is lost?

Badua But she is my child.

Osam And so what? Do you think Anowa will forgive you anymore for that? Please, leave her to live her life!

Badua Why are you always against me where Anowa is concerned?

Osam You have been against me too. Did I not tell you to . . .

Badua Make her a priestess . . . make her a priestess . . . Always. Why? Why did everyone want me to put my only child on the dancing ground? Since you want to see possessed women so much, why didn't you ask your sisters to apprentice their daughters to oracles?

Osam (*very angry*) Don't shout at me, woman! Who comes complaining to me about Anowa? . . . They say that that would have been to the good of us all. But now – there she is, as they said she might be, wandering . . . her soul hovering on the outer fringes of life and always searching for something . . . and I do not know what!

Badua (*quietly*) I don't know what you mean by all this. Who is not searching in life?

Osam I know you have just made up your mind never to understand me.

Badua (*bitterly*) Besides, that daughter of ours is doing well, I hear. Yes, for someone whose soul is wandering, our daughter is prospering. Have you heard from the blowing winds how their trade with the white men is growing? And how they are buying men and women?

Osam   Yes, and also how unhappy she is about those slaves, and how they quarrel from morning till night.

Badua   So! I didn't know she was a fool too. She thought it is enough just to be headstrong. (*Laughing drily.*) Before she walked out that noon-day, she should have waited for me to tell her how to marry a man . . .

Osam   Hmm.

Badua   A good woman does not have a brain or mouth.

Osam   Hmm. (*He coughs.*)

Badua   And if there is something wrong with their slaves, why don't they sell them?

Osam   That is not the problem. They say she just does not like the idea of buying men and women.

Badua   What foolishness. People like her are not content to have life cheap, they always want it cheaper. Which woman in the land would not wish to be in her place?

Osam   Anowa is not every woman.

Badua   *Tchiaa!* And who does she think she is? A goddess? Let me eat my food. (*She goes to sit down and places the food back on her lap.*)

Osam   And can I have some soup?

Badua   Yes. (*As she gets up again, the lights die on the courtyard.*)

Eight men in a single file carrying skins enter by lower right, move silently up and across the main stage and away lower left. **Kofi Ako** *follows closely behind them but stops in the centre of the lower stage. He is better dressed than before. He is carrying what seems to be a ridiculously light load. From off stage,* **Anowa**'s *voice is heard calling 'Kofi, Kofi'. He stops, she enters from the same direction, dressed as in the last scene although the lapse in time represents years. She is still barefooted. She is carrying nothing but a small stick which she plays with as she talks.*

Kofi Ako   What is the matter?

Anowa   Oh I just want you to wait for me.

Kofi Ako   Anowa, you walked faster when you carried loads which were heavier than mine.

Anowa   Well, *you* took the load off my head. But don't you complain about my steps. I cannot keep up with you. These days you are always with your men.

Kofi Ako (*smiles*)   Is that it? You know what? Let us sit down.

They move to their positions of the previous scene. Then as if he has remembered something, he moves some steps up towards the left and calls.

Boy!

Boy (*Running in*)   Father!

Kofi Ako   Tell the others that you are to sit down and rest a little.

Boy   Is our Mother coming to give us the food?

Kofi Ako   You can share it among yourselves, can you not?

Boy   We can, Father.

Kofi Ako   Then go and tell Yaako to share it up for you.

Boy   Yes, Father. (*He leaves.*)

Kofi Ako (*goes back to sit by* **Anowa**)   I think we should not come again with them. Yaako is very good and honest and he can manage everything.

Anowa (*quietly*)   Is that so?

Kofi Ako   I feel so.

Anowa (*quietly*)   Yes.

Kofi Ako   Why do you say that so sadly?

Anowa   Did I say that sadly? Maybe I am sad. And how not? I cannot be happy if I am going to stop working.

Kofi Ako   But why, Anowa?

Anowa   Men whom Odomankoma creates do not stop working . . . yes, they do but only when they are hit by illness or some misfortune. When their bodies have grown impotent with age.

Kofi Ako   Anowa, the farmer goes home from the farm . . .

Anowa (*gets up and starts walking before* **Kofi Ako**)   And the fisherman brings his boats and nets to the shore . . .

Kofi Ako   And if you know this already, then why?

Anowa   They return in the morning.

Kofi Ako   But we have finished doing all that needs to be done by us.

Anowa   Kofi, one stops wearing a hat only when the head has fallen off.

Kofi Ako (*irritably*)   Anowa, can one not rest a tired neck?

Anowa   Are we coming back after some time?

Kofi Ako   No.

Anowa   What shall we be doing?

Kofi Ako   Nothing. We shall be resting.

Anowa   How can a human being rest all the time? I cannot.

Kofi Ako   I can.

Anowa   I shall not know what to do with myself as each day breaks.

Kofi Ako   You will look after the house.

Anowa   No. I am going to marry you to a woman who shall do that.

Kofi Ako   You will not marry me to any woman. I am not sending you on that errand.

Anowa   See if I don't. One of these plump Oguaa mulatto women. With a skin as smooth as shea-butter and golden like fresh palm-oil on yam . . .

Kofi Ako (*jumping up and showing undue irritation*)   Anowa, stop that!

Anowa   Stop what?

Kofi Ako   What you are doing!

Anowa   What am I doing? (*Pause.*) *Ei*, master, let your heart lie cool in your chest.

Kofi Ako   Haven't I told you several times not to talk to me about marrying other women?

Anowa   Hmm, I am quiet. (*Pause.*)

Kofi Ako (*cooling down*)   And if I marry again what will become of you?

Anowa   Nothing that is unheard of. Ask your friends. What becomes of other women whose husbands have one, two, or more other wives besides themselves?

Kofi Ako   So what you want to be is my mother-wife?

Anowa   Yes, or your friend or your sister. Have we not enough memories to talk about from our working days until we get tired of them and each other, when we shall sit and wait for our skins to fall off our bones?

Kofi Ako   Your mood is on. (*He stretches his left arm forward and looks at it intently.*)

Anowa (*giggling*)   What mood? You are always funny. My nothing is on. It is just that when I throw my eyes into the future, I do not see myself there.

Kofi Ako   This is because you have no children. Women who have children can always see themselves in the future.

Anowa   Mm . . . children. It would be good to have them. But it seems I'm not woman enough. And this is another reason why you ought to marry another woman. So she can bear your children. (*Pause.*) Mm, I am only a wayfarer, with no belongings either here or there.

Kofi Ako   What? What are you saying? Wayfarer, you? But are you talking about . . . about slaves . . . and you. . . ? But, a wayfarer belongs to other people!

Anowa   Oh no, not always. One can belong to oneself without belonging to a place. What is the difference between any of your men and me? Except that they are men and I'm a woman? None of us belongs.

Kofi Ako   You are a strange woman, Anowa. Too strange. You never even show much interest in what the oracles say. But you are not at fault; they all say the same thing. Anowa, what makes you so restless? What occupies you?

Anowa   Nothing. Nothing at all.

Kofi Ako   (*walking away from her*)   Anowa, is it true that you should have been a priestess?

Anowa   O yes? But how would I know. And where did you hear that from? (*Looking genuinely lost.*)

Kofi Ako   Don't think about that one then. It doesn't matter. Still, there is too much restlessness in you which is frightening. I think maybe you are too lonely with only us men around. (*Pause.*) I have decided to procure one or two women, not many. Just one or two, so that you will have companionship of your kind.

Anowa   (*almost hysterical*)   No, no, no! I don't want them. I don't need them.

Kofi Ako   But why not?

Anowa   No! I just do not need them. (*Long pause.*) People can be very unkind. A wayfarer is a traveller. Therefore, to call someone a wayfarer is a painless way of saying he does not belong. That he has no home, no family, no village, no stool of his own; has no feast days, no holidays, no state, no territory.

Kofi Ako   (*jumping up, furious*)   Shut up, woman, shut up!

Anowa   Why, what have I done wrong?

Kofi Ako   Do you ask me? Yes, what is wrong with you? If you want to go and get possessed by a god, I beg you, go. So that at least I shall know that a supernatural being speaks with your lips . . .

Anowa's eyes widen with surprise.

Kofi Ako   I say Anowa, why must you always bring in this . . .

Anowa   What?

Kofi Ako   About slaves and all such unpleasant affairs?

Anowa   They are part of our lives now.

Kofi Ako   (*shaking his head*)   But is it necessary to eat your insides out because of them? (*Then with extreme intensity.*) Why are you like this? What evil lies in having bonded men? Perhaps, yes (*Getting expansive.*) in other lands. Among other less kindly people. A meaner race of men. Men who by other men are worse treated than dogs. But here, have you looked around? Yes. The wayfarer here belongs where he is. Consorts freely with free-born nephews and nieces. Eats out of the same vessel, and drinks so as well. And those who have the brains are more listened to than are babbling nobility. They fight in armies. Where the valiant and well-proven can become a captain just as quickly as anyone. How many wayfarers do we know who have become patriarchs of houses where they used only to serve?

Anowa   But in all this, they are of account only when there are no free-born people around. And if they fare well among us, it is not so among all peoples. And even here, who knows what strange happenings go on behind doors?

Kofi Ako (*irritated beyond words, he seizes and shakes her*)   Anowa, Anowa, where else have you been but here? Why can't you live by what you know, what you see? What do you gain by dreaming up miseries that do not touch you? Just so you can have nightmares?

Anowa (*still cool, she stares at him*)   It seems this is how they created me.

Kofi Ako   (*letting go of her*)   Hmm. How sad . . . And yet if I
gave you two good blows on your cheeks which flashed
lightning across your face, all this foolishness would go out of
your head. (*To himself*) And what is wrong with me? Any man
married to her would have by now beaten her to a pulp, a
dough. But I can never lay hands on her . . . I cannot even
think of marrying another woman. O it is difficult to think
through anything. All these strange words!

Anowa *continues to stare at him.*

Kofi Ako   Anowa, what is the difference? How is it you
can't feel like everybody else does? What is the meaning of
this strangeness? Who were you in the spirit world? (*Laughing
mirthlessly.*) I used to like you very much. I wish I could rid
you of what ails you, so I could give you peace. And give
myself some.

Anowa *still only stares at him.*

Kofi Ako   It is an illness, Anowa. An illness that turns to
bile all the good things of here-under-the-sun. Shamelessly,
you rake up the dirt of life. You bare our wounds. You are
too fond of looking for the common pain and the general
wrong.

Anowa *manages to look sad. She sighs audibly, then hangs down her
head as if ashamed. He looks down at her.*

Kofi Ako   Anowa, you are among women my one and only
treasure. Beside you, all others look pale and shadowless. I
have neither the desire nor wish to marry any other, though
we all know I can afford dozens more. But please, bring your
mind home. Have joy in our overflowing wealth. Enhance this
beauty nature gave you with the best craftsmanship in cloth
and stone. Be happy with that which countless women would ·
give their lives to enjoy for a day. Be happy in being my wife
and maybe we shall have our own children. Be my glorious
wife, Anowa, and the contented mother of my children.

Anowa's *answer is a hard grating laugh that goes on and on even after
the lights have gone out on them.*

The lights reappear after a little while. Enter 'The-Mouth-That-Eats-Salt-And-Pepper'. First, **Old Man**. *He walks up to the centre of the lower stage, and for a short while, stands still with his head down. Then he raises his head and speaks.*

Old Man My fellow townsmen. Have you heard what Kofi and Anowa are doing now? They say he is buying men and women as though they were only worth each a handful of the sands on the shore. *Ei*, Anowa and Kofi. Were those not the same who left Yebi like a pair of unwanted strangers? But peace creates forgetfulness and money-making is like a god possessing a priest. He never will leave you, until he has occupied you, wholly changed the order of your being, and seared you through and up and down. Then only would he eventually leave you, but nothing of you except an exhausted wreck, lying prone and wondering who you are.

Enter **Old Woman**.

Old Man Besides, there must be something unwholesome about making slaves of other men, something that is against the natural state of man and the purity of his worship of the gods. Those who have observed have remarked that every house is ruined where they take in slaves.
As you sit,
They grow
And before you know
Where you are,
They are there,
And you are not.
One or two homes in Abura already show this;
They are spilling over
With gold and silver
And no one knows the uttermost hedges of their lands.
But where are the people
Who are going to sit on these things?
Yes,
It is frightening.
But all at once,
Girl-babies die
And the breasts of women in new motherhood

Run dry.

Old Woman *tries to get in a word, thumping her stick and coughing.*

Old Woman She is a witch,
She is a devil,
She is everything that is evil.

Old Man (*raising his head and showing interest*) Who?

Old Woman Who else but that child of Abena Badua?

Old Man And what has she done now?

Old Woman Have you not heard? (*She is even more excited than ever. And for the rest of the scene makes an exhibition of herself, jumping, raising her stick in the air, coughing etc.*) She thinks the world has not seen the likes of her before. (*Now with feigned concern.*) I wonder what a woman eats to produce a child like Anowa. I am sure that such children are not begotten by normal natural processes.

Old Man (*with amused contempt*) But what?

Old Woman Ah! They issue from cancerous growths, tumours that grow from evil dreams. Yes, and from hard and bony material that the tender organs of ordinary human women are too weak to digest.

Old Man Are you not sure that you are seeing too much in too little?

Old Woman What are you saying? Am I wrong? What woman is she who thinks she knows better than her husband in all things?

Old Man A good husband would himself want advice from his wife, as the head of a family, a chief, a king, any nobleman has need of an adviser.

Old Woman But Anowa is too much. She is now against the very man who she selected from so many. She would rather he was poor than prospering. They say she raves hourly against our revered ancestors and sanctions their deeds in high tones. She thinks our forefathers should have waited for her to be born so she could have upbraided them for their misdeeds and shown them what actions of men are virtuous.

Old Man   I do not know if I can believe all this you say of the pitiful child. But certainly, it is not too much to think that the heavens might show something to children of a latter day which was hidden from them of old?

Old Woman *is so flabbergasted at this she opens her mouth wide and turns in the* **Old Man**'s *direction while he walks slowly away.*

Old Woman (*closing her mouth in a heavy sigh*)   But, people of
    Yebi, rejoice,
For Kofi Ako has prospered
And he is your son.
Women of Nsona house,
They say Kofi Ako can stand
On his two feet to dress up fifty brides
And without moving a step,
Dress up fifty more.
And where and when did this last happen
But in fables and the days of dim antiquity?
They say Kofi sits fat like a bullfrog in a swamp,
While *that* Anowa daily grows thin,
Her eyes popping out of her head like those of
A hungry toad in a parched grassland.
But she is the one
Who must not be allowed to step on any threshold here!
When was this infant born,
That would teach us all what to do?
Who is she to bring us new rules to live by?
It is good she said she was not coming back to Yebi,
But if she so much as crosses the stream
That lies at the mouth of the road,
We shall show her that
Little babies only cry for food
When hungry,
But do not instruct their elders how to tend a farm:
Besides,
As the sourest yam
Is better than the sweetest guava,

The dumbest man is
Always better than a woman.
Or *he* thinks he is!
And so Kofi shall teach Anowa
He is a man!

Old Woman *exits coughing and her throat wheezing.*

Phase Three

The big house at Oguaa.

*The upper stage is a big central hall. The furniture here is either consciously foreign or else opulent. There are beautiful skins lying on the richly carpeted floor. Other articles include a giant sideboard on which are standing huge decanters, with or without spirits, and big decorative plates. In the central wall is a fireplace and above it, a picture of Queen Victoria unamused. To the left of the Queen is a picture of **Kofi Ako** himself, and to the right, a large painting of the crow, the totem bird of the Nsona clan. In the centre of the room is a gilded chair with rich-looking cushions, and in front of it, a leopard skin. The lower stage represents here a path leading from the house into the town and outside generally.*

The lights blaze on both lower and upper stages to a tumult which at first is distant but draws nearer and nearer to lower right. First a group of women, any number from four, enter from the right dancing to no distinct form and with great abandon. Meanwhile they sing, or rather recite.

He is coming!
Nana is coming
He is coming.
The master of the earth is coming.
Give way,
O – o – give way!
For the Master of all you see around is coming
Turn your face, the jealous!
Close your eyes, the envious!
For he is coming,
Nana is coming!

*They pass on and away lower left, and after them, a lone man comes blowing **Kofi Ako**'s horn to the rhythm of just two lines.*

Turn your face, the jealous!
Close your eyes, the envious!

*The **Hornblower** stops on the stage while multitudes enter from the same direction and move away lower left. They are men and women*

*carrying raw materials, skins, copra, crude rubber and kegs of palm oil.
Controlling the exportation of the last product has made* **Kofi Ako** *the
richest man, probably, of the whole Guinea Coast. Other men and women
are carrying cheap silks and madras cloth, muskets, hurricane lamps,
knives and enamel ware.*

Kofi Ako *enters, borne by four brawny men in some kind of a
carrier chair, basket or sedan. He is resplendent in brilliant kente or velvet
cloth and he is over-flowing with gold jewelry, from the crown on his
head to the rings on his toes. He is surrounded by more hailing women
and an orchestra of horns and drums. As he passes, he makes the gestures
of lordship over the area. The procession goes off, lower left; the*
Hornblower *is the last man to leave.*

When the tumult has died down, **Anowa** *enters from upper left and
sits on one side of the chairs in the central hall. She looks aged and
forlorn in her old clothes. She is still bare-footed. She sits quietly for a
while, as though waiting for somebody, then she stands up and begins to
pace around, speaking to herself.*

Anowa (*as she speaks, she makes childish gestures, especially with her
hands, to express all the ideas behind each sentence*) I remember
once. I think I was very young then. Quite young certainly.
Perhaps I was eight, or ten. Perhaps I was twelve. My
grandmother told me of her travels. She told of the great
places she had been to and the wonderful things she had seen.
Of the sea that is bigger than any river and boils without
being hot. Of huge houses rising to touch the skies, houses
whose foundations are wider than the biggest roads I had ever
seen. They contained more rooms than were in all the homes
I knew put together. Of these houses, I asked:
Tell me Nana, who built the houses?
She said:
Why do you want to know?
The pale men.
Who are the pale men?
I asked.
You ask too many questions.
They are the white men.
Who are the white men?
I asked.
A child like you should not ask questions.

They come from far away.
Far away from beyond the horizon.
Nana, what do they look like?
I asked.
Shut up child.
Not like you or me,
She said.
But what do they look like Nana?
I asked.
Shut up child or your mouth will twist up one day with
    questions.
Not like you or me?
Yes like you or me,
But different.
What do they look like, Nana?
What devil has entered into you, child?
As if you or I
Were peeled of our skins,
Like a lobster that is boiled or roasted,
Like ... like ... but it is not good
That a child should ask questions.
Nana, why did they build the big houses?
I asked.
I must escape from you, child.
They say ... they said they built the big houses to keep the
    slaves.
What is a slave, Nana?
Shut up! It is not good that a child should ask big questions.
A slave is one who is bought and sold.
Where did the white men get the slaves?
I asked.
You frighten me, child.
You must be a witch, child.
They got them from the land.
Did the men of the land sell other men of the land, and
    women and children to pale men from beyond the horizon
    who looked like you or me peeled, like lobsters boiled or
    roasted?
I do not know, child.

You are frightening me, child.
I was not there!
It is too long ago!
No one talks of these things anymore!
All good men and women try to forget;
They have forgotten!
What happened to those who were taken away?
Do people hear from them?
How are they?
Shut up child.
It is too late child.
Sleep well, child.
All good men and women try to forget;
They have forgotten!

Pause.

That night, I woke up screaming hot; my body burning and sweating from a horrible dream. I dreamt that I was a big, big woman. And from my insides were huge holes out of which poured men, women and children. And the sea was boiling hot and steaming. And as it boiled, it threw out many, many giant lobsters, boiled lobsters, each of whom as it fell turned into a man or woman, but keeping its lobster head and claws. And they rushed to where I sat and seized the men and women as they poured out of me, and they tore them apart, and dashed them to the ground and stamped upon them. And from their huge courtyards, the women ground my men and women and children on mountains of stone. But there was never a cry or a murmur; only a bursting, as of a ripe tomato· or a swollen pod. And everything went on and on and on. (*Pause.*)

I was very ill and did not recover for weeks. When I told my dream, the women of the house were very frightened. They cried and cried and told me not to mention the dream again. For some time, there was talk of apprenticing me to a priestess. I don't know what came of it. But since then, any time there is mention of a slave, I see a woman who is me and a bursting of a ripe tomato or a swollen pod.

She now stares straight and sharply at the audience for a long time, and then slowly leaves the stage by upper right. Then suddenly, the voices of an unseen wearied multitude begin to sing 'Swing Low, Sweet Chariot'. The song goes on for a while and stops. Long pause while lights remain on. Then the lights go off on the lower stage only. **Girl** *enters from upper right. She resembles* **Anowa** *of a long time ago. She is dressed in a one-piece cloth wrapped around her. She too, looks like a wild one, and she is carrying a broom and a duster with which she immediately begins to dust and sweep. Then suddenly she stops and just stands dreamily. Meanwhile,* **Boy** *enters from upper right and quietly steals behind her and cries 'Hei!' She is startled.*

Girl (*turning round to face* **Boy**)   How you frightened me.

Boy   Have you just started working in here? And why were you standing there like that?

Girl   That is none of your business.

Boy   I don't know what is happening in this house. I am sure there are more people here than in Oguaa town. Yet nothing gets done.

Girl   But you!

Boy   I what? Is this the hour you were instructed to come and clean the place up?

Girl   Well, that is not my fault.

Boy   What is not your fault? Look at those arms. I wonder what they could do even if you were not so lazy. Listen, today is Friday and Father is going to come in here. And don't stand there staring at me.

Girl   And anyway, are you the new overseer? Why don't you leave me alone?

Boy (*playfully pulling her nose*)   I won't!

Girl   You!

She raises her arm to hit him, and causes one of the decorative plates to fall. It breaks. **Boy** *is furious.*

Boy   God, what is wrong with you? Look at what you've

done!

Girl Well, it's broken, isn't it? I wouldn't fuss so much if I were you.

Boy Doesn't anything bother you?

Girl Not much. Certainly not this plate. (*She bends down to pick up the pieces. Then she stands up again.*) This mistress will not miss it. After all, she has no time these days for things like plates.

Boy You are mad, that's all. I thought she said we should always call her 'Mother' and the master 'Father'.

Girl (*giggling*) Some Mother and Father, heh!

Boy I don't think I have said anything for you to laugh at.

Girl You are being very unfair. You know I like both of them very much. (*Earnestly.*) I wish I really was their child . . . born to'them. (*She pouts.*) As for her too.

Boy What has happened now?

Girl Nothing. Now she flits about like a ghost, talking to herself.

*They stop and listen. The **Boy** moves up to upper left and peeps.*

Girl Is she coming?

Boy (*not turning round*) No. (*Then he moves back towards **Girl**.*)

Girl Listen, they were saying at the fish-kilns that she went and stared at Takoa's baby so hard that the baby is having convulsions . . .

Boy (*shocked*) Ow!

Girl Takoa is certainly telling everyone that Mistress, I mean Mother, is swallowing the baby because she is a witch.

Boy Hei!

*The **Girl** is startled. The **Boy** moves closer to face her and begins hitting her lips with the fourth finger of his right hand.*

Boy   Don't let me catch you repeating any of the things those awful women say about Mother.

Girl   Yes, grandfather.

Boy   And you, where did you hear all these things from?

Girl (*petulantly*)   I said at the kilns. (*Throwing her mouth at him.*) Or are you deaf?

Boy   I am not deaf but people in this house talk too much.

Girl   It is because of this new affair. And the truth is, she herself talks more about it than anyone else. Whenever she thinks she is alone anywhere, she begins 'O my husband, what have I done, what have I done?' (*She imitates someone puzzled and asks the questions with her hands. Then she giggles.*)

Boy   Don't laugh. Have you seen how you yourself will end? (*He picks her duster up and begins to dust around.*)

Girl   *Ei*, don't turn wise on me. (*Noticing him working.*) Good. You should dust since you're keeping me from doing my work . . .

Boy   Huh! . . . And are you not a woman too?

Girl (*promptly and loudly*)   And if I am? (*She lets fall the broom, and looks up for some time without saying anything.*)

Boy   I did not say you can now rest.

Girl (*quietly and to herself*)   If I had more money than I knew what to do with, but not a single child, I should be unhappy. If my man refused to talk to me, I should soon start talking to myself; if he would not come to my room or allow me in his, I should pace around in the night. (*She now turns to look at the* **Boy**.) And after killing myself for him, he said to me one day, go away, and would not tell me why, I should then die of surprise!

Boy   People do not die of surprise.

Girl   See if I do not.

Boy (*whispering*)   What do you think is going to happen now?

Girl   Do I know? All I know is that if she goes away, I shall run away too.

Boy   I shall come with you.

Girl (*coyly*)   Not if you would be scolding me all the time ...

Boy (*drawing near her and trying to touch her breasts*)   No, I shall not.

The **Girl** *hits his hand away. They stand still for a moment. Then they resume working with vigour. The* **Boy** *begins to whistle some tune.*

Girl   And the way she carries on with everyone here ...

Boy   Playing with us as though we were her kinsmen?

Girl   Yes; perhaps that is why the master wants to send her away.

Boy   Maybe; and she certainly is more poorly dressed than some of us.

Girl   Yes, that is another thing. Can't she do something about herself?

Boy   What, for instance?

Girl   Ho, does she not see her friends, how they go around? All those new and fashionable nkabasroto and bubas? The sleeves blowing out in the wind, the full pointed shoes and the stockings ...

Boy   Of course, that is what *you* would like ...

Girl   Why, if I were her, what would I not do.
What would I not have?
As much as my eye will fancy
and the best my heart desires?

She forgets she should be working and lets fall the broom. Her eyes light up with joyful expectation and she acts out her dream to the amazed fascination of **Boy**.

Nkente to sit in for all my work days.
Velvets for visiting. Silks for Sundays.

Anowa *enters unnoticed and stands at the door. She looks as she did in the last scene, but wizened now and shabby. She is wearing her old cloth and is barefooted. Her hair is cropped close.*

Girl   O if I were her, and she were me
Jewels on my hair, my finger and my knee
In my ears the dangles, on my wrists the bangles
My sandals will be jewelled, my hair will be dressed;
My perfumes will be milled, my talcums of the best.
On my soups I will be keen
No fish-heads to be seen
O for her to be me
So that I could be free!

Anowa *glides out unseen. The* **Boy** *and the* **Girl** *stand looking at each other. The* **Girl***'s eyes glisten with unshed tears while the* **Boy** *breathes deeply and loudly a couple of times.*

Boy   Being a woman, of course, that's all you would think about. Though if I were you and so beautiful, I would not worry. Perhaps Father will take you for wife.

Girl   *Chiaa, aa,* that man who is afraid of women?

Boy   Listen, it is dangerous talking to you. How can you say a fearful thing like that?

Girl   But I am not lying . . . they say . . . they say . . .

Boy   Shut up.

He hits her on her buttocks, runs down lower right and away with the **Girl** *pursuing him, her broom raised. From upper left,* **Anowa** *re-enters the hall.*

Anowa   *(to the now disappeared* **Girl** *and* **Boy***)*   You said it right, my child. But the elders gave the ruling before you and even I came: 'The string of orphan beads might look better on the wrist of the leopard but it is the antelope who has lost his mother.'

She wanders round aimlessly humming to herself. Presently, **Panyin- na-Kakra** *enter. They are about eight years old. They run in from upper right with ostrich feather fans, stand on either side of the gilded* *chair and automatically begin fanning the chair. This goes on for some time without* **Anowa** *noticing it. When she does, she laughs out dryly.*

Anowa Poor children, I feel like picking them up and carrying them on my back.

Panyin-na-Kakra (*still fanning*) Mother please, we did not hear you.

Anowa It is all right, my children, I was not speaking to you. (*Aside.*) They are fanning that chair now so that by the time their lord enters, the space around it will be cool. I suppose this is one of the nice things Yaako is teaching them to do. Hmm ... woe the childless woman, they warn. Let someone go and see their mother, who is she? Where is she sitting while they stand here fanning an empty chair? Let someone go and see how she suffered bearing them. The nine months dizziness, when food tasted like dung and water like urine. Nine months of unwholesome desires and evil dreams. Then the hour of the breaking of the amnion, when the space between her life and her death wore thin like a needy woman's hair thread. O the stench of old blood gone hot ... Did she go through all that and with her rest at the end postponed so they (*Pointing at the boys.*) will come and fan an empty chair? To fan an empty chair? (*She gets up and listlessly goes to the picture of Queen Victoria and addresses it.*) Hei, sister, I hear you are a queen. Maybe in spite of the strange look of you, you are a human woman, too, eh? How is it with you over there? Do you sometimes feel like I feel, that you should not have been born? `Nana ... won't you answer? If you won't answer (*Making gesture of riddance.*) take your headache ... and I say, you don't have to look at me like that because I have seen your likes before. (*To herself.*) But I shall not cry. I shall not let him see the tears from my eyes. Someone should have taught me how to grow up to be a woman. I hear in other lands a woman is nothing. And they let her know this from the day of her birth. But here, O my spirit mother, they let a girl grow up as she pleases until she is married. And then she is like any woman anywhere: in order for her man to be a man, she must not think, she must not talk. O – o, why didn't someone teach me how to grow up to be a

woman? (*Then she remembers the children.*) *Hei*, Kakra, Panyin!
Stop fanning that chair.

Panyin-na-Kakra (*startled*)   But please, Mother, Yaako
said . . .

Anowa   I say. Stop fanning that chair Panyin, go and tell
Yaako that I have asked you to stop fanning the chair.

They put their fans on one of the stools and **Panyin** *goes out.* **Anowa**
puts her arms around **Kakra** *and moves down with him. When she sits
down he sits on a rug by her.*

Anowa   Kakra.

Kakra   Mother.

Anowa   Where do you and Panyin come from?

Kakra   The house in Tantri, Mother.

Anowa   No, I mean before that.

Kakra   Mother, I don't know.

Anowa   Kakra, am I growing old?

Kakra (*He turns to look at her and then looks away
bewildered*)   Mother, I don't know.

Anowa   No, you don't know. Go and play with your friends,
child.

Kakra *rises up and leaves.* **Anowa** *bows down her head.* **Kofi Ako**
enters on the arm of **Boy**. *He is bedecked as in the last scene.* **Anowa**
stares contemptuously at the two of them. **Boy** *leads him to the chair
and places him in it. Now and any other time in the rest of the scene,
when* **Kofi Ako** *silently examines his limbs, 'Asem yi se nea mokobo
tuo' or any African funeral march or drums should be played.*

Boy   Father, shall I go and fetch Nana the priest?

Kofi Ako (*hurriedly*)   Not yet. I shall call you and send you
with a message for him.

Boy   Yes, Father. (*He retires.*)

Awkward silence.

Anowa   I was told that you wanted to speak to me.

Kofi Ako   All I want to say Anowa, is that I do not like seeing you walking around the house like this.

Anowa   You don't like seeing me walk around the house like what?

Kofi Ako   Please, stop asking me annoying questions.

Anowa   Don't shout. After all, it is you who are anxious that the slaves should not hear us. What I don't understand, Kofi, is why you want to have so many things your own way.

Kofi Ako (*very angrily*)   And I don't think there is a single woman in the land who speaks to her husband the way you do to me. (*Sighs and relaxes.*) Why are you like this, Anowa? Why?

Anowa *laughs.*

Kofi Ako   Can't you be like other normal women? Other normal people?

Anowa *continues laughing, then stops abruptly.*

Anowa   I still don't know what you mean by normal. Is it abnormal to want to continue working?

Kofi Ako   Yes, if there is no need to.

Anowa   But my husband, is there a time when there is no need for a human being to work? After all, our elders said that one never stops wearing hats on a head which still stands on its shoulders.

Kofi Ako   I do not see the reason why I should go walking through forests, climbing mountains and crossing rivers to buy skins when I have bought slaves to do just that for me.

Anowa   And so we come back to where we have been for a long time now. My husband, we did not have to put the strength of our bodies into others. We should not have bought the slaves . . .

Kofi Ako   But we needed them to do the work for us.

Anowa *begins to pace up and down and from side to side and never stops for too long any time during the rest of the scene.*

Anowa As though other people are horses! And now look at us. We do nothing from the crowing of the cock to the setting of the sun. I wander around like a ghost and you sit, washed and oiled like a . . . bride on show or a god being celebrated. Is this what we left Yebi for? Ah, my husband, where did our young lives go?

Kofi Ako *(angrily)* Stop it, Anowa, stop it. And what is the meaning of all this strange talk? If you feel old, that is your own affair. I feel perfectly young.

Anowa Do you?

Kofi Ako *(fiercely)* Yes, I do. And you stop creeping around the house the way you do. Like some beggar. Making yourself a laughing stock. Can't you do anything to yourself? After all, you are my wife.

Anowa Am I your wife? What is there to prove it?

Kofi Ako I don't understand you.

Anowa Don't you? I am asking you what I do or what there is about me that shows I am your wife. I do not think putting on fine clothes is enough.

Kofi Ako Are you referring to the fact that we have not had children?

Anowa An adopted child is always an adopted child and a slave child, a slave . . . Perhaps I am the barren one. But you deserve a son; so Kofi, I shall get you a wife. One of these plump mulatto women of Oguaa . . .

Kofi Ako Anowa, stop that!

Anowa Besides, such women are more civilised than I, who only come from Yebi. They, like you, have learned the ways of the white people. And a woman like that may be attractive enough to be allowed into your bed . . .

Kofi Ako Anowa stop that! Stop it, stop it!

Anowa (*laughing*)   Stop what? Stop what?

Kofi Ako *sighs again and relaxes. He begins to examine his limbs as the funeral music or drums rise and fall, and* **Anowa** *plays at digging her toes into the skins or re-arranging the plates on the sideboard.*

Anowa   And what did the priest say the last time he was here?

Kofi Ako   What do you mean? What has that to do with you?

Anowa   Too much. I know all this has something to do with what he has been telling you.

Kofi Ako   You are speaking as if your head is not there.

Anowa (*screaming*)   What did his divination say about me?

Kofi Ako   I don't know. And anyway, listen. I thought you were just as good at this sort of thing as he is. You should know, should you not? Why don't you go and wash your mouth so you can be a priestess at last. I can't stand any more of your strange ways.

Anowa (*voice betraying nervousness*)   What are you talking about?

Kofi Ako (*laughing bitterly*)   What am I talking about!

Another awkward pause.

Anowa   Yes, what are you talking about?

Kofi Ako (*with an almost feigned fatigue*)   Please, just leave me alone. O God, Anowa did you have to destroy me too? What does someone like you want from life? Anowa, did you ... I mean did you make me just to destroy me?

Anowa   Kofi, what are you saying?

Kofi Ako   Anowa, Anowa, O, Anowa.

Anowa   So what did the priest say the last time he was here?

Kofi Ako   That has nothing to do with you.

Anowa   I think it has. Too much, I feel deep inside me that all this business about me leaving you has something to do with what he told you last week.

Kofi Ako   What mad talk!

Anowa (*hysterically*)   What did the priest's divination say about me?

Kofi Ako   Please stop walking up and down. It irritates me.

Anowa   Why are you sending me away from you?

Kofi Ako   Just leave me alone.

Anowa   What have I done wrong?

Kofi Ako   Nothing.

Anowa   Is it because I did not give you children. (*Silence. She moves up to him and changes her attitude to one of supplication.*) Do you want to take a new wife who would not like to see me around?

Kofi Ako   Anowa, why do you want to go on asking foolish questions to which you know I cannot give you answers?

Anowa   But they are not foolish questions.

Kofi Ako (*unconcerned*)   In fact, I thought you would be glad to get away. I don't know what you want, and even if I knew, I am not sure it would have been in my power to give it. And you can't give me the only thing I want from you, a child. Let us part, Anowa.

Anowa   But going away is one thing. Being sent away is another.

Kofi Ako   And by that you mean, as always, that you have a right to do what you like and as always I am to sit by and watch?

Anowa (*throws up her hands in despair*)   O the god of our fathers! Is there nothing I can open my mouth to say which cannot be twisted around my own neck to choke me?

Music or drums as **Kofi Ako** *examines his limbs.* **Anowa** *paces up and down. Then she speaks, almost to herself.*

Anowa   Did the priest say . . . what is there about me which he thinks will not bring you blessings now? I must have done something wrong. I must have done something. I'm not a child, Kofi, I know they say a man whose wife is constantly sleeping with other men does not prosper. Did the priest say I am doing something like that? Or anything as evil as that?

Kofi Ako (*a bitter smile on his lips*)   Just go away and leave me alone, woman.

Anowa (*sadly*)   I cannot, my husband. Because I have nowhere to go. I swore I would not go back to Yebi. And I can still live here, can I not? I would not disturb you. I can stay in my part of the house. Just don't send me away, we have not seen each other's beds for far too long for it to matter if we don't any more . . . (*She stares at him and utters her next words as though she has just made a discovery.*) Ahh – or is it a death you are dying? We are dying. Listen, my husband, did the priest say you are dying, I am dying, we are dying?

Kofi Ako   You are mad. I am very alive.

Anowa (*gets up and raises her voice*)   Boy!

Kofi Ako   Why are you calling him?

Anowa   It has nothing to do with you.

Boy (*running in*)   Mother, I am here.

Anowa   Boy, I am going to ask you a question. (*She resumes pacing up and down.*) Boy, you know your master says I must go away from here and never come back.

Boy *hangs his head down with embarrassment.*

Anowa   My feet are on the road already and if it were not that he has not yet told me what he has found wrong with me or what I have done wrong, I would already be gone. Boy, do you know why?

Boy   No, Mother.

Anowa   Boy, have you heard of a man who seeks to divorce his wife and will not say why?

Boy Mother, I have never known the customs of this land well.

Anowa What about where you came from? Did you hear of such a case before you were taken away?

Boy I do not remember that I did.

Anowa Boy, I thank you. Go call for me as many of the older men and women as are around . . . Bring everybody on whom your eyes fall.

Boy Yes, Mother. (*He leaves.*)

Kofi Ako (*furiously*) Anowa, what are you doing? Why must they know about this? You have never behaved like a child before – why are you behaving like one now?

Anowa I do not know why we must not bring them in. I need their help and they also came from places where men live, eat and die. Perhaps one is among them who can help me. And I am behaving like a child now because I have gained nothing from behaving like a grown-up all my life.

Kofi Ako (*surprised*) You are mad Anowa.

Anowa Not yet!

Boy (*from the doorway*) Are they to come?

Anowa Let them come.

Boy *re-enters followed by as many men and women as possible. The last pair is the twins. They all shuffle around looking wide-eyed.*

All Mother, we are here.

Anowa I see you. Listen. Has any of you heard of a woman whose husband wanted to divorce her but would not tell her why?

They look bewildered and answer 'No' as if it were a line in a musical round, sung softly: No, no, no, no, no, no . . . They all whisper aloud to each other.

Anowa Then please you may go . . .

They all turn round at once.

Anowa No wait . . . Eh – eh . . . I would like to send some of you. I am sending you to the oldest and wisest people on this land; go ask them if they have ever heard of a man who sought to divorce his wife and would not tell her why. (*Points at random to different people.*) You go to the bearded woman of Kwaakrom and you to the old priests of Nanaam Mpow. You over there to Bekoe, he whom dwarfs abducted and taught the mysteries of the woods. Go quickly and come back today and walk as you have never walked before. Come quickly, for already I hear too many noises in my head and you must come back before my mind flies and gets lost.

The crowd disperses through all available exits. Exhausted but still excited, **Anowa** *paces around* **Kofi Ako** *who is now very silent.*

Anowa I have known this was coming for weeks and I have feared. An old man said, 'Fear "It-is-coming" but not "It-has-come".' But for me 'It-has-come' has brought me no peace. Perhaps . . . Boy!

Boy (*running*) Mother, I am here.

Anowa I hear Nana Abakframpahene Kokroko is here. He and the other chiefs are meeting with the Governor. Go. Whisper in his ears that he is to come to me. Tell him it is urgent and he is to pardon us for not going to him ourselves. All shall be explained in time. He is to come but without his retinue.

Kofi Ako (*raising himself up*) Anowa, what are you doing all this for?

Anowa The times are past when our individual actions had to be explained to each other.

Boy *looks away in embarrassment.*

Kofi Ako Perhaps you are going out of your senses.

Anowa That should not mean anything to you.

Kofi Ako That is not what concerns me, but you shall not let this out before Nana. (*He stamps his feet.*)

Anowa Just sit there and look at me.

Kofi Ako (*shouts*) You may go away, Boy. Forget what your Mother told you.

Boy Yes Father. (*He retires.*)

Anowa Who are you to say what you shall allow and what you shall not allow me?

Kofi Ako (*loud with anger*) Nana is my friend and not yours.

Anowa That is why I am asking him to come.

Kofi Ako Anowa, you shall not disgrace me before him.

Anowa Darkness has overtaken us already, and does it matter if we hit each against the other? Are you not disgracing me before the whole world?

Kofi Ako Your strange speeches will not persuade me . . .

Anowa I am not trying to. It is a long time since my most ordinary words ceased to have any meaning for me.

Kofi Ako I say once more that Nana is the only man in this world I respect and honour.

Anowa My good husband, in the old days how well I knew you. That is why I want to consult him too.

Kofi Ako I should have known that you were always that clever.

Anowa And certain things have shown that cleverness is not a bad thing.

Kofi Ako Everyone said you were a witch. I should have believed them.

Anowa (*derisively*) Why, have I choked you with the bone of an infant?

Kofi Ako Stop all this show and just leave me alone, I say.

Anowa Then I shall ask advice of whom I please.

Kofi Ako Anowa, if you do not leave me quietly, but go

consulting anybody about this affair, I shall brand you a
witch.

Anowa (*shocked*)   No!

Kofi Ako (*brought suddenly to life by her exclamation*)   And if I do,
you know there is more than one person in the world who
would believe me.

Anowa (*screams*)   No, no, no!

Kofi Ako   And there will be those who would be prepared
to furnish proof.

Anowa   Kofi, I am not hearing you right.

Kofi Ako   And then you know what could happen. But, that
should not make much difference to you. Since you do not
care to live or behave like everybody else . . .

Anowa   But what have I done?

Kofi Ako   I just want you to leave me, that's all.

Anowa   O the Gods of my fathers, what is it? What is it?

Kofi Ako   I shall have the little house built for you, as I
promised, but in Yebi . . .

Anowa   But I cannot go and live there.

Kofi Ako   I will give you half of the trade and half of the
slaves, if you want them.

Anowa   I don't want anything from you.

Kofi Ako   Take away with you all the jewelry.

Anowa   I say I want nothing . . .

Kofi Ako   And you must leave immediately. I myself shall
come to Yebi, or send people you can respect to come and
explain everything to your family . . .

Anowa   No, no, no!

Kofi Ako   . . . I shall ask a few men and women to go with
you now, and carry your personal belongings.

Anowa But . . .

Kofi Ako Boy!

Anowa Stop!

Kofi Ako What?

Unknown to the two, not only **Boy** *but several of the slaves, men and women, appear.*

Anowa You cannot send me away like this. Not to Yebi, or anywhere. Not before you have told me why. I swore to Mother I was not returning. Not ever. (*Not shedding a tear but her eyes shining dangerously.*) No, I am not in rags. But . . . but I do not have children from this marriage. Ah! Yes, Kofi, (*She moves to him and whispers hoarsely and audibly.*) we do not have children, Kofi, we have not got children! And for years now, I have not seen your bed. And Kofi, (*Getting hysterical.*) now that I think back on it, you have never been interested in any other woman . . .

Kofi Ako What are you saying, Anowa?

Anowa Kofi, are you dead? (*Pause.*) Kofi, is your manhood gone? I mean, you are like a woman. (*Pause.*) Kofi, there is not hope any more, is there? (*Pause.*) Kofi . . . tell me, is that why I must leave you? That you have exhausted your masculinity acquiring slaves and wealth?

Silence.

Why didn't you want me to know? You could have told me. Because we were friends. Like brother and sister. You just did not want me to know? And the priest said it was my fault. That I ate your manhood up? Why did he say I did it? Out of envy? Did he not tell you that perhaps you had consumed it up yourself acquiring wealth and slaves?

Kofi *looks around and sees the peeping eyes. He is horrified. He gestures to* **Anowa** *who doesn't know what is happening and goes on talking. He makes an attempt to go away and then sits down again. The slaves disappear.*

Anowa Now I know. So that is it. My husband is a woman

now. (*She giggles.*) He is a corpse. He is dead wood. But less than dead wood because at least, that sometimes grows mushrooms . . . Why didn't you want me to know?

Long pause while they look at each other strangely. Then he gets up to leave.

Anowa   Where are you going? Kofi, don't leave. (*Pause.*) Let us start from the beginning. (*Long pause.*) No, I shall leave you in peace. (*Pause.*) I am leaving, Kofi. I am leaving. I shall leave you in peace.

He exits upper left. She watches his receding back until he disappears. She then shifts her gaze to the gilded chair. She stares at that for some time, after which her eyes just wander in general around the room. Then at some point she begins to address the furniture.

Ah, very soon the messengers will be coming back,
Rugs, pictures, you, chair and you, Queen,
Should they ask of me from you, tell them I am gone,
Tell them it matters not what the wise ones say,
For
Now, I am wiser than they.

*She fixes her eyes on the gilded chair again. Suddenly she jumps a step or two and sits in it and begins to dangle her legs like a child, with a delighted grin on her face. She breaks into a giggle. There is a sudden gun-shot off stage, followed by a stillness. As pandemonium breaks out off stage with women and men shrieking, **Anowa** begins to giggle again. The light dies slowly on her.*

*Lights come on both parts of the stage. Upper is still the great hall. In the centre is the gilded chair unoccupied. In the background can be heard funeral drums and wailing. A few women, led by **Badua**, who is weeping, troop in from upper right and sit down, **Badua** in the right hand corner nearest the lower stage. The women sit around the gilded chair as though it is the funeral bed. A little later, **Osam** enters from upper left to sit in the left hand corner facing **Badua**. All are in deep red mourning. The drum and wailing stops, but only to give way to Kofi's **Hornblower** who enters immediately after **Osam**, stands directly behind the chair, blows a sequence of the exhortation and stops. The lights go dim on the upper stage.*

'The Mouth-That-Eats-Salt-And-Pepper' enters. **Old Woman** *first and almost shrieking.*

Old Woman   *Puei, puei, puei*! This is the type of happening out of which we get stories and legends. Yebi, I wish you *dué, dué dué*. May all the powers that be condole with you. Kofi Ako shoots himself and Anowa drowns herself! This is too much. Other villages produce great men, men of wealth, men of name. Why should this befall us? What tabooed food have we eaten? What unholy ground have we trodden?

Old Man *enters, stands in the centre of the stage with his head down.*

Old Woman   O Kofi Ako! Some say he lost his manhood because he was not born with much to begin with; that he had been a sickly infant and there always was only a hollow in him where a man's strength should be. Others say he had consumed it acquiring wealth, or exchanged it for prosperity. But I say that all should be laid at Anowa's doorstep. What man prospers, married to a woman like Anowa? Eh, would even Amanfi the giant have retained his strength faced with that witch? They say she always worked as though she could eat a thousand cows. Let the gods forgive me for speaking ill of the dead, but Anowa ate Kofi Ako up!

Old Man *(looking at her keenly, chuckles)*   There is surely one thing we know how to do very well. And that is assigning blame when things go wrong.

Old Woman   What do you mean by that! I did not shoot Kofi Ako, did I?

Old Man   I never said you did.

Old Woman   Was it not that Anowa who made him shoot himself?

Old Man *(quietly and not looking at* **Old Woman***)*   Perhaps, perhaps, perhaps. And yet no one goes mad in emptiness, unless he has the disease already in his head from the womb. No. It is men who make men mad. Who knows if Anowa would have been a better woman, a better person if we had not been what we are?

Old Woman *glares at him, spits and wobbles out coughing harder than ever before.*

Old Man They used to say here that Anowa behaved as though she were a heroine in a story. Some of us wish she had been happier and that her life had not had so much of the familiar human scent in it. She is true to herself. She refused to come back here to Yebi, to our gossiping and our judgements. Osam and Badua have gone with the others to bring the two bodies home to Yebi. Ow, if there is life after death, Anowa's spirit will certainly have something to say about that!

He begins to walk away, while all the lights begin to die.

In the approaching darkness, we hear the single Atentenben wailing in loneliness.

Woza Albert!

Percy Mtwa, Mbongeni Ngema
and Barney Simon

Characters

Two actors (Percy Mtwa and Mbongeni Ngema in the original productions) must play a number of characters – switching roles between and sometimes within scenes – with the bare minimum of costume and prop.

The stage is lit by the house-lights. The set consists of two up-ended tea-chests side by side about centre stage. Further upstage an old wooden plank, about ten feet long, is suspended horizontally on old ropes. From nails in the plank hang the ragged clothes that the actors will use for their transformations. The actors wear grey track-suit bottoms and running shoes. They are bare-chested. Around each actor's neck is a piece of elastic, tied to which is half a squash ball painted pink — a clown's nose, to be placed over his own nose when he plays a white man.

Scene One

The actors enter and take their positions quickly, simply. **Mbongeni** *sits on the tea-chests at the point they meet in the middle.* **Percy** *squats between his legs. As they create their totem, the house-lights dim to blackout.*

On the first note of their music, overhead lights come on, sculpting them. They become an instrumental jazz band, using only their bodies and their mouths — double bass, saxophone, flute, drums, bongos, trumpet, etc. At the climax of their performance, they transform into audience, applauding wildly.

Percy *stands, disappears behind the clothes rail.* **Mbongeni** *goes on applauding.* **Percy** *reappears wearing his pink nose and a policeman's cap. He is applauding patronisingly.* **Mbongeni** *stares at him, stops applauding.*

Percy Hey! Beautiful audience, hey? Beautiful musician, né? Okay, now let us see how beautiful his pass-book is! (*To appalled* **Mbongeni**.) Your pass!

Mbongeni (*playing for time*) Excuse my boss, excuse? What?

Percy (*smugly, to audience with his back to* **Mbongeni**) Okay, I'll start again. You know you're a black man, don't you?

Mbongeni Yes, my boss.

Percy And you live here in South Africa?

Mbongeni (*attempting to sidle off-stage behind* **Percy**'s *back*) Yes, my boss.

Percy   So you know that you must always carry your pass.

Mbongeni   Yes, my boss.

Percy   Okay, now what happens if you don't have your pass?

Mbongeni   I go to jail, my boss.

Percy   And what happens if your pass is not in order?

Mbongeni (*nearly off-stage*)   I go to jail, my boss.

Percy (*wheels on* **Mbongeni**)   H-E-E-E-Y! Your pass!!!

Mbongeni (*effusively*)   OOOOhhh, my pass, my constable! (*Moves to* **Percy** *holding out his pass*.) Here's my pass my lieutenant.

Percy   Okay, now let's have a look. (*Examines the pass*.) Where do you work?

Mbongeni   I work here, my Captain.

Percy   You work here? If you worked here your passbook would be written 'Market Theatre, Johannesburg'. But look, it is written 'Kentucky Southern Fried'. Is this Kentucky Southern Fried? And look at the date. It tells me you haven't worked in four years. This is vagrancy, you're unemployed. (*To audience*.) Ja, this is what I call 'loafer-skap!'.

Mbongeni   No, my Colonel, I am a guitarist, I've been playing music for five years, my boss.

Percy   Hey, you lie, you fuckin' entertainer!

Mbongeni   It's true, it's true, my boss.

Percy   Can you show me where it is written 'musician'? Hey? Where's a guitar? Where's a guitar! Where's a guitar?

Mbongeni   Ag, nee – my Brigadier, I am self-employed!

Percy   Self-employed? (*Chuckling collusively to audience*.) Hell, but these kaffirs can lie, hey?

Mbongeni   Maar, dis die waarheid, but it is true – my General!

Percy   You know where you should be?

Mbongeni   No, my boss.

Percy   You should be in prison!

Mbongeni   No, my boss.

Percy   And when you come out of prison, do you know where you should go?

Mbongeni   No, my boss.

Percy   Back to the bush with the baboons. That's where you belong! Kom hierso! Section 29. (*To audience, pleasantly.*) Do you know about Section 29? That's a nice little law specially made for loafers like him. And I've got a nice little place waiting for him in Modder-B Prison. Kom jong! (*Pulls* **Mbongeni** *by his track-suit.*)

Mbongeni (*aside*)   Shit!

Percy (*threatening*)   What did you say? Wat het jy gesê?

Mbongeni   Nothing – my President!

*The policeman (**Percy**) chases the musician (**Mbongeni**) behind the clothes-rail.*

Scene Two

Enter both actors with prison blankets wrapped around their shoulders. Both are singing a prison song, a prisoner's fantasy of his woman's longing for him:

   Ha-ja-ka-rumba
   Ha-ja-karumba

(*Solo.*)
   Bath'uyeza – uyez'uyezana?
   Bath'uyeza – uyez'uyezana?
   Kuthima ngizule kodwa mangicabanga
   Yini s'thandwa sithando sami ye –

(*Chorus.*)

Hajakarumba – hajakarumba.
Hajakarumba – hajakarumba.

[They say he is coming. Is he really coming?
I am mad when I think of it.
Come back my love, oh my love.]

Under the song, **Mbongeni** *gives orders.*

Mbongeni   Modder-B Prison . . . prisoners – line up! Body
Inspection. Hey wena cell number 16. Inspection cell number
16. Awusafuni na? Awusafunukuvula vula hey wena we-
neloda. Vul'inggwza sisone. [Hey you, cell number 16.
Inspection cell number 16. Are you hiding anything? Don't
you want to show what is hidden – come on you men – show
me your arses!] Prisoners inspection!

Both (*doing 'Towsa' dance, revealing empty orifices and
armpits*)   Ready for body inspection, my Basie! Blankets clear,
my Basie! No tobacco! No money! No watch! My Basie!
Mouth clear! Ears clear! (*Open mouths wide.*) Hooo! Hooo! (*Pull
ear-lobes.*) Haaa! Haaa! My Basie!

Percy   Hands up!

Both (*raise arms*)   Arms clear, my Basie! (*Raise legs.*) Everything
clear, my Basie! Also arse, my Basie!

Mbongeni   Inspection! (*They pull down their trousers, display bare
backsides.*) See nothing hidden, my Basie! Prisoners! Lights out!
(*Lights dim.*)

Both (*lying on the floor covering themselves with blankets*)
Goodnight, Basie, goodnight. Dankie Baba, dankie. Beautiful
arse, my Baba. Nothing hidden, my Basie.

Lights dim on sleeping figures.

Scene Three

Percy (*singing in his sleep*)   Morena walks with me all the way
/ Watching over me all the day / When the night time
comes he's there with me / Watching over, loving me.

Mbongeni (*restless, stirring from sleep*)   Hey man uyangxola man – uyangxola man. [Hey man, you making noise man.]

The singing continues.

Hey! Hey, hey! Stop singing your bloody hymns man, you're singing in your bladdy sleep again! Morena! Morena hoo-hoo, there's no Morena here!

Percy (*dazed*)   I'm sorry. (*Silence. He begins to hum again.*)

Mbongeni (*kicks* **Percy**, *who jumps up, is chased*)   Hayi man – isejelela. [This is prison man.]

Percy (*cowering*)   Morena, the saviour, is watching over you too, my friend.

Mbongeni   Morena, the saviour, here in Modder-B Prison? BULLSHIT!

Lights up bright. Work yard. Actors holding picks.

Mbongeni   Prisoners! Work yard!

Both (*working and singing a work-song*)
Siboshiwe siboshel'wa mahala
Wen'utha senzenjani
Siboshiwe siboshel'wa mahala
Wen'utha senzenjani

[They arrested us for nothing
So whàt can we do?]

Mbongeni *hurts his hand, nurses it.*

Mbongeni   It's this bladdy hard labour!

Percy (*attempting comfort*)   Don't worry my friend. Morena is over there, he's watching over us.

Mbongeni   Morena. Here in prison?

Percy   He's watching over you too.

Mbongeni (*kicking at him, chasing him*)   Morena here?? BULLSHIT!!

Scene Four

Mbongeni   Prisoners! Supper!

Both (*running*)   Supper! Supper! Supper!

Transforms to supper-time. Prisoners racing around in a circle, carrying plates, handing them in for food. **Mbongeni** *bullies* **Percy** *out of the way*

Percy   Thank you, soup, Baba. Thank you, Baba.

Mbongeni   Soup, Baba. Thank you soup, Baba, thank you Baba.

Percy   Porridge, Baba. Little bit of sugar, Baba.

Mbongeni   Porridge, Baba! Porridge. A little bit of sugar, Baba. A little bit of sugar, Baba. Thank you, Baba.

Percy   A little bit sugar, Baba. Please, little bit, Baba. Thank you, Baba. Thank you, Baba, too much sugar, Baba.

Mbongeni   Sugar . . . (*Reaches for* **Percy**'*s food.* **Percy** *points to a guard, stopping* **Mbongeni** *who smiles to the guard.*) No complaints, my boss. Geen klagte nie.

Percy   No complaints, Baba.

Mbongeni *eats in growing disgust;* **Percy** *with relish.*

Mbongeni (*spits on the floor*)   Ukudla kwemi godoyi lokhu [This is food for a dog] – No, a dog wouldn't even piss on this food. Ikhabishi, amazambane, ushukela, ipapa, utamatisi endishini eyodwa – ini leyo? [Cabbage, potatoes, sugar, porridge, tomatoes in one dish – what is this?]

Percy (*eating unconcerned*)   Thank you Morena for the food that you have given me. Amen.

Mbongeni (*turns on him, furious*)   Hey uthini Amen? [What do you say Amen for?] – For this shit? Thank you Morena for this shit?

Percy *crawls away.* **Mbongeni** *beckons him back.*

Mbongeni   Woza la! [Come here!]

Percy *hesitates.* **Mbongeni** *moves threateningly; points to the ground at his feet.*

Mbongeni Woza *la!*

Percy *crawls over reluctantly.*

Mbongeni On your knees!

Percy, *terrified, gets down on his knees.*

Mbongeni Pray! My Bullshit, I'm getting out of here tomorrow. Pray to your Morena, tell him thanks for me. I'll never listen to your voice again!

Mbongeni *pushes* **Percy** *forward on to the floor.* **Percy** *goes down with a scream that becomes a siren.*

Blackout.

Scene Five

The siren transforms into train sounds. Lights up. Both men are sitting back-to-back on boxes, rocking as in a train. **Mbongeni** *is reading a newspaper,* **Percy** *a Bible.* **Mbongeni** *spits out of the window, sits again.*

Percy (*evangelically*) Blessed are those that are persecuted for righteousness' sake, for theirs is the Kingdom of Heaven. Blessed are ye when men shall revile ye and persecute ye and shall send all manner of evil against ye falsely, for thy sake. Rejoice, and be exceedingly glad for great is the reward of heaven. For so persecuted they—

Mbongeni (*turns on him, hits him on the head with newspaper*) Hey! Persecuted? Prosecuted! Voetsak! Voetsak! (*Recognises his former fellow prisoner.*) Hey, brother Bullshit! When did you come out of prison? They promised me they would keep you in for life!

Percy Be careful, my friend, of the anger in your heart. For Morena will return and bear witness to our lives on earth and there will be no place to hide. He will point his holy finger and there will be those who rise to heaven and those who burn in hell. Hallelujah! I hope you're not one of them!

Mbongeni   Rise to heaven? Where is heaven?

Percy   It is the Kingdom of God.

Mbongeni   Up there? Neil Armstrong has been there.

Percy   Neil Armstrong?

Mbongeni   Hallelujah! He's been right up to the moon and he found a desert, no god!

Percy   My brother, I don't care what you or your friend on the moon say, because I know that he will return to his father's kingdom on earth, even as I know that his father has heard your blasphemies and forgiven you!

Mbongeni   Where does his father live? In Jerusalem?

Percy   The Lord, our father, is everywhere.

Mbongeni   And Morena, the saviour, is coming to South Africa?

Percy   Hallelujah!

Mbongeni   How is he coming to South Africa? By South African Airways jumbo jet? (*He transforms into a photographer photographing the audience.*) And everybody will be waiting in Johannesburg at Jan Smuts airport. Pressmen, radiomen, South African television, international television, ABC, NBC, CBS, BBC, and they will all gather around – (*He turns to* **Percy**, *who has transformed into the Prime Minister with pink nose and spectacles.*) – our honourable Prime Minister!

Scene Six

Percy (*moving forward ingratiatingly into spotlight*)   Thank you very much, thank you very much. My people, Morena is back and South Africa has got him! I hope that the free world will sit up and notice whose bread is buttered and where! Let them keep their boycotts, their boxers, rugby players, and tennis racketeers. Stay home Larry Holmes! Stay home John McEnroe! We have got Morena! But there is already rumours going around that this is not the real Morena, but some cheap impostor. And to those that spread such vicious rumours I can only say, 'Tough luck friends! He chose us!' (*Raises his hands in V-signs, laughs.*)

Blackout

Scene Seven

Lights up on **Mbongeni** *wearing a Cuban army cap and smoking a fat cigar.*

Percy (*as announcer*)   And now ladies and gentlemen, on the hotline straight from Havana – the comrade from Cuba – Fidel Castro! Sir, have you got any comment to make on the impending visit of Morena to South Africa?

Mbongeni (*laughing*)   Morena in South Africa? Who's playing the part? Ronald Reagan?

Blackout.

Scene Eight

Lights up on **Percy** *playing cool bongo on boxes.*

Mbongeni (*dancing flashily*)   And now for you to see on Black TV – the face of Black South Africa! (*Enjoying the bongo, dancing up to the player.*) Beautiful music my brother, cool sound, man, cool! Real cool! Beautiful music, oh yeah, oh yeah. Now tell me, my brother – what would you say – if Morena – walks in – right through that door?

Percy (*making a rude finger-sign*)   Aay, fok off man!

Blackout.

Scene Nine

Lights up bright on **Percy**, *now a young street meat-vendor. The boxes are his stall. He is swatting flies with a newspaper held in one hand. His other hand holds a second newspaper as shade against the sun.*

Mbongeni (*enters, singing, as a labourer-customer*)
Siyitshil'igusha sayigqiba
Siyitshil'igusha sayigqiba
Muhla sitsh'igusha.
Wena wendoda wawuphina
Wena wendoda wawuphina
Muhla sitsh'igusha.
[We ate and finished a big sheep the other day.
Where were you when we blessed ourselves with a sheep?]

Mbongeni   Hullo, my boy.

Percy   Hello, Baba.

Mbongeni (*not tempted by the display*)   Ehhh, what meat can you sell me today?

Percy   I've got mutton, chicken, and nice sausages. (*Swats a fly on the sausages.*)

Mbongeni   Oh yeah ... the chicken does not smell nice, hey? Must get some cover, some shade from the sun, hey? (*Deliberating.*) Ehhh, how much are those chops?

Percy   It's two rand fifty, Baba.

Mbongeni   Two rand fifty? Are they mutton chops?

Percy   Ehhh, it's mutton.

Mbongeni   No pork?

Percy   No pork, Baba. I don't like pork.

Mbongeni   Okay my boy, give me mutton chops. Two rand fifty, hey? Where's your mother, my boy?

Percy   She's at work.

Mbongeni   She's at work? Tell her I said 'tooka-tooka' on her nose. (*Tickles the boy's nose.*) She must visit me at the men's hostel, okay? Dube hostel, room number 126, block 'B', okay? Bye-bye, my boy. 'B', don't forget. (*About to leave he turns astonished at sight of – invisible – TV interviewer.*)

Percy (*awed by TV-interviewer*) Hello, Skulu. I'm fine, thanks. And you? (*Listens.*) Morena? Here in South Africa? What shall I ask from Morena if he comes to South Africa? Baba, I want him to bring me good luck. So that the people that come will buy all this meat. And then? I want him to take me to school. Sub-A, uh huh. (*Watching the interviewer leave.*) Thank you, Baba. Inkos'ibusise [God bless]. Yeah, Baba . . . Au! TV!

Blackout.

Scene Ten

Lights up, dim, on **Mbongeni** *as Auntie Dudu, an old woman, wearing a white dust-coat as a shawl. She is searching a garbage bin (upturned box). She eats some food, chases flies, then notices the interviewer. She speaks very shyly.*

Mbongeni Hey? My name is Auntie Dudu. No work my boy, I'm too old. Eh? (*Listens.*) If Morena comes to South Africa? That would be very good. Because everybody will be happy and there will be lots and lots of parties. And we'll find lots of food here – (*Indicates bin.*) – cabbages, tomatoes, chicken, hot-dogs, all the nice things white people eat. Huh? (*Receives tip.*) Oh, thank you, my boy. Thank you, Baba. Inkos'ibusise. [God bless.] God bless you. Bye bye, bye bye . . .

A fly buzzes close. She chases it.

Fade.

Scene Eleven

Lights up bright on a barber's open-air stall. **Percy** – *the barber* – *is sitting on a box,* **Mbongeni** – *the customer* – *between his knees. Auntie Dudu's shawl is now the barber's sheet.*

Percy   Ehh, French cut? German cut? Cheese cut?

Mbongeni   Cheese cut.

Percy   Cheese cut – all off!

Mbongeni (*settling*)   That's nice ... How much is a cheese cut?

Percy   Seventy-five cents.

Mbongeni   Aaay! Last week my cousin was here and it was fifty cents.

Percy   Hey, you've got very big hair my friend. (*He begins cutting hair.*)

Mbongeni (*squirming nervously during the – mimed – clipping, relaxing at the end of a run*)   That's nice. What machine is this?

Percy   Oh, it's number ten ...

Mbongeni   Number ten? Ohhh.

Percy   Though it's a very old clipper.

Mbongeni   That's nice. (*More cutting, more squirming.*) That's nice. Where's your daughter now?

Percy   Ohh, she's in university.

Mbongeni   University? That's nice. What standard is she doing in university?

Percy (*clipping*)   Ohhh, she's doing LLLLLB. I don't know, it's some very high standard.

Mbongeni   Oh yeah, LLB.

Percy (*confirming with pleasure*)   Uh huh, LLB.

Mbongeni   That's nice! I remember my school principal failed seven times LLB!

Percy   Ohhh, I see! I understand it's a very high standard.

Mbongeni   Tell me my friend, but why don't you apply for a barbershop? Why do you work in the open air where everyone is looking?

Percy (*continuing clipping*) Aaahh, don't ask me nonsense. I had a barbershop. But the police came with the bulldozers during the Soweto riots.

Mbongeni Ooohh, 1976?

Percy Uh huh. During the times of black power. Everything was upside down . . . (*To the invisible interviewer as he enters.*) Oh, hello, Skulu. I'm fine, thanks. And you? (*Listens.*) Morena? Here, in South Africa?

Mbongeni That's nice.

Percy (*clipping, talking excitedly*) Well now, I want him to build me a barbership in a very big shopping centre in Johannesburg city, with white tiles, mirrors all over the walls, and customers with big hair!

The clipper gets caught in **Mbongeni**'s *hair. He struggles.*

Mbongeni EEEEeeeeiiiiii!

Blackout.

Scene Twelve

Lights up. **Percy** *and* **Mbongeni** *are coal-vendors, soot-stained sacks on their heads. They are climbing on to boxes – a coal lorry – taking off.*

Both Hey! Firewood for sale! Coal for sale! Smokeless coal for sale! Firewood for sale! (*They make the sound of the lorry's engine revving. The lorry moves off.*)

Percy *Coal for sale!* Hey wena, Auntie Ma-Dlamini, phum'endlini. [Hey, you, Aunt Dlamini, come out of your house.] (*He spies a young girl, gestures.*) Dudlu – mayemaye, the sugar the pumpkin. [Hallo there, hi hi, you are the sugar, the pumpkin.]

Mbongeni Red light! Hey wena! [Hey you!] Driver – awuboni irobbot? [Can't you see the red light?]

Percy Don't you see the red light?

Mbongeni Awuboni la uyakhona? [Don't you see where you're going?]

Percy He hasn't got a licence.

Noise of the lorry revving. They discover the invisible interviewer below, turn to him impatiently.

Percy What? Morena here in South Africa? You're talking rubbish! (*Lorry sounds again. It jerks forward.*) Smokeless coal for sale! Firewood for sale! (*Looks back.*) Putsho putshu ikaka kwedini. You're talking shit, boy.

Mbongeni Inkanda leyo-kwedini-iyashisa he? [Your prick is hot, boy – heh?]

Percy *looks back contemptuously and makes a rude sign with his finger as the lorry drives off.*

Fade.

Scene Thirteen

Lights up on **Mbongeni** *entering as a fragile, toothless old man. He sings throughout the following action. He settles on the boxes, attempts to thread a needle. His hands tremble but he perseveres. He succeeds on the third, laborious attempt and begins to sew a button on his coat.*

Mbongeni (*humming*)
  Bamga-lo-kandaba bayimpi
  Heya we-bayimpi izwelonke
  Ngonyama ye zizwe
  Ohlab'izitha
  UNdaba bamgwazizwe lonke okazulu
  Amambuka nkosi
  [The soldiers of our enemies have come to attack the king
  They are coming from the four corners of the world to
    attack the Lion
  We must kill the enemies
  They are attacking him from all over the world, the son of
    Zulu
  These strangers from another place attack our King.]

Mbongeni *becomes aware of the (invisible) interviewer. Laughs knowingly.*

Mbongeni (*speaking*) Eh? What would happen to Morena if he comes to South Africa? What would happen to Morena is what happened to Piet Retief! Do you know Piet Retief? The big leader of the white men long ago, the leader of the Afrikaners! Ja! He visited Dingane, the great king of the Zulus! When Piet Retief came to Dingane, Dingane was sitting in his camp with all his men. And he thought, 'Hey, these white men with their guns are wizards. They are dangerous!' But he welcomed them with a big smile. He said, he said, 'Hello. Just leave your guns outside and come inside and eat meat and drink beer.' Eeeeii! That is what will happen to Morena today! The Prime Minister will say, just leave your angels outside and the power of your father outside and come inside and enjoy the fruits of apartheid. And then, what will happen to Morena is what happened to Piet Retief when he got inside. Dingane was sitting with all his men in his camp, when Piet Retief came inside. All the Zulus were singing and dancing . . . Bamya-lo-Kandaba payimpi . . . (*Repeats snatches of the song.*) And all the time Dingane's men were singing and dancing, (*Proudly.*) they were waiting for the signal from their king. And Dingane just stood up . . . He spit on the ground. He hit his beshu and he shouted, Bulalan'abathakathi. Kill the wizards! Kill the wizards! Kill the wizards! And Dingane's men came with all their spears. (*Mimes throat-slitting, throwing of bodies.*) Suka! That is what will happen to Morena here in South Africa. Morena here? (*Disgusted.*) Eeii! Suka!

Blackout.

Scene Fourteen

Lights flash on: **Percy,** *an airport announcer, is standing on a box, calling out.*

Percy Attention, please! Attention, please! Now this is a great moment for South Africa! The Lord Morena has arrived! The jumbo jet from Jerusalem has landed! Now lay down your blankets, sing hosanna, hosanna, lay down your presents. Hey, you over there, move away from the tarmac! (*More urgently.*) Move away from the runway! Move away!

Mbongeni (*rushing in as a photographer*)   Hosanna! Hosanna! Son of God! 'Hosanna nyana ka thixo!' ['Son of God.'] Hey, what will you say if Morena comes to you? (*To a member of the audience.*) Smile, smile! (*He turns to* **Percy** *then back to the camera crew.*) Sound! Rolling! Slate! Scene twenty-seven, take one. And action . . .

Scene Fifteen

Percy *wearing his pink nose and flash sunglasses, alights from the plane (box).*

Mbongeni (*approaching him with a mimed microphone*)   Happy landings, sir.

Percy (*flattered by this attention*)   Oh, thank you. Thank you.

Mbongeni   Well sir, you've just landed from a jumbo jet!

Percy   Eh, yes.

Mbongeni   Any comments, sir?

Percy   I beg your pardon?

Mbongeni (*arch interviewer*)   Would you not say that a jumbo jet is faster than a donkey, sir?

Percy   Eh, yes.

Mbongeni   Aaahh. Now tell me, sir, where have you been all this time?

Percy   Around and about.

Mbongeni   And how is it up there in the heavens?

Percy   Oh, it's very cool.

Mbongeni   Cool! (*Laughs artificially loud.*) So, I'm to understand that you've been studying our slang, too!

Percy   Right on!

They laugh together.

Mbongeni   Now tell me, sir, in the face of all boycotting moves, why did you choose South Africa for your grand return?

Percy   I beg your pardon?

Mbongeni   I mean, uuuh, why did you come here, sir?

Percy   To visit my Great-aunt Matilda.

Mbongeni   Excuse me, sir?

Percy   Yes?

Mbongeni   Your name, sir?

Percy   Patrick Alexander Smith.

Mbongeni   You mean you're not Morena, sir?

Percy   Who?

Mbongeni   Morena.

Percy   Morena?

Mbongeni   Are you not Morena? (*To film-makers.*) Cut!!! Morena! Where is Morena?

Percy *minces off, insulted. Stage dim,* **Mbongeni** *wanders across stage, calling disconsolately.*

Mbongeni   Morena! Morena! Morena! M-o-o-o-r-e-e-e-n-a-a-a! . . .

Lights dim. **Percy** *begins to join the call, alternating, from behind the clothes rail. He emerges calling and addressing a high and distant Morena. As he talks, the lights come up.*

Scene Sixteen

Percy Morena! Morena-a-a! Where are you? Come to
Albert Street! Come to the Pass Office! We need you here
Morena! Ja, Morena, this is the most terrible street in the
whole of Johannesburg! Ja, Morena, this is the street where
we Black men must come and stand and wait and wait and
wait just to get a permit to work in Johannesburg! And if
you're lucky enough to get the permit, what happens? You
wait and wait and wait again for the white bosses to come in
their cars to give you work. (*Turns back to* **Mbongeni**.) But
I'm lucky! I've got six months special! (*Shows his pass-book.*)
Qualified to work in Johannesburg for six months!

Mbongeni How many months? Eh?

Percy Six months!

Mbongeni Six months? Congratulations. (*Laughs, slaps*
Percy's *back, shakes his hand.*) Eh! Six month special!

Percy Three weeks in a queue!

Mbongeni But you're still their dog! (*Moves upstage to urinate,
with his back to the audience.*)

Percy Aaahh, jealous! You jealous!

Mbongeni Have you got a job? Have you got school fees
for your children? Have you got money for rent? Have you
got bus fare to come to the Pass Office? Oh, come on man,
we've all got specials but we're still their dogs!

Car sounds.

Percy (*leaps up*) Hey! There's a car! A white man! (*Moves to
the car at the front edge of the stage, follows it as it moves across.*) Are
you looking for workers, my boss? Ya, I've got six-month
special, qualified to work in Johannesburg.

Mbongeni *moves forward trying frantically to distract the driver. Car
sounds continue, actors alternating.*

Mbongeni Boss, I've got fourteen-day special. This is my last
chance. This is my last chance. Take two boys, my boss, two!

Percy   Messenger boy, tea boy, my boss. One! I make nice tea for the Madam, my boss. Bush tea, China tea, English tea! Please, Baba. Lots of experience, Baba. Very good education, my boss. Please my boss. Standard three, very good English, Baba.

Mbongeni's *sound of a departing car transforms into a mocking laugh.*

Mbongeni   I told you, you're still their dog! (*Laughs, mocks.*) Standard three, bush tea, China tea – where do you get China tea in Soweto?

Percy   Aah voetsak! I've got six months special!

Mbongeni (*shows* **Percy** *his pass-book*)   Hey, look at my picture. I look beautiful, heh?

Percy (*laughs bitterly*)   How can you look beautiful in your pass-book?

Car sounds again. **Mbongeni** *rushes forward to the stage edge, follows the car,* **Percy** *behind him.*

Mbongeni   One! One, my boss! Everything! Sweeper, anything, everything, my boss! Give me anything. Carwash? Yeah, always smiling, my boss. Ag, have you got work for me, my boss? I'm a very good nanny. I look after small white children. I make them tomato sandwich. I take them to school, my boss. Please, my boss. Please.

Car leaves. **Mbongeni** *wanders disconsolately upstage.* **Percy** *watches him.*

Percy (*laughing*)   Ja! Who's a dog? Don't talk like that! This is South Africa! This is Albert Street. (*Laughs.*) Nanny, nanny, tomato sandwich!

Car sounds again.

Both (*confusion of requests from each*)   Six-month special, my boss. Fourteen-day special, Baba. This is my last chance. Hey man, this is my corner! Very strong, Baas. Ek donder die kaffers op die plaas. [I beat up the kaffirs on the farm.] One, my boss. Two, my boss. Anything, my boss. Have you got anything for me, Baba?

Percy   Basie, he's a thief, this one.

Mbongeni   He can't talk Afrikaans, this one, my boss.

Percy   He's lying, Basie. Hy lieg, my baas!

The third car pulls away.

Percy (*confronting* **Mbongeni** *angrily*)   Hey, this is my corner, these are my cars. I've got six months special.

Mbongeni   Hey! Fuck off! I stand where I like, man.

Percy   You've got fourteen-day special. There's your corner.

Mbongeni   Hey! You don't tell me where to stand!

Percy   You've got fourteen-day special. You're not even qualified to be on Albert Street.

Mbongeni   Qualified? Qualified? Wenzani uthath'a ma shansi hey uthatha ma shansi. [What are you trying to do? You taking chances. Hey? You taking chances.]

Mbongeni *kicks* **Percy**. **Percy** *turns on him.*

Percy   Baas Piet! Baas Piet! I'll tell Baas Piet you got forgery.

Mbongeni (*mimes picking up stone*)   Okay, okay. Call your white boss! I've got friends too!

Percy   Baas Piet!

Mbongeni (*beckons his friends, wildly picking up stones*)   Hey Joe! We Joe! Zwakala – sigunu mfwethu. (*To* **Percy**.) Angihlali eZola mina – angihlali eMdeni mina – Joe zwakala simenze njalo. [Joe come here – it's happening. I don't live in Zola – I'm not from Mdeni – Joe come here let's work on him.]

Mbongeni *quietens, struck by something in the audience.*

Percy (*muttering sulkily*)   These are my cars, man. I've got six-month special, these are mine. This is my corner – That's the temporal corner! I'll tell Baas Piet!

Mbongeni (*now totally stunned by what he is watching*)   Heeey, heeey! Ssh man, ssh.

Percy (*cautious*)   What?

Mbongeni (*indicating the audience*)   Morena . . .

Percy   Aaay, fok off!

Mbongeni   It's Morena – that one there with the white shirt.

Percy (*doubtfully*)   Morena? Ay, nonsense . . . Is it Morena?

Mbongeni   It's him – I saw him in the *Sunday Times* with Bishop Tutu. It's him!

He sidles forward to the edge of the stage. **Percy** *shyly eggs him on.*

Percy   Hey, speak to him.

Mbongeni (*nods with the invisible Morena*)   Excuse. Are you not Morena? Yiiiii! Hosanna! Morena!

The actors embrace joyously. Then follow Morena, frantically showing their passes and pleading.

Both Actors   Morena, look at my pass-book!

Percy   I've got six-month special but I can't find work.

Mbongeni   I've been looking here two months, no work. Take us to heaven, Morena, it's terrible here.

Mbongeni *follows Morena.* **Percy** *falls behind.*

Percy   Temporary or permanent is okay Morena!

Silence as **Mbongeni** *converses with Morena. He comes back exhilarated.*

Percy   Hey, what does he say?

Mbongeni   He says let us throw away our passes and follow him to Soweto!

Percy   Hey! He's right! Morena! Morena!

Both (*sing, exhorting the audience*)
   Woza giya nansi inkonyane ye ndlovu –
   Aph'amadoda sibabambe sebephelele.
   Wozani madoda niyesaba na?

[Come on join this child of an elephant
Where are the men? Let us face them!
Come men, are you afraid?]

Percy (*under the song*)   Morena says throw away your passes and follow him to Soweto.

Mbongeni   We are not pieces of paper, man! We are men!

Percy   Ja! Let them know our faces as Morena knows our faces!

Mbongeni   Morena says no more passes!

Percy   Ja!!

Mbongeni   We don't have numbers any more!

Percy   Ja!

Mbongeni   Let them look at our faces to know that we are men.

Percy   Ja! When we follow Morena we walk as one!

The actors throw away their passes and their song transforms into train sounds.

Scene Seventeen

The actors mime standing beside each other at a train window. They wave to people outside.

Percy   Hey madoda! Sanibona madoda! May God bless them! Ja, you've got a very good imagination. I really like your stories. But you must go to church sometimes – Hey, there's a train coming! (*Looks to one side.*)

Flurry of their faces and noises as they mime watching adjoining train pass. Then they pull their windows up. Siren. **Mbongeni** *moves downstage.* **Percy** *stands on a box, begins Regina Mundi Song:*

Somlandela – somlandela u Morena
Somlandela yonke indawo
Somlandela – somlandela u Morena

Lapho eyakhona somlandela.

[We shall follow – we shall follow Morena
We shall follow him everywhere
We shall follow – we shall follow Morena
Where-ever he leads – we shall follow.]

While the song continues:

Mbongeni (*joyous siren*)   Ja, madoda, hundreds of thousands
will gather at the Regina Mundi Church in the heart of
Soweto. And people will sing and dance. There will be bread
for all. And wine for all. Our people will be left in peace,
because there will be too many of us and the whole world will
be watching. And people will go home to their beds. (*He joins
in the song for a few phrases.*) These will be days of joy. Auntie
Dudu will find chicken legs in her rubbish bin, and whole
cabbages. And amadoda – our men – will be offered work at
the Pass Office. The barber will be surrounded by white tiles.
The young meat-seller will wear a nice new uniform and go
to school, and we will all go to Morena for our blessings.

Song subsides. **Percy** *lies on boxes as sleeping woman. Lights dim.*

And then … the government will begin to take courage again
… The police and the army will assemble from all parts of
the country … And one night, police dogs will move in as
they have done before. There will be shouts at night and
bangings on the door …

Percy (*banging on a box*)   Hey! Open up, it's the police! Maak
die deur oop! Polisie!

Mbongeni (*ducking down by the boxes as if hiding beside a
bed*)   … There will be sounds of police vans and the crying
of women and their babies.

Percy (*turns over on the boxes as an old woman waking in bed, starts
crying and calling in Zulu*)   We Jabulani, hayi-bo-hey-hey-we-
Nonoza, akenivule bo nanka amaphoyisa esesihlasele, we
Thoko akenivule bo. Auw-Nkosi-Yami, ezingane ze-Black
Power! [Hey, Jabulani, Hey no, hey-hey, Nonoza, open the
door can't you hear the police are here. They've come to

attack us. Thoko, please open the door. Oh my God, these children of Black Power!]

He goes to open the door. Throughout **Mbongeni** *tries to stop him.*

Mbongeni   Sssh Mama! Tula Mama! Mama! Mama! Leave the door! (*He gives up, stands silent, transfixed, hiding.*) They'll start surrounding our homes at night. And some of our friends will be caught by stray bullets. There will be road-blocks at every entrance to Soweto, and Regina Mundi Church will be full of tear-gas smoke! Then life will go on as before.

He throws his arms up in the air in disgust, cries out.

Scene Eighteen

Lights flash on. Bright daylight. Coronation Brickyard. **Mbongeni,** *as* **Zuluboy,** *is singing.*

Mbongeni (*singing*)   Akuntombi lokhu kwabulala ubhuti ngesibumbu kuyamsondeza. [This is no woman. She killed my brother with a fuck and she never lets him go.]
(*He calls out towards the street.*) Hey Angelina – sweetheart! Why are you walking down the street? Come here to Coronation Brickyard! Zuluboy is waiting for you with a nice present! (*Points to his genitals, laughing.*)

Percy (*enters as Bobbejaan – Baboon – Zuluboy's fellow brickyard worker*)   Hey! Zuluboy, forget about women. Start the machine!

Mbongeni *sings on.*

Percy   Hey! The white man is watching us. Boss Kom is standing by the window! Start the machine.

He makes machine sounds as he attempts to start it. He pulls the starter cord abortively, flies backwards across the yard.

Mbongeni (*laughs*)   Hey Bobbejaan! Start the machine!

Percy   You laugh and I must do all this work! I'll tell Baas Kom. Baas Kom! Basie! Baas Kom!

Mbongeni Ssshhhhhh! Bobbejaan! Bobbejaan ... ssh – I want to tell you a secret.

Percy What secret?

Mbongeni (*whispers*) We don't have to work so hard any more. Because Morena, the saviour, is coming here.

Percy Huh? Morena here? Hau! Baas Kom!

Mbongeni Hau, no Bobbejaan! Listen – I was there on Thursday by the Jan Smuts Airport. We were delivering bricks. People were coming with taxis, bikes, trains, trucks, others on foot. There were many people, Bobbejaan. They were singing and crying and laughing and dancing and sweating and this other woman was shouting: Morena, give me bread for my baby. The other woman was shouting: Morena, my son is in detention. The other man: Morena, give me a special permit to work in Johannesburg city. The little girl, standing next to me: Morena, give me a lollipop. The big fat Zulu – the driver from Zola Hostel – Morena, give me a Chevrolet Impala! And me – I was there too—

Percy What did you say?

Mbongeni Morena, come to Coronation Brickyard tomorow morning! And he's coming here.

Percy To Coronation Brickyard? Morena?

Mbongeni Hau – Bobbejaan, at the wedding, long ago – ten thousand years ago – he take a bucket of water, he make wine.

Percy (*smugly*) Ja, everybody knows that!

Mbongeni He take one fish, he make fish for everybody! Fried fish!

Percy Hau!

Mbongeni He take one loaf of brown bread, he make the whole bakery! Here at Coronation Brickyard, you will see wonders. He will take one brick, number one brick, and throw it up in the air. And it will fall down on our heads, a million bricks like manna from heaven!

Percy   Hey! You're talking nonsense. Morena? Here at Coronation Bricks? Start the machine. I'll tell Baas Kom!

Percy *goes off.* **Mbongeni** *begins rolling a cigarette, singing his Zuluboy song.* **Percy**, *as Baas Kom with pink nose and white dustcoat, enters quietly from behind the clothes rail and creeps up on him.* **Mbongeni** *spits, just missing* **Percy** *who leaps back.*

Mbongeni   Oh, sorry, Boss. Sorry, sorry . . . (*He runs to start the machine.*)

Percy   Sis! Where were you brought up?

Mbongeni   Sorry Boss!

Percy   Ja Zuluboy! And what are you sitting around for?

Mbongeni   Sorry, Boss. Sorry.

Percy   Are you waiting for Morena?

Mbongeni   No, Boss. No.

Percy   Ja, I've been listening. I've been watching. You're waiting for Morena. Ja. Did you not listen to the Prime Minister on the radio today?

Mbongeni   I don't have a radio, Boss.

Percy   We don't like Morena anymore. And everybody who's waiting for Morena is getting fired.

Mbongeni   Oh, very good, Boss. Me? I'm Zuluboy – ten thousand bricks in one day!

Percy   Ja. Where's Bobbejaan?

Mbongeni (*attempting to start the machine*)   He's gone to the toilet.

Percy   Call him. Call him, quickly!

Mbongeni   Hey! Bobbejaan! (*He makes motor sounds as the machine kicks over but does not 'take'.*) Bobbejaan!

Percy (*still as Baas Kom, with* **Mbongeni** *watching over his*

shoulder)   Now listen. I want two thousand bricks for Boss
Koekemoer. Two thousand bricks for Baas Pretorius. Two
thousand bricks for Mrs Dawson.

Mbongeni *indicates his pleasure in Mrs Dawson.* **Percy** *cautions
him:*

Percy   Zuluboy! Six thousand bricks for Boss Van der
Westhuizen. Two thousand bricks for Boss Koekemoer. Two
thousand bricks for Baas Pretorius. Two thousand bricks for
Mrs Dawson.

Mbongeni   Baas, sorry, I'm confused.

Percy   What confused? What confused? You're bloody lazy,
man! See to these orders and push the truck. (*He indicates the
truck on the side of the stage.*)

Mbongeni   Hey! This truck is too heavy, Baas!

Percy   Get other people!

Mbongeni   People have gone to lunch.

Percy   Get Bobbejaan!

Mbongeni   Ten thousand bricks, Boss!

Percy   Hey! Get Bobbejaan!

Mbongeni   Bobbejaan! Uyahamba laphe khaya.. [They'll fire
you.] Bobbejaan! (*Mumbling.*) Two thousand bricks Mrs
Dawson . . . Hau! (*Laughs with pleasure.*) Mrs Dawson! Ten
thousand brick Baas van Des-des-destuizen . . . Too much! (*He
starts the engine. Engine 'takes'. Shouts.*) Bobbejaan!

Percy (*off-stage, as Bobbejaan*)   I'm coming, man! (*He enters.*)
Hey, hey. Where's Morena?

Mbongeni   No Morena. Hey, shovel the sand, Baas Kom is
firing everybody that's waiting for Morena.

Percy (*laughing*)   Ja! I've been telling you! Hey, bring down
the pot.

They alternate shovel and motor sounds, as they mime shovelling.
Mbongeni *begins to sing and dance his Zuluboy song.*

Percy   Hey, stop dancing. Stop dancing!

Mbongeni   Hey! I am boss-boy here! (*He switches off the engine.*)

Percy   Lunch time!

Mbongeni   No Bobbejaan. First push the truck.

Percy   Hau! Ten thousand bricks! Hau! Lunch time!

Mbongeni   Baas Kom said, push the truck! Get Bobbejaan, push the truck. PUSH!

Percy *joins him reluctantly. They start to chant while they mime pushing the heavy truck.*

Both (*chanting*)
   Woza kanye-kanye! [Come together!]
   Abelungu oswajini! [Whites are swines!]
   Basibiza ngo-damn! [They call us damns!]

   Woza kanye-kanye! [Come together!]
   Abelungu oswajini! [Whites are swines!]
   Basibiza ngo-damn! [They call us damns!]

They finally stop, exhauted.

Percy (*holding his back, moaning*)   Oh, oh, oh, yii, yii! Lunch time! Hayi ndiva kuthi qhu. [My back is breaking.]

Mbongeni   Hayi suka unamanga. [Hey you lie.] (*He squats to examine the truck.*) It has gone too far. Reverse!

Percy   Reverse?! Reverse?

Muttering, he joins **Mbongeni**. *They pull the truck back again, chanting.*

Both (*chanting*)
   Woza emuva! [Come reverse!]
   Phenduka ayi. [Change now.]
   Abelungu oswayini! [Whites are swines!]
   Basibiza ngo-damn! [They call us damns!]

Percy   Hayi. (*Goes off.*)

Mbongeni   Bobbejaan, come back, it stuck in ditch.

Percy (*off-stage*)   Hayi, xelel'ubaas Kom ukuba sifuna
i-increase. [Tell Baas Kom we want increase.]

Mbongeni   We . . . kuyintekentekana lokhu okuwu-
Bobbejaan. [Hey man, Bobbejaan is too weak.] Come back,
Bobbejaan! Uyahamba laphe khaya. [They'll fire you.]
Where's my cigarette? (*Mimes lighting a cigarette. Talks to himself,
starts praise-chant.*)

Percy (*enters as Baas Kom*)   And now? And now? (*Mocking
praise-chant:*) Aaay, hakela, hakela. What the bloody hell is
that? Huh? Push the truck! Come!

Mbongeni   Having rest, baas. Still smoking.

Percy   Do you think I pay you for smoking? (*Glances at the
truck.*) Hey, push the truck!

Mbongeni   We pushed the truck! Ten thousand bricks! Boss,
there's too much work for two people. Me and Bobbejaan
start the engine. Me and Bobbejaan shovel the sand. Me and
Bobbejaan load the bricks. Me and Bobbejaan push the truck!
Aaay suka! We need other people!

Percy   There's no jobs!

Mbongeni   There *is* jobs!!! Ten thousand bricks! This
morning there were many people at the gates standing there
looking for work. And you chased them away!

Percy   Zuluboy, you're getting cheeky, huh?

Mbongeni   I'm not getting cheeky. It's true.

Percy   Ja! I'm cutting down your salary. I think you're
getting too much. Ja! Ja!

Mbongeni   The boss can't cut salary.

Percy   Ek gaan dit doen! [I'm going to do it.]

Mbongeni   That's not showing sympathy for another man.
The cost of living is too high. There is too much inflation.

Percy   Zuluboy! Zuluboy! You sit around waiting for

Morena and then you come and tell me about the cost of living? You talk about inflation? What do you know about inflation? I've got you here, just here. One more mistake, once more cheeky, and you're fired!

Mbongeni   Okay. All right boss. Let's talk business like two people.

Percy (*bangs on the box*)   He-ey! Push the truck, man!

Mbongeni, *furious, bangs on the box.* **Percy** *retreats towards his office space.*

Mbongeni   Hey! You must listen nice when another man talks!

Percy   Okay. Talk, talk.

Mbongeni *advances.*

Percy   No – talk over there, talk over there!

Mbongeni (*backs away*)   All right. Okay, okay. The people want increase. Where's the money for the people?

Percy   Increase?

Mbongeni   Increase!

Percy   Don't I give you free food? Free boarding and lodging?

Mbongeni   The people don't like your free food! They want money. There is too big families to support. Too many children.

Percy   I don't give a damn about your too many children. Don't you know about family planning?

Mbongeni   Family planning? What is that?

Percy   Don't you know that you must not have too many children? You must have two, three, and stop your fuck-fuck nonsense! Too many pic-a-ninnies! Too many black kaffir babies all over the country. (*Sharing this with the audience.*) Their kaffir babies cry 'Waaaaa! Waaaaa!' Just like too many piccaninny dogs!

Mbongeni (*threatening*) Hey!

Percy Zuluboy!

Mbongeni Whose children cry 'Waaa, waaa'?

Percy Zuluboy!

Mbongeni Whose children is piccaninny dogs?

Percy Bring your pass-book!

Mbongeni Why?

Percy You're fired! Bring your pass-book. I'm signing you off.

Mbongeni You can't sign me off!

Percy I'm calling the police! I'm calling the government buses and I'm sending you back to your homelands. Ek stuur julle na julle fokken verdomde, donorse, bliksemse plase toe! [I'm sending you to your fucking, cursed, useless farms.] You don't like my work? You don't like my food! Go back to your bladdy farms! Go starve on your bladdy farms!

Mbongeni I must starve?

Percy Ja!

Mbongeni My children must starve?

Percy Ja!

Mbongeni Go on strike!!!

Percy Hey! Bring your pass-book!

Mbongeni (*pulls out his knobkerrie from behind the box*) Here's my pass-book!

Percy Zuluboy!

Mbongeni (*advancing*) Here's my pass-book.

Percy (*ducking behind the rack of clothes at the back of the stage*) Bobbejaan!

Mbongeni Here's my pass-book! Stay away – hlala phansi

wena ngane ka Ngema. Hlala wena ngane ka Madlokovu –
hlala. Wena dlula bedlana inkunzi engena mona, hlala phansi
mfana – Hlala! Pho – kuhlala ba. [Stay away – sit down you
son of Ngema. Sit down son of Madlokovu. Sit. You fuck and
you never feel jealous. Sit down great son. Sit. So who am I
– the greatest!] (*Mutters to himself.*) Stay away. Go on strike. My
children cry 'Waa-waa'. (*Suddenly he sees Morena approaching. He
wipes the sweat from his eyes, shakes his head in disbelief. Falls to his
knees.*) Hey. Hey! Morena! So you've come to Coronation
Bricks! Come, Morena. Did you listen to the radio today?
Everybody's waiting for you, and everybody is fired. Come, sit
down here, Morena. (*Offers a box.*) Sit down. Sit down Morena.
(*Calls out.*) Bobbejaan!

Percy (*entering as Bobbejaan, angrily*)   Hau! One minute
'Bobbejaan!' One minute 'Bobbejaan!' (*He sees Morena, stops
complaining and turns away shyly.*)

Mbongeni (*laughs*)   Bobbejaan, who is this? Who is this!!!

Percy (*backs away smiling shyly*)   Hey. I don't know him. Who
is it?

Mbongeni   Who is this? I win the bet. Give ten rands.

Percy   Who is he?

Mbongeni   Give ten rands!

Percy   Who is he?

Mbongeni   Morena!

Percy   Hey! Morena?!

Mbongeni   He's from heaven. He has come now. He
landed at Jan Smuts Airport on Thursday by the airline from
Jerusalem.

Percy   Hey Morena! (*Clapping hands.*) I saw your picture in
the paper. Morena, I could not believe you're coming. I
thought you're coming back by the clouds. (*He sits on the floor.*)

Mbongeni   The clouds are too hot now. It's summer. He
flies air-conditioned. Excuse, Morena, this is Bobbejaan.

Bobbejaan, shake hands with Morena.

Percy *stands, embarrassed, backs away.*

Mbongeni   Shake hands with the Son of God! Shake hands, Bobbejaan!

Percy *ducks behind the Zuluboy on the box. Zuluboy laughs.*

Mbongeni   Bobbejaan is shy! We are working together here, Morena. When I say, 'Morena, come to Coronation Brickyard', I mean you must make bricks like you make bread and wine long ago. I mean you must make bricks to fall down like manna from heaven—

Percy   Like you made fried fish!

Mbongeni   Ja! But now, I say no! Stay away! No! You must not make bricks for Coronation Brickyard! You must go on strike like me and Bobbejaan! Angithi Bobbejaan? [Isn't it so, Bobbejaan?] We work hard here. We sweat. Sweating for one man!

Percy   Boss Koekemoer!

Mbongeni   Every Friday, Boss Koekemoer, seven thousand bricks—

Percy   Boss Pretorius!

Mbongeni   Boss Pretorius ten thousand bricks!

Percy   Van de Westhuizen!

Mbongeni   Boss Van-des-destuizen, eleven thousand bricks! Where do we stay?

Percy   In a tin!

Mbongeni   In a tin! Like sardine fish!

Percy   In a tin, Morena!

Mbongeni   Where do the bricks go to!? The bricks go to make a big house, six rooms, for two people. A white man and his wife! Angithi Bobbejaan? [Isn't it so, Bobbejaan?] Our fingers are breaking Morena! Is nie good kanjalo man. [That's not good like that, man.]

Percy   Ten thousand bricks!

Mbongeni   Ten thousand bricks! Me and Bobbejaan must push the truck. Aaay suka! Stay away! No bricks for Coronation Bricks! (*He puts out his cigarette and clears his nose – to* **Percy***'s embarrassment.*) Are you hungry, Morena? Are you hungry? I've got nice food for you, I've got a packet of chips. (*Mimes.*) It's very good this one. There's lots of vinegar and salt – I bought them from the shop just around the corner.

Percy   That's potatoes, Morena.

Mbongeni   I've got half-brown bread. Whole-wheat. You made this long ago, huh? I've been telling Bobbejaan, you made plenty in the wedding – He's got power, this one! (*Mimes.*) This is Coca-cola, Morena.

Percy   It's cold drink.

Mbongeni   For quenching thirst.

Percy   Ha, Morena, there's no Coca-cola in heaven?

Mbongeni   What do you drink up there?

They listen, then laugh uproariously.

Percy   These two!

Mbongeni   You and your father! Skelm! [Mischief-makers!]

He mimes opening a Coke bottle.

Percy   (*looks upstage, then calls in Baas Kom's voice, as if from off-stage*)   Bobbejaan! (*Then as Bobbejaan again.*) Baas Kom! Morena, I must go! One minute 'Bobbejaan!' One minute 'Bobbejaan!' (*Going off.*) Hey Zuluboy, I want my chips!

Mbongeni   (*drinks from the mimed Coke bottle, burps, offers it to Morena*)   Yabhodla ingane yenZule ukuba okungu – MSuthu ngabe kudala kuzinyele. [There burps the son of a Zulu; if it was a Sotho he would be shitting.] Did you hear that man who was shouting 'Bobbejaan'? That's our white boss. Boss Kom. He's not good. But don't worry . . .

Percy (*off-stage in Baas Kom's voice*)   Bobbejaan!

Mbongeni   Lots of vinegar . . .

Percy (*enters as Baas Kom, stops at sight of Morena*)   En nou! En nou? Who is this? Who is sitting around eating lunch with my kaffirs? That's why you're getting cheeky, hey? Ja, you sit around and have lunch with terrorists!

Mbongeni   Hau! He's not a terrorist, Baas! He's a big man from heaven!

Percy   This man is a communist, jong! Ek het van jou nonsense gehoor. Die hele land praat van you. [I've heard of your nonsense. The whole country is talking about you.]

Mbongeni   Excuse. He cannot understand Afrikaans.

Percy   What? Cannot understand Afrikaans?

Mbongeni   Right.

Percy   Cannot understand Afrikaans? Stay where you are! (*Retreats to his office behind the clothes.*) I'm calling the police. Fuckin' agitator!

Mbongeni   Aay suka!! Don't worry, Morena, don't worry. (*He proffers the Coke bottle.*) He does not know who you are. He does not know who your father is.

Percy (*as Baas Kom, offstage*)   Hello? Hello? Lieutenant Venter? Ja! Now listen here. There's a terrorist here who's making trouble with my kaffirs. Ek sê daar's 'n uitlander hier wat kak maak met my kaffirs. [I say there's a foreigner here who's making shit with my kaffirs.] Ja. Hello? Hello? Ag die fuckin' telephone! Bobbejaan! (*As Bobbejaan:*) Ja, Basie? (*As Baas Kom:*) Kom, kom, kom. (*As Bobbejaan:*) Ja, Basie? (*As Baas Kom:*) You see that man eating with Zuluboy? (*As Bobbejaan:*) Ja, Basie. (*As Baas Kom:*) He's a terrorist! (*As Bobbejaan:*) A terrorist, Basie? That's Morena! (*As Baas Kom:*) It's not Morena – Now listen here. Listen carefully. I'm writing down this message. You take this message to the police station and I'm going to give you a very nice present. A ten rand increase, okay? (*As Bobbejaan:*) Ja, thank you Basie, thank you Basie. (*As Baas Kom:*)

Ja, go straight to the police station and don't tell Zuluboy. (*As Bobbejaan*:) Ja Basie, ja. (*As Baas Kom*:) Go to the police station and you get the ten rand increase!

Mbongeni Did you hear that, Morena? (*He listens.*) What? Forgive a man seventy times seventy-seven? Aikhona Morena! This is South Africa. We fight! Bobbejaan is very dangerous. (*Listens to Morena.*) Okay, you win. Wait and see, Morena.

Percy (*enters as Bobbejaan, putting on his shirt*)   Morena, I'm going to the shop, just around the corner.

Mbongeni Bobbejaan, your chips are here.

Percy Give them to Morena.

Mbongeni Morena is not hungry.

Percy Eat them yourself.

Mbongeni I'm not hungry either. Where are you going, Bobbejaan?

Percy To the shop!

Mbongeni Why, Bobbejaan?

Percy I'm going to buy hot-dogs for Baas Kom.

Mbongeni Where's the money?

Percy I've got it here.

Mbongeni Show it to me.

Percy Why?

Mbongeni Ja. You Judas, Bobbejaan!

Percy What are you talking about?

Mbongeni You betray Morena, Bobbejaan.

Percy Haw! Morena, do you hear that?

Mbongeni Bobbejaan, you betray Morena, Bobbejaan! You Judas, Bobbejaan!

Percy I'm going to buy hot-dogs for Baas Kom!

Mbongeni   You . . . you . . . you take a message to the
police. And you get ten rands increase Bobbejaan!

Percy   Aay Morena. Morena, do you hear that?

Mbongeni   Morena, shhh. Keep quiet. This is South Africa.
Ten rands increase. (*He reaches for the knobkerrie.*)

Percy   Baas Kom! (*He runs off.*)

Mbongeni   (*mimes his knobkerrie being grabbed by
Morena*) Morena, leave it! Leave it! Morena! Morena, leave it!
Morena! He has run away now. Bobbejaan, sodibana nawe
wena. [Bobbejaan, you and I will meet again.] A man hits
this cheek you give him the other. Aikhona, Morena! They're
calling the police to arrest you now! Okay, come. Let me hide
you there by the trees – quickly – (*Siren sounds. He stops.*)
There's one, two, three . . . there's thirteen police cars. Huh?
Forgive them, they do not know what they are doing?
Aikhona, Morena! They know! They know! (*He sings and
performs a Zulu war dance, which ends with him thrusting his knobkerrie
again and again at the audience in attack.*)

> Quobolela njomane kandaba heya-he
> soze sibajahe abelungu he ya he.

> [Be ready you horses of the black warriors
> Time will come when we'll chase these whites away.]

Scene Nineteen

The lights come up on the actors wearing military hats and pink noses.
Percy *has a bloody bandage under his hat.*

Mbongeni   Address! Ssshhhooo! Attention!

They drill in unison.

Percy   (*saluting*)   Reporting sir! John Vorster Squad, sir!

Mbongeni   What have you to report, Sergeant?

Percy   Operation Coronation, sir!

Mbongeni Meaning, Sergeant?

Percy We have finally captured Morena, sir!

Mbongeni You've what? Attention! One-two-three-one-two-three-one! (*They march to each other, shake hands.*) Excellent, Sergeant! Excellent!

Percy Thank you, sir.

Mbongeni And now, what's happened to your head, Sergeant?

Percy A mad Zulu, sir.

Mbongeni A mad Zulu?

Percy Yes sir. He struck me with the branch of a tree, sir.

Mbongeni A branch of a tree?

Percy They call it a knobkerrie, sir.

Mbongeni Ah! When, Sergeant?

Percy During Operation Coronation, sir.

Mbongeni You mean Morena was with a bunch of mad Zulus?

Percy No, sir.

Mbongeni What does he mean, this stupid sergeant?

Percy He was with one mad Zulu, sir!

Mbongeni One mad Zulu?

Percy Yes, sir!

Mbongeni And how many men did you have, Sergeant?

Percy Thirty, sir!

Mbongeni And where are they now, Sergeant?

Percy In hospital, sir!

Mbongeni And the mad Zulu?

Percy He got away, sir!

Mbongeni   God! Wat gaan aan?! [God! Whàt's going on?!] Where is Morena now, Sergeant?

Percy (*pointing proudly above the audience*)   He's upstairs, above us, sir. On the tenth floor of John Vorster Square Prison, sir!

Mbongeni   Aaaahhh! (*Looking up.*) And you've provided ample guard, Sergeant?

Percy   Yes, sir. One hundred and twenty, sir.

Mbongeni (*moving forward, watching the tenth floor, mesmerised*)   Are you sure he's on the tenth floor, Sergeant?

Percy (*following his gaze nervously*)   Yes, sir.

Mbongeni   Then what is that I see?

Percy (*moving behind him, also mesmerised, both eye-lines travelling above the audience*)   I'm sorry sir.

Mbongeni   Why are you sorry, Sergeant?

Percy   I see two men floating, sir.

Mbongeni   Then why are you sorry, Sergeant?

Percy   I'm afraid one of them is Morena, sir.

Mbongeni (*moving in, nose-to-nose, menacingly*)   Precisely, Sergeant! And-who-is-the-other?

Percy   The Angel Gabriel, sir.

Mbongeni (*despairing*)   Ha! Gabriel!

Percy   I'm sorry, sir. I never thought of air flight, sir.

Mbongeni   Eeeeeiiiii! One-two-three-four-one-four! Attention! Dismissed, Sergeant!

Scene Twenty

Lights find both actors travelling beside each other on a train.

Mbongeni (*laughing*)   Jaaa. And where do we go from there? After a miracle like flying men, I'm telling you the government will be real nervous. And they won't start nonsense with him for a long time. In fact, they will try very hard to please Morena. He will be taken to all the nice places in the country. Like the game reserve where he can lie down with a leopard and a lamb. (*They cuddle.*) And then – (*They mime a high-speed lift.*) – they will take him right up to the high spots of Johannesburg City – Panorama Wimpy Bar, Carlton Centre, fiftieth floor! And then, on a Thursday they will take him down – (*They mime going down, pink noses on their foreheads like miners' lamps.*) – the gold mines to watch. (*They mime deafening drills.*) And then, on a Sunday the mine dancers. (*They perform a short dance routine.*) And – (*Hand to ear.*) – aah, the government gardens in Pretoria. (*Doves cooing.*) And then, they will take him on a trip to SUN CITY – (*Stage radiantly light.*) – THE LAS VEGAS OF SOUTH AFRICA, where they will build him a holy suite and President Lucas Mangope, the puppet, will offer him the key to the homeland of Bophutatswana! And then what will happen? They will take him past the good-time girls.

Standing on a box, **Percy** *mimes.*

Mbongeni   And the gambling machines.

Percy *transforms into a one-armed bandit,* **Mbongeni** *works him, wins triumphantly.*

Mbongeni   And when television cameras turn on him, will he be smiling? Will he be joyous? No. He'll be crying. And when all the people shout—

Both   Speech! Morena, speech!

Mbongeni   —Morena will say, 'No.'

Percy (*miming holding a mike*)   No, speak up.

Mbongeni   No! Morena will say, what key is this? What place is this? This place where old people weep over the graves of children? How has it happened? How has it been permitted? I've passed people with burning mouths. People buying water in a rusty piece of tin, and beside them I see people swimming in a lake that they have made from water that is here!

Percy   Be careful, there are police spies here.

Mbongeni   What spies? Morena will say, I pass people who sit in dust and beg for work that will buy them bread. And on the other side I see people who are living in gold and glass and whose rubbish bins are loaded with food for a thousand mouths.

Percy   Hey! That's not your business. There are security police, man.

Mbongeni   What security police? Morena will say, I see families torn apart, I see mothers without sons, children without fathers, and wives who have no men! Where are the men? Aph'amadoda madoda? [Where are the men?] And people will say, Ja, Morena, it's this bladdy apartheid. It's those puppets, u Mangope! u Matanzima! u Sebe! Together with their white Pretoria masters. They separate us from our wives, from our sons and daughters! And women will say, Morena there's no work in the homelands. There's no food. They divide us from our husbands and they pack them into hostels like men with no names, men with no lives! And Morena will say, come to me, you who are divided from your families. Let us go to the cities where your husbands work. We will find houses where you can live together and we will talk to those who you fear! What country is this? (*Spits on ground.*)

Percy *starts to sing and march on the spot.* **Mbongeni** *joins him. They mime carrying a banner.*

Both (*sing a Zulu song and march*)
Oyini oyini madoda
Oyini oyini madoda
Sibona ntoni uma sibon'u Mangope
Siboni sell-out uma sibon'u Mangope
Sibona ntoni uma sibon'u Gatsha
Siboni puppet uma sibon'u Gatsha
Khulula khulula Morena
Khulula khulula Morena
Sibona ntoni nang'u Matanzima
Sibon'u umbulali nang'u Matanzima

[What is this, what is this men
What is this, what is this men
What do we see when we see Mangope
We see a sell-out when we see Mangope
What do we see when we see Gatsha
We see a puppet when we see Gatsha
Help us – Help us Morena
Help us – Help us Morena
What do we see – there is Matanzima
We see a killer when we see Matanzima.]

Percy (*interrupted*)   Hey! Tear gas!

They struggle, continuing the song, throwing stones, sounding sirens, dogs barking. Lights go down as they are subdued.

Both   Morena-a-a-a! Morena-a-a-a!

Scene Twenty-one

Spotlight finds **Percy** *as Prime Minister, pink nose, spectacles.*

Percy   My people, as your Prime Minister I must warn you that we stand alone in the face of total onslaught. Our enemies will stop at nothing, even to the extent of sending a cheap communist magician to pose as the Morena, and undermine the security of our nation. But let me assure you that this cheap impostor is safely behind bars, from which he cannot fly. Peace and security have returned to our lovely land.

Scene Twenty-two

Lights come up on **Mbongeni** *squatting on a box, wrapped in a prisoner's blanket.*

Mbongeni (*knocking*)   Cell number six! Morena! (*Knocking.*) Cell number six! Morena! Bad luck, hey! I hear they got you again. They tell me you're in solitary confinement just like us. From Sun City to Robben Island! (*Laughs ruefully.*) You've made us famous, Morena. The whole world is talking about us. Hey bayasiteya labedana bamabhunu man! [Hey they are riding us these white boys.] Morena, I sit here just like you with this one light bulb and only the Bible to read! Ja! And the New Testament tells me about you, and your family, and your thoughts. But why do they give us your book to read, Morena? They must be bladdy mad, Morena. This book only proves how mad they are. Listen. (*Knocking.*) Cell number six! For people like us, to be locked here like this is just rubbish. So what do you want here? What does your father know? What does he say? Come on Morena, man! (*Knocking.*) Cell number six! You've got all the power! How can you let these things happen? How can you just sit there like that, Morena? Okay, okay, I know you don't like miracles, but these are bladdy hard times, Morena. Morena, I must tell you, now that I've gone into your book, I really like you, Morena. But I'm getting bladdy disappointed. How long must we wait for you to do something? Morena, I must tell you, I'm among those who have stopped waiting. One day we'll have to help you! Phambiti neri-hondo! [Power to the people!] Can you hear me Morena? Cell number six!! (*'Sarie Marais' being whistled off-stage. Knocking more cautiously.*) Cell number six!! Morena! Morena . . . Cell number six . . .

Scene Twenty-three

Percy *enters whistling 'Sarie Marais'. He is a soldier, pink nose, camouflage hat. Mimes carrying rifle.*

Mbongeni (*enters similarly dressed*)   Two three! Morning Corporal!

Percy   Morning Sergeant!

Mbongeni   How are things going, Corporal? (*He rests on a box.*)

Percy   I'm tired, Sergeant.

Mbongeni   Oh, God. To be a guard on bladdy Robben Island!

Percy Ja, ever since they brought Morena out here to Robben Island everything has been upside down.

Mbongeni All those bladdy interviews, that's what's killing us!

Percy I'm sick of having my photograph taken.

Mbongeni I know. The next photographer I see, I shoot to kill!

Percy *Daily News.*

Mbongeni *Sunday Times.*

Percy *Time Life.*

Mbongeni *Pravda.*

Percy *London Observer.*

Mbongeni *New York Times.*

Percy All those bladdy communists!

Mbongeni You know, I got a letter from a woman in Sweden. She saw my photograph in her newspaper. And my wife was chasing me with a frying pan! I told her I never knew the woman, but she didn't believe me.

Percy I wish they had kept him in John Vorster Square or Pretoria Central.

Mbongeni Come on, Corporal. You know what happened at John Vorster Square. Gabriel got him out of there in ten seconds flat! Only Robben Island has got the right kind of AA missiles.

Percy AA? What is that?

Mbongeni Anti-Angel.

Percy Anti-Angel? I never heard of that!

Mbongeni He'll never get away from Robben Island!

Percy (*distracted, points into the audience*) Hey! Sergeant! What's that you said? Just look over there! Just look over there!!!

Mbongeni (*moves lazily toward him singing 'Sarie Marais'*)   My
Sarie Marais is so ver van my hart . . . (*Suddenly he looks into the
audience, horrified.*) God! Hey! Fire! Fire!

They riddle the audience with machine-gun fire.

Percy   Call helicopter control, quick!!!

Mbongeni   Hello? Hello? Radio one-two-five-four CB?
Over. Hello? Radio one-two-five-four . . .

Scene Twenty-four

Lights reduce to spot-light the boxes. Actors turn their hat brims up.
Mbongeni *spins his hand above his head. Helicopter sounds. They are
in a helicopter, looking down.*

Percy (*mimes radio*)   Radio one-two-five-four CB receiving,
over. What? That's impossible! Are you sure? Okay, over and
out. Hey, what do you see down below?

Mbongeni (*miming binoculars*)   Oh, it's a beautiful day down
below. Birds are flying, swimmers are swimming, waves are
waving. Hey! Morena's walking on water to Cape Town! Ag
shame! His feet must be freezing! Hey, I wish I had my
camera here!

Percy   This must be the miracle of the decade!

Mbongeni   Ag, I always forget my camera!

Percy   Down! Down! Radio one-two-five-four CB receiving,
over. Yes, we've got him. Yeah, what? Torpedo? Oh no, have
a heart! He's not even disturbing the waves! Ja, I wish you
could see him, he looks amazing!

Mbongeni (*nodding frenetically into mike*)   Ja jong, ja! [Yes man,
yes!]

Percy   What? Bomb Morena? Haven't you heard what they
say? You start with Morena and it's worse than an atom
bomb! Over and out! Hey, this is a shit bladdy job! You pull
the chain.

Mbongeni   No, you!

Percy   No! You pull the chain!

Mbongeni   No, man!

Percy   This man is mos' happy, why blow him up?

Mbongeni   No come on, come on. Fair deal! Eenie, meenie, minie moe. Vang a kaffir by the toe. As hy shrik, let him go. Eenie, meenie, minie, moe! It's you!

Percy   Okay! This is the last straw! I think I'm resigning tomorrow!

Mbongeni   Ready ... target centre below ... release depth charges ... bombs ... torpedoes ... go!

They watch. The bombs fall. A moment of silence and then a terrible explosion. They separate, come together detonating each other. Light reduces to stark overhead shaft.

Both   Momeeeee! Aunti-i-i-eee! He-e-e-l-l-p!

Blackout.

Scene Twenty-five

South African television news theme is proclaimed in darkness.

Mbongeni   News!

Lights on.

Percy (*in pink nose, proudly holds a cardboard TV screen shape around his face*)   Good evening. The United Nations Security Council is still waiting further information on the explosion which completely destroyed Capetown and its famous Table Mountain. (*Bland smile.*) United Nations nuclear sensors have recorded distinct signs of nuclear disturbance in the Southern African sector. Investigators have suggested a strong possibility of a mishap to a SAA Military Helicopter carrying a nuclear missile over the bay. However, Mrs Fatima Mossop, domestic servant, Sea Point, a freak survivor of the calamity, insisted that the explosion emanated from a human figure walking across the bay from the Island, supporting the superstition that the nuclear-type explosion was an inevitable result of a bomb attack on Morena. The Prime Minister himself continues to deny any relationship between Morena and the agitator imprisoned on the Island. Mrs Fatima Mossop is still under observation by the state psychiatrists. Well, that is all for tonight. Goodnight. (*Fade on fixed smile.*)

Scene Twenty-six

The graveyard. **Mbongeni** *in a hat and dust-coat is weeding and singing Zuluboy's songs from Scene Eighteen.* **Percy** *is sleeping on the boxes.* **Mbongeni** *sees him, rouses him.*

Mbongeni   Hey! Hey! Hey! This is not a park bench. It's a tombstone. This is a cemetery, it's not Joubert Park.

Percy (*groggy*)   I'm sorry, I should know better.

Mbongeni   You want Joubert Park? You want Joubert Park? You catch the number fifty-four bus. Or you want Zola Park? You catch a Zola taxi. Or you want to have a look at the ducks? Go to the Zoo Lake. But don't sit on my tombstones. Please.

Percy   Okay, I'm sorry about that. Can I have a look around?

Mbongeni   Oh, well if you want to have a look around, look around, but don't sit around! The dead are having a hard enough time. These tombstones are bladdy heavy!

Percy   Aaahh, tell me, do you keep your tombstones in alphabetical order?

Mbongeni   Yeah. What do you want?

Percy   Where's 'L'?

Mbongeni   You want 'L'?

Percy   Ja.

Mbongeni Serious? Okay. Right there. That whole line is
'L'. By that big tombstone. See? Livingstone . . . Lamele . . .
Lusiti . . . Lizi . . .

Percy Have you got any Lazarus here?

Mbongeni Lazarus? Lazarus? Oh, Israel Lazarus? That was
a very good man! You mean that one? American Half-Price
Dealers? That was a very good man, I used to work for him
in 1962. But he's not dead yet! Why are you looking for his
grave here?

Percy I'm just looking for something to do.

Mbongeni But this face I know. Are you his son?

Percy No, not his.

Mbongeni Then who are you?

Percy Morena.

Mbongeni You? Morena? Aaay suka! They killed him.
That is his tombstone.

Percy Oh no, Baba. Have you forgotten? I will always
come back after three days, bombs or no bombs.

Mbongeni Hay! Morena! Aawu nkulunkulu wami! [Oh my
God!]

Percy Ssssshhhh! Please, don't shout my name.

Mbongeni Do you remember me?

Percy Who are you?

Mbongeni Zuluboy from Coronation Brickyard!

Percy Hey! Zuluboy! (*They embrace.*) What are you doing
here?

Mbongeni I'm working here at the cemetery. I'm disguised
from the police! Lazarus . . . Lazarus . . . aaaahhh! Now I
understand! Morena, you're looking for people to raise!

Percy Ja!

Mbongeni But why didn't you ask me?

Percy How would I know?

Mbongeni I know exactly who my people want! Come, let us look at these tombstones.

Mbongeni *leads* **Percy** *in a dance around the cemetery, singing.*
Mbongeni *stops,* **Percy** *beside him. He points to a corner of the audience.*

Mbongeni Morena! Here's our 'L' – ALBERT LUTHULI – the Father of our Nation! Raise him Morena!

Percy Woza Albert! [Rise up Albert!]

Mbongeni *falls over, stunned then ecstatic.*

Both (*singing*)
Yamemeza inkosi yethu
Yathi ma thambo hlanganani
Oyawa vusa amaqhawe amnyama
Wathi kuwo

[Our Lord is calling.
He's calling for the bones of the dead to join together.
He's raising up the black heroes.
He calls to them . . .]

Mbongeni (*addressing the risen but invisible Albert Luthuli*) Hey, Luthuli uyangibona mina? U Zulu boy. Ngakhula phansi kwakho e-Stanger. [Hey, Luthuli, do you remember me? I'm Zuluboy. I grew up in Stanger.]

They dance on, repeating the song.

Both (*singing*)
Yamemeza inkosi yethu
Yathi ma thambo hlanganani
Oyawa vusa amaqhawe amnyama
Wathi kuwo

[Our Lord is calling.
He's calling for the bones of the dead to join together.

He's raising up the black heroes.
He calls to them . . .]

Mbongeni *stops,* **Percy** *beside him.*

Mbongeni Morena! Robert Sobukwe! He taught us Black
Power! Raise him!

Percy Woza Robert!

Mbongeni (*ecstatic*) Hau Manaliso! Manaliso!

They dance on.

Both (*singing*)
Yamemeza inkosi yethu
Yathi ma thambo hlanganani
Oyawa vusa amaqhawe amnyama
Wathi kuwo

[Our Lord is calling.
He's calling for the bones of the dead to join together.
He's raising up the black heroes.
He calls to them . . .]

Mbongeni Lilian Ngoyi! She taught our mothers about
freedom. Raise her!

Percy Woza Lilian!

Mbongeni (*spins with joy*) Woza Lilian! – Hey Lilian, uya
mbona uMorena? Uvuswe uMorena. [Come Lilian – hey
Lilian, do you see Morena? It's Morena who raised you.]

They dance on.

Both (*singing*)
Yamemeza inkosi yethu
Yathi ma thambo hlanganani
Oyawa vusa amaqhawe amnyama
Wathi kuwo

[Our Lord is calling.
He's calling for the bones of the dead to join together.
He's raising up the black heroes.
He calls to them . . .]

Mbongeni   Steve Biko! The hero of our children! Please
Morena – Please raise him!

Percy   Woza Steve!

Mbongeni   Steve! Steve! Uyangikhumbula ngikulandela e
Kingwilliamstown? [Steve, do you remember me, following
you in Kingswilliamstown?]

Both (*dancing*)   Woza Bram Fischer! . . . Woza Ruth First! . . .
Woza Griffith Mxenge . . . Woza Hector Peterson . . . (*They
stop, arms raised triumphantly.*) WOZA ALBERT!!!

Blackout.

The Other War

Alemseged Tesfai
translated by Paul Warwick,
Samson Gebregzhier and
Alemseged Tesfai

Characters

tetiyesus, *an Eritrean mother*
Astier, *her daughter*
Assefa, *Astier's husband, an Ethiopian cadre*
Hiwot, *an old friend of Letiyesus*
Solomie, *Astier's daughter from a previous marriage with an Eritrean*
Kitaw, *Astier and Assefa's son*

Act One

The curtain opens and we see **Hiwot**, *a woman of about forty-five,
moving around the stage. Centre stage there is a table, covered with a
clean cloth, and chairs. To the left is a cupboard which contains glasses
and other household objects. On the right there is radio-cassette player. On
the left, by the entrance, there is a hatstand. The house is clean and
well-kept, it is the house of a middle-income family in Asmara.*

As the play starts, **Letiyesus**, *a woman of around fifty, enters
slowly. Although she is tired, her movements seem distraught. She has
come from her village. Leaving her bag by the door, she says, 'How are
you,* **Hiwot***?', while she arranges her netsela.* **Hiwot** *seems shocked,
but runs to greet her friend.* **Letiyesus** *is so happy to have come home
that she doesn't notice that* **Hiwot** *seems disturbed.*

Letiyesus (*sitting on a stool, down stage*) Oufff . . . Yesus,
Mariam and Yosef, I'm so tired! On my way here I called in
at your house but they told me you were here.

Hiwot Why are you late . . . did you come on the night
bus?

Letiyesus Mbwa! I left this morning but because of all
these checkpoints it took all day. Oh, what a terrible life . . .
and those men at the checkpoints! Tell me, are they human
beings, or animals? Shameless people! (*Grabbing her breasts and
imitating their voices and gestures.*) What have we got here . . .
huh? What have you hidden here? They wouldn't spare
anyone, even old women.

Hiwot You're lucky it stopped at that . . . (*She opens her mouth
as if to speak urgently, but glancing furtively around the house she gets
nervous and says nothing.*)

Letiyesus (*not noticing* **Hiwot***'s behaviour, she speaks
despairingly*) What can we do?

Hiwot How was the village? (*She begins to prepare coffee.*)

Letiyesus (*biting her lower lip and shaking her head*) They are

---

* See Glossary on p. 300 for translations of Tigrinyan and Amharic words and phrases.

searching the heavens for a drop of rain. But there isn't any.
Years ago, I remember, Mariam herself used to hear our
pleas. She used to respond immediately. But now? I don't
know what's wrong with her. On my way here – people must
have thought I was crazy – I was arguing aloud, provoking
her: (*Looking up.*) 'What's wrong with you?' I asked her. 'Have
you deserted us now? Are you taking sides with THEM?!'

Hiwot (*laughing*)   So, you've started fighting with saints as
well?

Letiyesus   Mbwa! My argument is full of love, not hatred. I
was hoping that, from all the voices directed towards her, she
would single out my own, as a mother would do at the cry of
her own child. But, in vain!

They laugh together.

Hiwot (*looking about her, she whispers*)   Have you heard anything
about your son Miki-el?

Letiyesus   Oh, the answer is always the same. 'He is in
Sahel.' Then, when I ask how he is, 'Nebsi, nebsi!' 'He is
fine, mother, don't worry.' That's all you ever get from these
fighters!

Hiwot   'Nebsi'? What does that mean?

Letiyesus   'Nebsi' means . . . er . . . I think it means OK,
good or something. But then they've changed everything: the
way they speak, their hairstyles – do you know they have
even changed our marriage ceremony?

Hiwot (*surprised*)   There were fighters marrying in the middle
of your village?

Letiyesus   Of course!

Hiwot   Didn't they come?

Letiyesus (*sarcastic*)   Who, those 'lions' from the checkpoint?
They are only brave around their own den. Listen, I'm trying
to tell you about this wedding. The bride was wearing shorts
right up to here (*She touches the top of her thighs.*) and her hair
was curled like a hermit's, falling locks that covered half her

face. A boy hardly older than them was to marry them. He said: 'Attention! Relax!' ... then 'Awet Nahafash!' and that was that, they were married. In all my visits to them, I'd not seen a marriage before, I've never seen anything like it. I just sat there, stunned. It's amazing, times really are changing.

Hiwot *is laughing.* **Letiyesus** *continues her story, while going to remove her netsela.*

Letiyesus Then they started to dance, with their guns slung over their shoulders.

Letiyesus *demonstrates the way that fighters dance the cuda – they both laugh throughout.*

Suddenly, **Letiyesus** *stops dancing, she has noticed that her house is not as she had left it, things are rearranged.* **Hiwot** *immediately stops laughing. She looks nervously from side to side, she cannot look* **Letiyesus** *in the face.* **Letiyesus** *stands frozen and looks carefully around her home. The cheerful laughing has been succeeded by a heavy silence.*

Letiyesus Who has disturbed my home? Whose radio is that?

Hiwot (*avoiding the question*) Please sit down, have some coffee.

Letiyesus (*sitting*) Have those kebeles sent others to share my house?

Hiwot Not kebeles. The day before yesterday your daughter Astier came here with her husband and children. She demanded your key and I gave it to her. They moved into those two rooms and put all your things in the store outside. (*She avoids the angry glare of* **Letiyesus** *by fiddling with the jebena and cups.*) He has been transferred from Addis. They both said that they wanted to live with you, their mother.

Letiyesus (*staring at* **Hiwot**, *shocked and angry*) How can this be, Miki-el's home becoming a shelter for an Amhara? Why didn't you tell them that you didn't have the key?

Hiwot I thought Astier was alone, that's why I gave it to her. I didn't know he was with them. Later, I came to speak with her and I heard them saying: 'Anchi manchi, anchi manchi!' I couldn't believe my ears. Since then, I have left my house every day and waited for you here. I wanted to warn you.

Letiyesus (*unable to control her feelings, she closes her eyes and shakes with rage*) Oh, wicked daughter! What will people call me now? Whose mother-in-law? Some enemy! Some Amhara!

Hiwot (*consoling her*) Please, please, my sister. Letiyesus calm down, put it out of your mind. After all, he seems like a kind boy, he's always smiling . . .

Letiyesus (*shouting*) There's no such thing as an Amhara who doesn't smile. Nonsense! Even at the checkpoints, they were grinning and smirking while they groped and pawed us. (*Pointing to her breasts.*)

There is a noise outside and they look at each other.

Hiwot Here they come. (*She puts her hand on* **Letiyesus'** *shoulder.*) Please Letiyesus, my sister, hide your feelings and show them a happy face.

Letiyesus (*not listening, but looking to the heavens*) Oh, Mariam, what evil have I ever done, what is my sin?

A girl, fifteen or sixteen years old, enters first, followed by **Astier** *with a baby, and then* **Astier** *'s husband,* **Assefa**. *The girl,* **Solomie**, *runs to her grandmother and hugs her while she remains seated.*

Solomie Grandma! Grandma!

Letiyesus Let me stand, let me stand. (*She looks at* **Solomie** *and joy spreads over her face.*) Oh my child, you have grown. (*She looks her up and down.*) Oh Solomie, my grandchild, I think you are destined to be short for ever.

Astier *and* **Assefa** *are waiting to be greeted, but* **Letiyesus** *does not turn to face them. This makes* **Hiwot** *uneasy and she shuffles around the stage.*

Astier I think that's enough for you Solomie, now it's our turn to be welcomed, Mother.

Unwillingly, **Letiyesus** *greets* **Astier** *with insincere kisses. She doesn't kiss* **Assefa,** *but shakes his hand. He holds her hand with both of his, bowing his head respectfully.*

Assefa *(still bowing)*   Endemin Alu, Em-Mama. Endemin Alu?

Letiyesus   Dihan, Wedei, Tzibuq. I'm well, and I have God to thank for it. *(She goes to offer* **Assefa** *a seat.)*

Assefa   No, no, no, I'll do that, please sit down, Em-Mama. *(He arranges the seats and they all sit down.)* Endemin Allu? *(Then he speaks to* **Astier***.)* Oh, she looks nothing like her photograph, in real life she is more beautiful and younger. Wait a moment, is this your mother or your sister?

There is no answer, a heavy silence fills the room.

Astier   Did you understand him mother? He said that you are young and beautiful. He thinks you look more like my sister than my mother. *(She laughs uneasily.)*

Letiyesus *(unconvinced and with a tinge of sarcasm)*   Really? Maybe he is trying to flatter me. Your mother is old enough, girl.

Again there is uncomfortable silence. To break it, **Hiwot** *moves things around noisily.*

Hiwot   He is right you know. You are still young.

No one responds to her attempt to make conversation. She feels even more uncomfortable and returns to her fidgeting.

Assefa *(to* **Astier,** *in Amharic)*   I think she's tired, when did she get home . . . how do you say that in Tigrinya? Me-as . . . Metu . . . Gebu . . .

Astier *(helping him)*   Me-as Atitkhen?

Assefa   Good! Ma-as Atikhin?

Letiyesus   I arrived just before you.

Assefa *(standing, anxious to escape the uneasy gathering)*   No wonder she looks tired. I am tired myself. I want to get some rest. I'll leave you two to carry on chatting, you have a lot to catch up on. (*He goes into the next room.*)

Astier   Solomie, fetch him some warm water for his feet.

Solomie *obeys reluctantly.*

Hiwot   Well, I think I'll have to go back too. My house has been locked up all day.

Astier   Why don't you stay with us Mother Hiwot, let's have dinner together.

Hiwot   No, I must go, it's getting late. (*To* **Letiyesus**.) Besides, I think you have missed your daughter and I should give you a chance to be together. Goodnight. (*She gets up to leave.*)

Letiyesus   Goodnight, Hiwot, goodnight.

Silence.

Astier (*looking at the baby, then at her mother*)   Mother, aren't you going to look at Kitaw?

Letiyesus   And what is Kitaw?

Astier   Our son! It's not just Solomie any more, I have a son, Kitaw.

Letiyesus (*very insincerely*)   Oh, how forgetful of me! Of course I'll see him.

Astier *offers the baby to her mother.* **Letiyesus** *doesn't move from her seat, but just glances briefly at the child and then leans back. She picks up a cup of coffee and starts to drink it.*

Yes, a handsome child, what did you say his name was?

Astier   Kitaw. Assefa chose the name. In Amharic it means 'punish them'.

Letiyesus (*irritated*)   And who does he intend to punish?

Astier (*still looking at the baby*)   What about all the secessionists of course?

Letiyesus cannot control herself, she throws the cup to the floor.

Astier Mother, why did you do that, aren't you happy that we have come here?

Letiyesus (*angry, heavily sarcastic*) Oh yes, I'm glad. My child and her children are with me again and I am very happy.

Astier But only your words sound nice. Your face says something else. From the moment we stepped into this room you have been wearing this gloomy face that is making me uneasy. What wrong have I done you?

Letiyesus (*still slightly sarcastic*) Me? You haven't done me any wrong.

Astier (*smiling*) So, why don't you joke and laugh as usual? (*She nods her head and smiles knowingly.*) I know what you're thinking Mother. I know your heart, too. You're angry because I married an Amhara. But Assefa is not like the other Amharas. He's kind and besides, he is a brilliant cadre. In time, as you get used to him, you will grow to like him. (*She laughs uncomfortably.*) He is so funny . . . you will see . . . you will not miss your son, Miki-el any more.

Letiyesus (*unable to control her anger any longer, she erupts*) Remember Miki-el is the same Miki-el who is your own brother.

Astier Yes, that's what I am trying to tell you. Assefa is not just a husband to me. He is also like a brother. In the same way, he will be like a son to you.

Letiyesus *stares at her daughter, amazed. She cannot think of anything to say, feeling her daughter is lost to her. She remains silent. Unconcerned,* **Astier** *continues to rock the baby. Enter* **Solomie**.

Solomie Mama, Gashie Assefa wants you.

Astier (*holding* **Kitaw** *tightly to her, she gets up*) I'm coming Assie.

Exit **Astier**, **Solomie** *and* **Kitaw**.

Letiyesus (*staring at* **Astier** *until she is out of sight, she addresses the audience, very agitated and confused*) Gashie . . . Assie . . . am I dreaming?

Act Two

The same room except there is now a telephone near the table. Two months have passed and the newcomers have had an effect on the' family's life. **Letiyesus** *is forced to cook, take care of the children, etc. We see* **Letiyesus** *sweeping the floor, folding the children's clothes and performing the daily household chores. On the wall is a banner bearing the slogan of a Dergue campaign for a conservation programme.* **Solomie** *sits at the table and does her homework.*

Letiyesus Solomie, my child, please come and help me fold these clothes.

Solomie OK, Grandma, just let me finish what I'm doing.

Letiyesus *is arguing to herself and gesturing with her hands.*
Solomie *sees her and leaves her writing to go towards her.*

Solomie Grandma, why are you always talking to yourself?

Letiyesus *and* **Solomie** *begin folding up sheets together.*

Letiyesus (*smiling*) I am not talking to myself.

Solomie So who are you talking to?

Letiyesus To Mariam. I'm asking her to keep my grandchild Solomie safe and to help her with her studies.

Solomie (*laughing*) Grandma, don't treat me like a child, how can you be praying when you are in such an angry mood? (*Frowns seriously.*) You know, sometimes I do the same thing – I talk to myself, just like you do.

Letiyesus Mbwa! You little brat! However could you be talking to yourself like I do? You are too young!

Solomie But Grandma, I have no one to talk to. (*She starts crying.*) At school nobody will come near me, the other students all chat together, but when I try to join in they walk away and leave me on my own. They have even given me a nickname.

Letiyesus What nickname? What do they call you.

Solomie   'Chairwoman's daughter'.

Letiyesus (*consoling her*)   So, what is there to be upset about? Isn't it true? Hasn't your mother become Chairwoman of our kebele?

Solomie   Don't try to fool me. I saw you the day she was elected. You were so mad, you had one of your headaches. You even had to tie a band around your head.

Letiyesus (*pretending to hit her*)   Little girl, you are going to cause me plenty of problems. Never repeat what you have just said. Go now, go and finish your ho-wek.

Solomie   Not ho-wek, it is homework. Anyway, I've already finished it. (*She sits on a stool near* **Letiyesus** *and looks her in the face.*) Grandma, Aya Miki-el . . . what does he look like?

Letiyesus (*frightened, but touched*)   What, how do you know about Miki-el, why do you ask about him?

Solomie   I only want to know what he's like!

Letiyesus   Tall, fair-skinned, handsome (*Teasing.*), not like you! . . . His teeth are chipped because he once fell over, playing with your mother when they were little.

Solomie   You love him very much, don't you Grandma?

Letiyesus (*smiling tenderly*)   What do you think? I even love you, ugly little thing.

Solomie   Mama used to love him too. Whenever my father came home drunk and beat her up, she would say to me, 'If my brother Miki-el were here, your father would not dare treat me like this.' But after they divorced and she started seeing Gashie Assefa, she always spoke ill of you and Miki-el. She used to upset me so much. I hated her.

Letiyesus   Come now, Solomie. You are only a child. Aren't you taking on too much for someone your age?

Solomie   But what am I supposed to do or feel? Grandma, it is only here, in this house with you that I am laughing again. In Addis . . . ? (*Pensively and reluctantly.*) When my mother and father were fighting, which was almost all the time, I used to hide under the bed so I would not see them. When he left us, she started to beat me just as he used to beat her. She really beat me, Grandma, and took all her anger out on me. Then Gashie Assefa came, actually he treated me quite well, but then neither of them were ever at home. They would go out, leave me all alone in a big house . . . I would feel lonely . . . so lonely, I would cry . . . Oh, how I cried, Gran . . . (*She cannot control her tears any longer and starts to cry.*)

Letiyesus   What are these tears for? (*She fakes hitting her again, with a spoon or a fan.*) I don't like tears and weepy weaklings. My nerves can't stand them.

Solomie *is full of remorse and hangs her head.* **Letiyesus** *is touched, she feels sorry for her and hugs her.*

Letiyesus   Oh, dear child. Shame on those who cause this suffering. Come, no more sadness, no more tears. The time will come for you to be happy. Don't worry, the Virgin Mariam will not forsake us.

She straightens out **Solomie** *who, stopping her crying, wipes her eyes.*

Go on, finish your ho-wek.

Solomie   Not ho-wek, it's *homework*, Grandma!

Letiyesus *laughs and jokingly threatens her with a stick.* **Solomie** *giggles and is running towards the table when she suddenly stops and looks uneasy.* **Astier** *has entered, home from work.*

Astier (*scowling at* **Solomie**)   Where is Kitaw?

Solomie   He's asleep.

Astier   Didn't I tell you to watch him even when he is sleeping? What if he wakes up alone and gets upset?

Solomie   Let me do my homework first.

Astier   What have you been doing all morning, chatting with her? (*Meaning* **Letiyesus**. *She picks up the telephone.*) Oh, all this chatter (*Dialling.*), hurry along, take your books to your room and do your homework in there.

Exit **Solomie**.

Astier   Ah, hello . . . Ato Zenebe? . . . Good afternoon . . . Astier here . . . fine . . . look, there were four women who were late coming to the meeting today, we shall send them to you for punishment . . . Oh, take whatever measures you think necessary.

Letiyesus *has been listening attentively.* **Astier** *finishes talking, replaces the telephone and sits down near* **Letiyesus**.

Astier   How are you Mama?

Letiyesus   How are you Astier? Did you have a fine day?

Astier   How could I have a fine day? These women are becoming a pain.

Letiyesus   But it's only your second week on the job. Isn't it a bit too early for them to be a pain and for you to be dealing out punishment?

Astier   No, no, no, no (*Shaking her head and trying to persuade her mother.*) . . . You don't understand, Mama, if we are to work effectively we must have strict control right from the start. If things are not set right now, they never will be. For your information, Adei Hiwot is among those to be punished.

Letiyesus (*confused*)   Hiwot? Our Hiwot?

Astier   Yes, Adei Hiwot herself. Why don't you come late to a meeting and see if you will be spared?

Letiyesus (*drawling, deliberately*)   If you are not worried about preparing your own meals, so be it, I'll accept your punishment.

Astier   Meals cannot be a problem. We can all eat in restaurants. But what I simply cannot understand is how it is that you find plenty of time for coffee gatherings and braiding each other's hair, and have no time at all for meetings. This is simply unacceptable.

Letiyesus (*rubbing her forehead and eyes*)   Astier, my dear daughter, please listen to me. Let us, for once, try to discuss

things calmly. Is this it? Are we to remain antagonistic as
though we were not mother and daughter?

Astier   Why do you think this is so, Mother? Well, I'll tell
you. Our hearts are in different places. Yours is with Miki-el,
and whether you like it or not *mine* is right here. *I* am right
here and here I shall remain.

Letiyesus (*shaking her head*)   How would you ever know what
is in my heart? You frighten me, Astier, you truly frighten me
. . . and nothing is more terrible than to be afraid of one's
own child.

Astier   Why should you be afraid? (*With a dramatic wave of the
hand.*) There's plenty of democracy here. You have the right to
speak freely. Let's talk.

Letiyesus (*picking up some courage and adjusting her dress*)   All
right, then, listen to me. The fact that you are the
chairwoman of this kebele would not have mattered to me. I
know how the elections are conducted and I know a lot of
good people are compelled to serve in such posts. I would
have found some excuse for you too. I would have said that
you were nominated, unwillingly elected . . . But, as soon as
you sat on that chair, you overwhelmed everyone with your
enthusiasm. You've been penalising people, picking quarrels
with everyone within your reach. How do you expect to
benefit from fighting against your own family, your own
people?

Astier (*her face flushed with rage*)   My family? Who are my
family and my people? Don't you realise that you and father,
especially father, have left me with a scar (*Touching her heart.*) I
will never be able to get rid of, all my life?

Letiyesus (*jumping up, uncontrollably angry*)   What? What did
you say? You unfeeling, cruel child! Didn't your father raise
you and your brother the best way he knew and shower upon
you both the unselfish love that only he was capable of
giving? Didn't he go through hell, sacrificing his own pleasure
and fighting against the illness that finally consumed him in
order to build this house, this shelter for you? How dare you

desecrate his memory in my presence? There is a limit to everything. There must be a limit even to my fear of you. Or have I totally lost you?

Astier If you think you are losing me now, you are mistaken Mother. Remember that day, when I was only a child, when I could not tell good from bad, when the taste of knowledge was still fresh in my mind . . . remember when you married me off to Zecharias? That's when you lost me. Yes, Mother, you and father gave me to a drunkard, just because his parents had money and some fancy titles. You didn't even notice that I was only half his age. Now, who are you to give me any advice?

Letiyesus So you are settling accounts, are you now? One person, Zecharias, did you wrong and you are wreaking your anger on your own people in revenge? Have you no conscience at all?

Astier (*shaking with rage and shouting*) Conscience? What conscience? Listen, Mother. I was beaten up, trodden on by Zecharias so much that I thought it would never end. My face was constantly swollen. Look at the marks under my eyes. I spent my youth, lying in bed, crying endlessly, waiting for him to come back drunk and use or misuse me, as he saw fit. Now, Mother, you are asking me why I am so enthusiastic about these people here? And why shouldn't I be? Zecharias locked me behind bars, Assefa opened the door and my eyes to the world. My heart was full of hatred, Assefa filled it with love. I was ignorant, today I am a chairwoman. (*She puts her hands on her hips.*) Now, what do you have to say? Who are my people? You or them? Answer me . . . say something . . . I thought you wanted to talk.

Letiyesus (*speechless, she cannot control her tears*) I have no answer, my daughter. Nothing to say. Besides, am I not weeping? Aren't my tears enough?

Astier The truth is bitter, isn't it, Mother? You can't swallow it. Why else would Letiyesus weep? Since when did you weep, Mother?

Letiyesus   But I shall weep! I am a mother! When I see
you, my own daughter, choosing the way to destruction, to
the abyss you are too blind to see, wouldn't my womb revolt?
Wouldn't my motherhood scream? No, don't be under any
illusions. It is not your 'truth' that's making me weep, Astier.
You have no truth.

Astier (*sarcastically*)   Really?

Letiyesus   Yes . . . and if you think you are going to find
the truth among these unwelcome strangers, we shall see,
Astier. (*Drying her tears and speaking slowly, in measured tones.*) Time
will show.

Assefa *arrives home from work and puts his coat on the table.*

Assefa   I'm hungry! I am starving!

Assefa *notices* **Letiyesus**' *eyes are red from crying. He seems shocked
and looks from one to the other for an explanation.*

Assefa   Endiye! What's going on here? Is she crying? (*He
kneels beside* **Letiyesus** *and puts his hand on her shoulder. She doesn't
like this.*) What's wrong, Em-Mama? Why are you crying like a
child?

Letiyesus   I'm all right, my son. It is my old migraine . . . it
must be the smell of coal . . . just a headache.

Assefa (*to* **Astier**)   Another one of your quarrels? And what
have you said to her this time? What kind of a person are
you, anyway? Please calm down, Em-Mama. Are we to have
no peace in this house? (*He takes* **Astier***'s hand and goes towards
the door.*) Come into the bedroom. I want to talk to you about
this.

They exit and **Solomie** *comes out of their bedroom. She goes to her
grandmother.*

Solomie (*whispering*)   I overheard everything she said to you.
But don't cry, Grandma. Tears don't suit you . . . I love you
more when you are laughing and cheerful.

Letiyesus (*wiping her tears*)   You're right, Solomie. You're
right, dear child. What's the point of weeping? Our tears give

pleasure to the enemy. One day all this will change and Mariam will show me their misery. I know it, I feel it.

Solomie (*hugging her tight*)   That's how I like you. Your own daughter saying those terrible things to you! If I spoke to her like that, she'd kill me, she would . . .

Astier *appears from her room.* **Solomie** *stops talking and releases her grandmother from her embrace.*

Astier   Get the lunch ready!

Act Three

The scene is the same as before. On the table there are empty bottles and unwashed glasses and plates. The house is in a mess as there has been a party. **Letiyesus** *ties a cord around her head [traditional Eritrean cure for a headache] and after putting a cloth around her waist she reluctantly begins to tidy up. Enter* **Hiwot** *from outside. The banner on the wall is now about the 'Red Star' campaign.*

Hiwot   Good morning, Letiyesus.

Letiyesus *(looking up)*   Yes, who is it? . . . Ah, how are you Hiwot?

Hiwot *(looking at the mess in disgust)*   What is this? What's been happening here? It looks like donkeys have been let loose the whole night.

Letiyesus *(looking at the bedroom)*   Ssh, they are sleeping. Talk softly, they may hear us.

Letiyesus *pulls* **Hiwot** *downstage towards the fornello and they sit as* **Letiyesus** *prepares tea.*

Letiyesus   You're right, my house was full of donkeys all night.

Hiwot   What was the gathering for?

Letiyesus   A party, another party. Every night, partying, drinking, brawling, dancing . . . but last night was something else. *(Imitating their toasts and being funny about it despite her headache.)* 'Victory to the Red Star Offensive!' . . . 'Yes, victory, victory!' . . . Glasses of cognac down throats. 'Bandits will vanish! . . . Yes, vanish, vanish . . .' Glasses of whisky into bellies. I am sheltering beasts in this house, my dear Hiwot.

Hiwot   But what can you do?

Letiyesus   What can't I do? I am not that desperate, you know. I sat here the whole night and condemned them to God, damned them all to hell. 'E . . . h!' I said throughout the night. *(Patting the floor [asking God to condemn someone].)*

'E . . . h, E . . . h!' When they said, 'We shall triumph,' I
responded, 'You'll be defeated,' and when they shouted,
'Destroy the bandits!' I said, 'You'll be destroyed.'

Hiwot (*laughing sympathetically*)   Poor Letiyesus! At least you
consoled yourself, gave yourself some relief. These people
thrive on crimes and sins, my sister. Your condemnations and
damnation will not bother them.

Letiyesus   I didn't do it to bother them. I was not
addressing them, no. I closed my eyes and sent all my prayers
and wishes straight to heaven and I know they got there.
These people will neither destroy us, nor win. The Mother of
Christ is up there. (**Hiwot** *laughs.*) I am telling you, I mean all
this. (**Letiyesus** *pauses for a while and then, recalling the previous
night's events, shows her disgust.*) Oh, the frivolity, the immorality I
witnessed last night. And the girls . . . (*She imitates their
movements.*) . . . dressed in sickening colours, their faces covered
in powder – up-and-down, in-out, swing-sway – Oh! (*She shakes
with even more disgust.*) They brought on my migraine and here
I am.

Hiwot (*trying to change the subject and half-whispering*)   What
about Astier? Has she become one of them?

Letiyesus   To tell you the truth, she is much better than
the others. She is reserved, you know, none of the frivolity
and immorality of the others.

Hiwot   Ah, this is a mother talking, a mother thing, isn't it?

Letiyesus   No, the mother thing comes only when there is a
child thing to match it, my dear Hiwot. My daughter has
taken me out of her heart. She has closed the gates to me.
She is driving me against her. But my womb, my motherhood
fears this confrontation.

Hiwot   In fact, I came here to tell you about her, Letiyesus.
Everyone in this kebele hates her and they are plotting against
her. Every man and woman has already been fined and there
is a rumour going around that she is taking kebele money for
herself. She may even go to jail.

Letiyesus   So be it. Let her get what she deserves if that's the case. I have neither the intention nor the inclination to stand up for a cursed child.

Hiwot   But consider this, if she goes to jail it will be all the worse for you. You will be stuck here, raising her son. No, I'll talk to her. Fall on my hands and knees and beg her to return to her senses.

Letiyesus   You'll lick cement, eat dust for nothing. Do you want to invite trouble onto yourself? As for her son, I am raising him whether she is here or not. So, what difference will your gesture make? Or do you want another penalty? Just pray that I shall be spared all this suffering.

Hiwot (*standing to leave*)   All right then, as you wish. How painful for you to have such a daughter. How did she ever become so heartless?

Letiyesus (*sitting and staring into the audience, half lost in thought*)   She always was a strong, stubborn girl, even when she was little. But, I am afraid we also had some responsibility for what happened. After she gave birth to Solomie, she told us she wanted to divorce Zecharias. We would not hear of any such thing – her father and I. She insisted, cried, screamed ... but, we forced her to be patient and look after her family. We had no idea she would be driven to this, no idea whatever that someday she would betray her own country and people.

Hiwot   Let me go before they wake up. Goodbye.

Letiyesus   Goodbye, Hiwot.

Hiwot *exits and* **Letiyesus** *continues her work. Enter* **Solomie**, *from outside, carrying the child.*

Letiyesus   Where did you take that child in this cold weather?

Solomie   I met a school friend and we were just chatting by the door. (*She kisses the child.*) Grandma, I overheard those other children talking about fighting in Sahel. They said that a lot of Tor-Serawit were killed. Are you listening?

Letiyesus (*scolding*)   Nosy child! You have no business listening to other people's conversation.

Solomie   They were talking right next to me!

Letiyesus (*interested*)   So, who did they hear this from?

Solomie   From the radio of the fighters. From Dimtsi Hafash.

Letiyesus   Wo ... If you repeat that again, they will strangle you. Nowadays, even your Gashie is hostile towards you. I can see it in his eyes.

Assefa *comes from his room, wearing pyjamas. He rubs his forehead with his right hand: he has a headache. Slowly he pulls up a stool and sits with* **Letiyesus**. **Solomie**, *carrying the child, moves around the room.*

Assefa (*to* **Letiyesus**)   Em-Mama, how are you this morning?

Letiyesus   Fine, thank you – and you?

Assefa   Ouff, I have a pain in my head ... Hey Solomie, give me two of those aspirins over there.

Solomie *brings the aspirins and after* **Letiyesus** *hands him some water, he swallows the pills.* **Astier** *enters in her nightgown.*

Astier (*kissing her son*)   Has he eaten his breakfast?

Solomie   Yes, early.

Astier   What time is it? (*She looks at her watch.*) ... Oh, ten o'clock. (*Moving towards* **Letiyesus**.) It's a good thing that today is Sunday. Good morning, Mother ... Oh, those headaches, why do you tie your head up, didn't I tell you not to?

Letiyesus (*holding her head between her hands*)   Oh, I feel like my head will burst and this pressure helps it.

Astier (*laughing, to* **Assefa**)   This is known as a Letiyesus-ism around here.

Assefa   Bakshin ... Stop your little jokes.

Letiyesus *is pouring tea and ignoring them.*

Assefa   Em-Mama, could you warm some water for my feet?

While **Letiyesus** *puts a container of water on the fire,* **Astier** *whispers something to* **Assefa** *and he nods his head, he seems impatient to speak to* **Letiyesus** *while she works. He drinks tea and then speaks eagerly and passionately to* **Letiyesus** *in broken Tigrinya.*

Assefa   Em-Mama, Astier and I want to talk to you about Mika-el.

Letiyesus *is so startled she drops what she is holding on the floor.*

Assefa *(noticing her reaction)*   It's all right, it's all right. It's good news, don't be afraid.

Astier   Yes, Mother, he wants to tell you something good for Miki-el and for all of us. Just listen to him carefully.

Letiyesus *looks ready to hear something bad.*

Assefa   The Revolutionary Army is annihilating the bandits. Mika-el is Astier's brother and this makes him my brother too. I don't want him to lose his life for a worthless cause. We have to bring him back here. Help us to do so.

Letiyesus *(confused)*   What are you saying to me, my son?

Assefa *(to* **Astier***)*   Please tell her.

Astier *(politely)*   Mother, what he's trying to tell you is about all of Miki-el's comrades. All the gedli are surrounded, they are in a critical situation. If you know where he is, or if you can send a relative to him as a messenger, tell him to surrender. Without being in any danger, or being harmed or imprisoned, he can come home to you. Mother, Assefa can do anything, everyone respects him.

Assefa   Yes, I can bring him to Asmara by helicopter.

Letiyesus *(she despises their whole behaviour, her headache gets worse and she presses her temples with both hands)*   How am I supposed to know where he is? I don't even know whether he is dead or alive and I know of no relative who is in contact with him.

Assefa   Em-Mama, don't you want Mika-el to be here with us?

She doesn't answer.

Assefa   Send a relative and try to contact him.

Still no answer.

Assefa   Em-Mama, we are doing all this for your benefit, Endiye! (*He gets angry and moves closer to* **Letiyesus***.*) Don't you feel sorry for your own son?

Letiyesus *is also losing her temper and she fidgets in her chair.* **Assefa***'s polite manner has disappeared and he starts shouting.*

Assefa   Em-Mama, your son will be eaten by vultures!

Letiyesus *looks* **Assefa** *full in the face.*

Letiyesus   Why don't you just leave me alone? What do you want of me?

Assefa (*shouting*)   Your son will be eaten by vultures! VULTURES!

Letiyesus (*angry*)   So he will be eaten by vultures! What of it? Is he any better than all his comrades?

Assefa *cannot believe what is happening. He glares furiously from* **Letiyesus** *to* **Astier***.* **Solomie** *is standing behind* **Astier***, still with the child in her arms. She is frightened and angry and she is biting her lower lip.* **Astier** *quickly tries to calm the situation.*

Astier   Oh, Mother . . .

Letiyesus   You be quiet, too, I have a headache.

Assefa (*extremely angry, to* **Astier***)   Just ignore her! We are being too soft on this woman. (*Pointing his finger at* **Letiyesus***.*) It looks as if you yourself are a bandit, just like your son. (*He sits down scowling.*) You, Solomie, come and wash my feet!

Astier *is staring wildly at her mother.* **Solomie** *gives* **Astier** *the child and brings boiling water. Without adding any cold water she gives it to* **Assefa***.* **Assefa** *and* **Astier** *are so involved with* **Letiyesus** *that they do not notice what* **Solomie** *is doing.*

Assefa (*muttering to himself in exaggerated agitation*)   I don't believe it! Such ingratitude! Pure arrogance! (*While he speaks he puts his feet into the water, without looking.* **Solomie** *is at his feet, ready to wash. He screams.*) Aaah! This little bitch has burnt me! (*He slaps her face and she falls over.*)

Letiyesus *jumps up, but when she sees that* **Solomie** *is all right, she sits down on her stool again.*

Astier   Are you OK, Assie? (*To* **Solomie**.) You idiot, you want to burn him with hot water? (*She kicks out at* **Solomie** *from her seat but she cannot reach.*)

Assefa (*almost speechless with pain and anger*)   Astier, bring me the water yourself. (*He heads towards the bedroom, looking malevolently at* **Letiyesus** *and* **Solomie**.) So, it's you and I now. So you are messing around with me? All right, we'll see. You don't know what you're up against. (*He limps out.*)

Astier (*to* **Solomie**)   Get up, take the child.

Solomie *snatches her brother.*

Astier   Careful, or I'll thrash you! (*While looking at* **Letiyesus***, she pours cold water into the container of hot water.*) As if you haven't done me enough harm, are you now destroying my happy family? Do you consider yourself a real mother? You are even turning Solomie against me.

Letiyesus   Turning Solomie . . . I am turning Solomie against you? Aren't you giving her enough reasons to hate   . you for yourself. Can you point to a single moment when you gave her motherly love? Besides, not just Solomie, every person in this kebele is against you. They are all after you. Ask yourself where you are, where you are heading.

Astier   Stop this, Mother! Stop provoking me! Stop cornering me or God knows what I'm going to do to you! (*She snatches up the container, spilling some water and goes towards the bedroom. She meets* **Solomie***, who is carrying the child and anxiously listening.*) Out of my way!

Exit **Astier**. **Letiyesus** *and* **Solomie** *stay behind, looking at each other.*

Letiyesus (*examining* **Solomie**'s *cheek*)   Are you all right?

Solomie *doesn't answer, but begins laughing.*

Letiyesus   Why are you laughing, did you do that on purpose?

Solomie   Yes, he had no right to insult you, calling you a bandit.

Letiyesus (*jokingly putting her fingers round* **Solomie**'s *throat*)   He'll strangle you like this. (**Solomie** *shrugs,* **Letiyesus** *looks at* **Kitaw** *in disgust.*) Ouff, what a nose. I hate noses like that.

Solomie   No, he's handsome, Grandma.

Letiyesus (*going to her fornello*)   He doesn't look like us. He is not one of us.

Act Four

The 'Red Star' banner has been replaced by a slogan about 'The Foundation of the Civilian Party' or something else that followed after the Sixth Offensive, implying that it has failed. **Letiyesus** *is cleaning the table and* **Solomie** *is sweeping the floor.*

Solomie (*working*) Grandma, who were those two women that I met at Mother Hiwot's house? When they met me they kissed and hugged me and one started to cry.

Letiyesus They are my sisters. The dark one was my cousin and the one who cried is my younger sister.

Solomie Adei Zaid?

Letiyesus Yes, she's Zaid.

Solomie Because of Mama everyone hates us, even our family no longer come here.

Letiyesus No, don't say that. Nobody hates us. They were not crying because they hate us. It is just they don't get the chance to see you as much as they like.

Solomie Grandma, you always treat me like a child who doesn't understand. But I think a lot and I know more than you realise. Why do women of this kebele frown whenever they see me on the streets? Because I'm her daughter, that's why. Nowadays I am starting to hate being in this house. I just feel like running away, disappearing.

Letiyesus Mbwa! Crazy girl, where would you go to?

Solomie To the field, to be a Tegadelit.

Letiyesus Ah, rubbish, child – it's only talk. When the first thorn pricks your foot you'll beg them to bring you back home.

Solomie I would never beg to come home. (*Pause.*) Grandma, did Adei Zaid tell you anything about Miki-el?

Letiyesus Must you bring this up every time? Why don't

you simply keep your mouth shut?

Solomie (*stops sweeping*)   And why don't you tell me? Must you keep hiding things from me? I know a girl at school who tunes in to their radio, the Dimtsi Hafash every morning. She told me that thirty thousand Tor have been killed. The Red Star Offensive has failed, the Tegadeli have won, Grandma. I know you think about them all the time, that all your heart and soul is with them. I also realise that this is the cause of your quarrels with Mama. So, Grandma, I am not a child any more. I think, I know and I'm with you. Mama hates me because I am on your side. Now, Grandma, tell me, how is Aya Miki-el?

Letiyesus (*deeply touched, she puts her hand on* **Solomie***'s shoulder and looks her in the eyes*)   Oh, what times have befallen us, dearest Solomie? Girls your age are flirting around and here you are consoling me, caring and thinking. Oh, what would I do without you? (*She holds* **Solomie** *and strokes her hair.*) Miki-el is fine, he is alive and well. He has sent a letter and as you said, they have won a great . . .

Assefa *enters and they immediately separate. His face is dark with anger. He hangs up his coat, puts his pistol on the table and looks at them.*

Assefa (*still standing*)   Continue to talk. Why do you stop?

They don't answer.

Assefa   Solomie, come here. You stopped when I came into the room. Why? What were you talking about?

Solomie   Nothing.

Assefa (*shouting*)   Speak, tell me the truth!

Solomie (*shaking with fear*)   Nothing, I was just telling her about my studies.

Assefa (*shouting*)   Does anyone talk about school while they are hugging each other? You were consoling each other, telling each other to be courageous. Isn't that so?

Solomie *is frightened.* **Letiyesus** *goes back to her fornello and* *begins cooking.*

Assefa   Em-Mama, come here.

She comes to him.

Assefa   Please sit down. Solomie, go and look after Kitaw.

She exits.

Assefa   Em-Mama, do you know where your daughter Astier is right now?

Letiyesus   All I know is she left this morning. She said she had a meeting.

Assefa   Didn't Adei Hiwot come round for a gossip as usual?

Letiyesus *(calmly).* Hiwot comes here to drink coffee, not to gossip.

Assefa   Who are the worst gossips of this kebele? Who brings word of the terrorist Wembedie?

Letiyesus   I don't know.

Assefa   Isn't Hiwot one of them?

Hiwot   Not when she's with me.

Assefa *(moving slowly and menacingly towards her)*   What about you Em-Mama?

Letiyesus   I'm not that type of person, my son.

Assefa   Have you never met with Wembedie, Em-Mama?

Letiyesus *(calmly, trying to pacify him)*   Listen, Assefa. Ever since you, yourself, told me that all the Wembedie have been destroyed, that my own son would be eaten by vultures, I have given them up. How can I meet with those who are dead and destroyed?

Assefa *(shaking his head and smiling)*   Em-Mama, you are a strong and cunning woman. You are no fool. *(Smiling again.)* Sorry, Em-Mama, I was talking in anger . . . In this kebele many are jealous of Astier, she is a committed revolutionary, but lots of people are working against her. Do you understand?

Letiyesus   Yes.

Assefa   Now, although she is innocent, some people in the kebele have ganged up to accuse her of things she had nothing to do with. She is being held by the police for investigation.

Letiyesus   Are you saying she is in prison? (*She doesn't seem to understand.*)

Assefa   Yes, that's why I am angry. That's why I said to you that there are some Wembedie in this kebele. They are smearing the names of committed revolutionaries by inventing false accusations.

Letiyesus   (*nodding her head pensively*)   So she is under arrest? Which station is she in? I must take her some food.

Assefa   There's no need to send her any food. I have spoken to the Colonel, he will release her. You think Astier will disappear that easily?

Letiyesus   (*standing, lost in thought and as if to herself*)   I don't know, I just . . . don't know.

Assefa   Wait, Em-Mama, sit down. You felt nothing when I told you about her imprisonment. Had you already heard?

Letiyesus   No, I hadn't.

Assefa   Astier is your daughter, you don't feel shock or sorrow when your child is imprisoned?

Letiyesus   What will my shock and sorrow achieve? But she's my child and I'm obviously distressed by what has happened.

Assefa   But you are not sorry, you are not even surprised.

Solomie *enters, with* **Kitaw**, *but when she sees what's going on, she goes out again.*

Assefa   Stay there, Solomie, stand still. (*She obeys.*) Listen,

Em-Mama, if Solomie was imprisoned you would pull your
hair out.

Letiyesus (*patiently*)   They are all my children and equal in
my eyes.

Assefa (*looking into her eyes*)   I don't believe you. If Mika-el
was imprisoned you'd commit suicide, you'd hang yourself.
Am I right? Eh, what would you do? What? What?

Letiyesus (*fearless*)   I don't know, my son. I don't know what
I would do.

Assefa *is furious again. He paces round the room slowly, looking in
turn at* **Solomie** *and* **Letiyesus**.

Assefa   Well, I'll tell you what you'd do. You would die of
sorrow. But Astier's imprisonment has not moved you one bit.
Why? (*No answer.*) Because she is my wife? (*Silence.*) Or because
she's a revolutionary? (*He bangs his fist on the table and points to*
Solomie *and* **Kitaw**, *shaking with anger.*) They are both Astier's
children. You love Solomie, but you don't care if Kitaw is
alive or dead. Why?

Letiyesus (*angry*)   I'm taking care of him, changing his
nappies, cleaning his messes. What do you mean, I don't care
whether he lives or dies?

Assefa (*pointing at* **Letiyesus**)   I'm not talking about nappies
and messes. I am talking about love. The love you have for
Solomie is obvious. I can read it in your face. But your heart
has no place for Kitaw. Both of them come from your
daughter's womb. Why is Solomie favoured over Kitaw?

Letiyesus   If you have something else in mind, say it
straight. I am an old woman. I am not a child to sit here and
be interrogated as to whom I love best.

Assefa   Why shouldn't you be interrogated? You think I
don't understand? Don't you know that I realise that you love
Solomie more because she was born from your countryman?
I'm not stupid. But you hate Kitaw because he is the son of
an Amhara. (*Sniggering.*) As far as you are concerned,
everything that comes out of Eritreans is good, and anything

mixed with Amhara is bad. Eh? Am I right?

Letiyesus   These are your words, not mine.

Assefa (*hoarse and breathless with extreme rage*)   Em-Mama, I know what is in your mind and in the minds of all the mothers of the Wembedie. You send your children to the field and expect them to come back to you carrying a flag. But that is a dream, Em-Mama, a fantasy! Your son Mika-el and all his likes are gone . . . disappeared . . . exterminated. The new Eritrean generation is Ethiopian at heart. There is simply no place for Wembedies here in Eritrea. Don't waste your time, Em-Mama.

Letiyesus (*calmly, but with a touch of irony*)   I'm always here, I always have time. It seems you're the one that's wasting time. You should be at work, you know.

Assefa (*looking at his watch*)   I will not leave until I'm finished . . . Let me remind you once again that your son Mika-el has been destroyed . . . he's gone! But Kitaw is alive and here. Your daughter, Astier, comes from that Eritrean womb you are so proud of. I, Assefa, planted my seed in your own daughter's womb. Kitaw was born. Kitaw walks on this earth, just like your Mika-el. My roots are firmly planted in Eritrea and no power can ever pull them up. So, get this straight. Eritrea no longer belongs to the Mika-els, it belongs to us, (*Pointing at* **Kitaw**.) to the Kitaws.

Throughout this discussion, **Solomie** *has been following every sentence, reacting with fear, shock and surprise.*

Letiyesus (*standing up confidently, looking at* **Assefa** *in the eyes*)   Good, I think I understand what you mean. Now it is your turn to listen to me. We were so naive that when you told us that the war was in Sahel, somewhere in the mountains, we used to believe you. But today you taught me a good lesson. So, another war is going on in our daughters' wombs? (*With mixed sarcasm and consternation.*) I thought you loved and embraced Kitaw as your son. I had no idea he was just bullets and bombs to you.

Assefa   Stop ridiculing me, I don't like . . .

Letiyesus (*interrupting*)   I'm not ridiculing you, I'm not used to doing that. You forced me to speak.

Assefa (*picking up his pistol*)   Enough! Everything has a limit. All the year, I tried to be a son to you. I waited for you to look upon me as your own, but you ignored all my efforts. At first I thought it was your mother love, maybe also some sympathy for Mika-el, that was keeping us apart. But I was wrong. It's not just love or a little sympathy – you are, yourself, a Wembedie! (*He gets still angrier.*) And you have won Solomie to your side.

He threatens her with his pistol and she is frightened. **Solomie** *holds the child tight and hides behind her grandmother.*

Assefa   Listen, Em-Mama, from this moment on, if you and Solomie do anything or go anywhere without my permission, you will pay for it. Assefa Jembere is not going to harbour Wembedies in his own house! (*Shakes his head and laughs. He inserts the pistol in its holster and puts on his coat, staring at both of them. The telephone rings and he answers.*) Hello . . . yes . . . how are you Comrade Colonel . . . Tomorrow afternoon? What's wrong, Colonel? Is it that serious? . . . Is that so? . . . All right, then. Let's meet in the afternoon . . . Yes, comrade, goodbye. (*To* **Letiyesus**.) Astier will be released tomorrow. She'll be here in the evening. Until then, none of you is to leave the house. I won't be home tonight, don't wait for me. (*He exits.*)

Letiyesus (*immediately*)   Please, Solomie, my daughter, put the child to bed and call Mother Hiwot quickly. I'll be waiting and packing clothes.

Solomie   Whose clothes are you packing? What are you planning to do, Grandma?

Letiyesus   Mine and yours. Hurry up . . . we have to leave while we still have time.

Solomie (*happy*)   Are we going to the village? (**Letiyesus** *nods.* **Solomie** *pauses, then apprehensively.*) What about Kitaw? What will happen to him?

Letiyesus (*surprised*)   That's his business, we will leave him here.

Solomie   How can you say 'That's his business'? Kitaw is my brother and besides he is only a child. I like him too, we must take him or I won't go.

Letiyesus (*angry*)   Are you joking, go and put him to bed now and call Mother Hiwot . . .

Hiwot *enters.*

Letiyesus   . . . Oh, I was just telling her to call you, it's good you came.

Solomie *exits with the child.*

Hiwot   I was waiting for Assefa to leave. When he did, I thought you would be alone and I came. Why are you packing your clothes?

Letiyesus   I've had enough, my sister. I'm taking Solomie to the village . . . from there? Only Mariam knows!

Hiwot   It's about time. You are a woman of dignity. You've put up with them far longer than you should have done.

Letiyesus   But today, he surpassed himself. He pointed his pistol at me and said 'The seed I planted in your daughter's womb has given us Kitaw. This land does not belong to Mika-el. It's mine and Kitaw's . . .' That's what he said.

Hiwot (*scornfully*)   And what does he think having a child means? What a cruel thing to say! Has he no manners?

Letiyesus   Why should he have? Why should he, Hiwot? He has this mare of a woman, who does whatever he wants, who gives us his Kitaws. What kind of creatures do we have here? (*Pauses, then laughs, mockingly.*) Oh, you should have seen him. As if having a child is the ultimate in heroism, an act of special bravery, he puffed himself up and (*Hands on hips, she repeats his puffs and grunts*) . . . It was ridiculous. What indignity, Hiwot? Like the lion whose mane has been shorn off, I felt naked . . . and all because of her.

Hiwot   You are still respected, your honour and identity are still intact. I wish everyone could be like you.

Letiyesus   Oh, you've made me forget my business. Solomie! Solomie! (**Solomie** *does not appear. To* **Hiwot**.) I am in a dilemma. She is insisting that Kitaw goes with us. She's adamant.

Hiwot   Solomie said that?

Letiyesus   Who else? Please my sister Hiwot, tell her we can't.

Hiwot (*thinks for a moment*)   Letiyesus, why don't you take him?

Letiyesus   You, too? Are you mad? I have burned inside because of this child – and now you want me to take him! If I have to bring him up, I might as well do it here, you know.

Hiwot (*holding* **Letiyesus**' *hand and speaking with a great deal of feeling*)   Don't block your mind. Think, Letiyesus. He told you he is going to rule this land through his son, didn't he? He dared to say to you that this land belongs to Kitaw, and not to Miki-el. Well, then, brace up! Take the child away from them. Snatch him, Letiyesus. He is your flesh and blood too. Burn them inside, just as they burned you. Don't let them use our own wombs to rule us!

Letiyesus (*looking at* **Hiwot** *with amazement. The whole idea is new to her*)   Mbwa! I honestly wouldn't mind burning them, breaking their hearts, as they did mine. But, it is a strange thought . . . too much for me, now . . . No, they'll murder us all.

Hiwot (*passionately*)   Come, Letiyesus. Once you are out in your village and disappear with our children fighters, these people won't find you. Your sister Zaid will go now and take the child with her through the check-point on the Dekemhare road. You, Solomie and I will go by Adi Sego, then we meet at Ala. Let's pack quickly. (*Excited.*) When they return and find the house empty, they will fight each other!

Letiyesus (*grabbing* **Hiwot**)   You are not leaving on my account, where will you go?

Hiwot   What do I have here except two or three jelebia? No, for better, for worse, I'd rather live with my brothers in the village. Anyway, if I stay here they'll make me pay for having been your friend: question me, maybe put me in prison. Don't you worry, I have nothing to leave behind here. Let me go, don't delay me. (*She exits.*)

Letiyesus *is thinking hard, when* **Solomie** *enters from her room and looks at her expectantly.* **Letiyesus** *glances at her.*

Letiyesus   Why do you stand there, go and pack the baby's clothes.

Solomie (*very happy*)   Oh, Kitaw's clothes?

Letiyesus (*with a glimmering of a smile*)   Don't you 'Kitaw' him! Don't ever call him Kitaw again. Call him 'Awet' . . . that means victory, you know . . . Awet.

Solomie *jumps up and down with happiness and kisses* **Letiyesus**, *who pushes her away, muttering inaudible words, like 'Go, go' or 'Don't be a nuisance!' – all in good humour. When she is alone, she goes centre-stage and searches the skies.*

Letiyesus   I don't know what you're saying about all this, Mother of Christ, but I am doing what I think is right. Help me! (*She goes back to packing and exits with her packed bags.*)

Act Five

Astier *and* **Assefa** *are sitting by a table. The latter, in his shirt with his collar undone and his tie loose, is on the telephone.* **Astier** *is sitting at his side and seems very anxious. The atmosphere is very tense. Their speech and actions reflect anxiety and depression.*

Assefa Hello . . . Ato Berhe . . . Good evening! This is Assefa Jembere . . . have you heard anything about them? . . . It's been four days since they left now! OK, I'll wait for you to make contact . . . please . . . God keep you! (*He hangs up and looks at* **Astier**, *speaking in a desperate tone.*) He says he has sent someone to Dekemhare. He'll call as soon as he gets word.

Astier (*her voice is sad and weak*) If he sends a messenger to Dekemhare, we shall get the reply soon. If she went straight to our village we shall bring her back easily, it is near Dekemhare. What I'm afraid of is . . . (*She stops and cracks her knuckles.*)

Assefa Why are you saying that over and over again? What are you afraid of? What is the reason for your fears? Do you know something? Do you suspect anything? Speak out! I want my son right here!

Astier (*fearful and pleading*) Please, Assie, don't you think I want my child back too?

Assefa I don't know, everything is confusing me.

He shakes his head and looks at her, with wide eyes, full of suspicion and hate. She watches him, afraid. The heavy silence is broken by the ring of the telephone. Both go to pick it up, but **Assefa** *gets there first.*

Assefa Hello . . . Major . . . How are you today . . . nothing . . . ? All right . . . thank you, Major.

He slowly hangs up, staring at **Astier**, *then bangs his fist on the table.* **Astier** *is startled. He says nothing and exits to his bedroom.* **Astier** *gets up slowly, clutching her abdomen. Fear, frustration and depression can all be read in her face. The telephone rings and, scared, she runs to answer. Then she stops, afraid, and stares at the telephone. Finally she* *gets up enough courage to pick it up.*

Astier (*with a stressed, broken voice*)   Hello Aya Berhe . . . Yes, this is Astier. Really? Aya Berhe, he didn't succeed . . . Did he call you? . . . So what did he say? Where are they? . . . At Ala? . . . (*She wants to cry.*) What about Kitaw? Is he with her? . . . (*She controls her tears*) . . . What is she doing in Ala?

Assefa *enters, smoking a cigarette. Seeing her state, he controls his rage and stands in front of her.*

Astier   So Aya Berhe, couldn't they bring them back . . . ? (*She is greatly shocked by the response, which shows in her face. She lets the telephone fall and is silent, eyes closed.*)

Assefa (*snatching the telephone, he hangs up and breathes heavily*)   What did he say? Can't you speak?

Astier (*trembling, she has to lean on the table to support herself. She speaks in a low voice, sad and scared*)   My relatives met her . . . she will not come, Assie. She has . . . she's taken Kitaw and Solomie and crossed over . . . to them. She's going to Sahel, to join the Wembedie. (*Her voice fades away and she sits because she can no longer stand up.*)

Assefa, *bewildered and unable to believe what he has heard, holds his cigarette with his right hand and inhales a lungful. With the forefinger of his left hand, he points at* **Astier** *and shaking it threateningly, he squints.*

Assefa   It cannot be possible. This cannot be happening.

Astier *looks up at* **Assefa**, *who regards her with hatred and suspicion, which frightens her even more.*

Astier   Assie, why are you looking at me like that?

Assefa (*moving closer to her, pointing his finger*)   You knew about this?

Astier (*it is her turn not to believe what she has just heard*)   How could I know?

Assefa (*enraged, throwing his cigarette on the floor and stamping on it*)   Why not?

Astier   Assie, you are not going to suspect me now, are you?

Assefa   How can I not suspect you? (*Stressing every word, or counting with his fingers.*) Your mother, your brother, your daughter and now my son. (*Shouting.*) MY SON KITAW! They have all become Wembedie! How do you expect me to believe you?

Astier (*looking into his face and pleading*)   Assie, just calm down a little . . . please. They may have gone but I am here with you.

Assefa (*grabbing his pistol from the table and pointing it at **Astier**'s forehead*)   With me, eh? You are with me? I don't know who to believe here. No, speak the truth before I spill your blood. The truth! Now!

Astier (*paralysed with fear*)   Assie, I'm telling you the truth. I'm not lying to you. I have given my body and all I have to you. You opened my eyes and I have devoted my life to the revolution. If you shed my blood, you'll be shedding the blood of an innocent woman who loves you. Assie . . . please . . . Assie! (*She holds his arms with trembling hands.*)

Assefa (*shaking her hands off and loading his pistol*)   Don't touch me!

*He aims the pistol and **Astier** freezes. Holding her cheeks with both hands and pressing her temples with her fingertips, she awaits her death in absolute panic.*

Astier (*weak with fear*)   Oh, dearest mother, what have I done to you to deserve this?

Assefa (*changes his mind and lowers the gun*)   No, death is all too quick and simple. Don't even think of leaving the house. I'm not finished with you yet. I'll send a guard immediately. You are not to leave the house.

Assefa *straps on his gun belt and starts to leave.* **Astier** *follows him, pulling at his coat.*

Astier   Assie, Assie . . . don't leave me alone. Don't shut me out. I left my family and relatives for you. You are the only person I have. Assie, have pity on . . .

Assefa *interrupts her with a heavy blow. She falls to the ground.*

Assefa   Do I care?

Astier *follows him out with her eyes. She looks around the room, then at the audience. She looks everywhere. She starts pulling her hair out. Finally, she puts her head in her hands and cries bitterly, shaking all over. No one is there to hear her.*

Glossary

Amharic was the official language of the Ethiopian Empire which the ruling Amhara ethnic group sought to impose on everyone, including Eritreans. The Amhara only constitute 20–25% of the Ethiopian population, and there are around 60 languages spoken in Ethiopia. The Eritreans saw, and referred to their enemy, often not as Ethiopians but specifically as Amhara.

Tigrinya is one of nine indigenous languages in Eritrea. It is the language of the capital, Asmara, and of many of the educated people.

One of the distinguishing traits of and jokes against Assefa is that he cannot speak Tigrinya fluently and often makes mistakes in his pronunciation.

Both Amharic and Tigrinya are written in an ancient script which comprises of a syllabary rather than an alphabet. The renderings given here are therefore phonetic approximations and not written as they would be in Ethiopia or Eritrea.

Adei   a common title for older women, 'mother'
'Anchi manchi, anchi manchi!'   how Amharic sounds to a Tigrinyan
'Awet Nahafash!'   an EPLF slogan meaning 'Victory to the masses!'
Aya   Eritrean version of 'Gashi'
Bakshin   Amharic for 'please'
cuda   traditional Tigrinya celebration dance
'Dihan, Wedei, Tzibuq'   'OK, friend, good'
Dimtsi Hafash   EPLF radio station
donkeys   Eritreans mockingly referred to Amharas as donkeys. The Dergue tried to discourage the word, so this would be very funny to an Eritrean audience
'Endemin Allu?'   formal greeting in Amharic
'Endiye!'   Amharic expression of surprise, similar to the Tigrinyan 'Mbwa!'
fornello   a small metal stove filled with hot coals and used for heating a jebena

Gashie   Amharic title of respect

gedli   literally 'struggle', but sometimes, as here, 'one who struggles' (strictly 'tegaladai')

jebena   a small clay pot used for making coffee

jelebia   traditional dress of a Tigrinya woman

kebeles   Asmara was organised into 'kebeles' (sub-sections) by the Dergue. (The Dergue was the Ethiopian military junta regime, 1974–1991, led by Mengistu Haile-Mariam.) Each kebele was run by a cadre

'Mbwa!'   a common Tigrinya exclamation, used to show surprise, disgust, exasperation, etc.

netsela   a thin white shawl worn over the shoulders and head. Traditional dress for Tigrinya men and women

Red Star campaign   the Dergue's sixth and largest military offensive, launched in 1982

Sahel   region in northern Eritrea and base for the EPLF

Tor-Serawit   Ethiopian infantry soldiers

Wembedie   Amharic term for EPLF fighters, meaning 'bandits'

Death and the King's Horseman

Wole Soyinka

Dedicated
in Affectionate Greeting
to my Father, Ayodele
who lately danced, and joined the Ancestors

Author's Note

This play is based on events which took place in Oyo, ancient Yoruba city of Nigeria, in 1946. That year, the lives of Elesin (Olori Elesin), his son, and the Colonial District Officer intertwined with the disastrous results set out in the play. The changes I have made are in matters of detail, sequence and of course characterisation. The action has also been set back two or three years to while the war was still on, for minor reasons of dramaturgy.

The factual account still exists in the archives of the British Colonial Administration. It has already inspired a fine play in Yoruba (*Oba Wàjà*) by Duro Ladipo. It has also misbegotten a film by some German television company.

The bane of themes of this genre is that they are no sooner employed creatively than they acquire the facile tag of 'clash of cultures', a prejudicial label which, quite apart from its frequent misapplication, presupposes a potential equality *in every given situation* of the alien culture and the indigenous, on the actual soil of the latter. (In the area of misapplication, the overseas prize for illiteracy and mental conditioning undoubtedly goes to the blurb-writer for the American edition of my novel *Season of Anomy* who unblushingly declares that this work portrays the 'clash between old values and new ways, between western methods and African traditions'!) It is thanks to this kind of perverse mentality that I find it necessary to caution the would-be producer of this play against a sadly familiar reductionist tendency, and to direct his vision instead to the far more difficult and risky task of eliciting the play's threnodic essence.

One of the more obvious alternative structures of the play would be to make the District Officer the victim of a cruel dilemma. This is not to my taste and it is not by chance that I have avoided dialogue or situation which would encourage this. No attempt should be made in production to suggest it. The Colonial Factor is an incident, a catalytic incident merely. The confrontation in the play is largely metaphysical, contained in the human vehicle which is Elesin and the universe of the Yoruba mind – the world of the living, the dead and the unborn, and the numinous passage which links all: transition. *Death and the King's Horseman* can be fully realised only through an evocation of music from the abyss of transition.

W.S.

Characters

Praise-Singer
Elesin, *Horseman of the King*
Iyaloja, *'Mother' of the market*
Simon Pilkings, *District Officer*
Jane Pilkings, *his wife*
Sergeant Amusa
Joseph, *houseboy to the Pilkings*
Bride
H.R.H. the Prince
The Resident
Aide-de-Camp
Olunde, *eldest son of Elesin*
Drummers, Women, Young Girls, Dancers at the Ball

The play should run without an interval. For rapid scene changes, one adjustable outline set is very appropriate.

Scene One

A passage through a market in its closing stages. The stalls are being emptied, mats folded. A few women pass through on their way home, loaded with baskets. On a cloth-stand, bolts of cloth are taken down, display pieces folded and piled on a tray. **Elesin Oba** *enters along a passage before the market, pursued by his drummers and praise-singers. He is a man of enormous vitality, speaks, dances and sings with that infectious enjoyment of life which accompanies all his actions.*

Praise-Singer Elesin o! Elesin Oba! Howu! What tryst is this the cockerel goes to keep with such haste that he must leave his tail behind?

Elesin (*slows down a bit, laughing*) A tryst where the cockerel needs no adornment.

Praise-Singer O-oh, you hear that my companions? That's the way the world goes. Because the man approaches a brand-new bride he forgets the long-faithful mother of his children.

Elesin When the horse sniffs the stable does he not strain at the bridle? The market is the long-suffering home of my spirit and the women are packing up to go. That Esu-harassed day slipped into the stewpot while we feasted. We ate it up with the rest of the meat. I have neglected my women.

Praise-Singer We know all that. Still it's no reason for shedding your tail on this day of all days. I know the women will cover you in damask and alari* but when the wind blows cold from behind, that's when the fowl knows his true friends.

Elesin Olohun-iyo!

Praise-Singer Are you sure there will be one like me on the other side?

Elesin Olohun-iyo!

Praise-Singer Far be it for me to belittle the dwellers of that place but, a man is either born to his art or he isn't. And

---

* See Glossary on p. 383 for translations of Yoruba words.

I don't know for certain that you'll meet my father, so who is going to sing these deeds in accents that will pierce the deafness of the ancient ones. I have prepared my going – just tell me: Olohun-iyo, I need you on this journey and I shall be behind you.

Elesin   You're like a jealous wife. Stay close to me, but only on this side. My fame, my honour are legacies to the living, stay behind and let the world sip its honey from your lips.

Praise-Singer   Your name will be like the sweet berry a child places under his tongue to sweeten the passage of food. The world will never spit it out.

Elesin   Come then. This market is my roost. When I come among the women I am a chicken with a hundred mothers. I become a monarch whose palace is built with tenderness and beauty.

Praise-Singer   They love to spoil you but beware. The hands of women also weaken the unwary.

Elesin   This night I'll lay my head upon their lap and go to sleep. This night I'll touch feet with their feet in a dance that is no longer of this earth. But the smell of their flesh, their sweat, the smell of indigo on their cloth, this is the last air I wish to breathe as I go to meet my great forebears.

Praise-Singer   In their time the world was never tilted from its groove, it shall not be in yours.

Elesin   The gods have said No.

Praise-Singer   In their time the great wars came and went, the little wars came and went; the white slavers came and went, they took away the heart of our race, they bore away the mind and muscle of our race. The city fell and was rebuilt; the city fell and our people trudged through mountain and forest to find a new home but – Elesin Oba do you hear me?

Elesin   I hear your voice Olohun-iyo.

Praise-Singer   Our world was never wrenched from its true course.

Elesin   The gods have said No.

Praise-Singer   There is only one home to the life of a
river-mussel; there is only one home to the life of a tortoise;
there is only one shell to the soul of man; there is only one
world to the spirit of our race. If that world leaves its course
and smashes on boulders of the great void, whose world will
give us shelter?

Elesin   It did not in the time of my forebears, it shall not in
mine.

Praise-Singer   The cockerel must not be seen without his
feathers.

Elesin   Nor will the Not-I bird be much longer without his
nest.

Praise-Singer (*stopped in his lyric stride*)   The Not-I bird,
Elesin?

Elesin   I said, the Not-I bird.

Praise-Singer   All respect to our elders but, is there really
such a bird?

Elesin   What! Could it be that he failed to knock on your
door?

Praise-Singer (*smiling*)   Elesin's riddles are not merely the
nut in the kernel that breaks human teeth; he also buries the
kernel in hot embers and dares a man's fingers to draw it out.

Elesin   I am sure he called on you, Olohun-iyo. Did you
hide in the loft and push out the servant to tell him you were
out?

Elesin *executes a brief, half-taunting dance. The drummer moves in and
draws a rhythm out of his steps.* **Elesin** *dances towards the market-
place as he chants the story of the Not-I bird, his voice changing
dexterously to mimic his characters. He performs like a born raconteur,
infecting his retinue with his humour and energy. More* **Women** *arrive
during his recital, including* **Iyaloja**.

Elesin
  Death came calling
  Who does not know his rasp of reeds?
  A twilight whisper in the leaves before
  The great araba falls? Did you hear it?
  Not I! swears the farmer. He snaps
  His fingers round his head, abandons
  A hard-worn harvest and begins
  A rapid dialogue with his legs.

  'Not I,' shouts the fearless hunter, 'but –
  It's getting dark, and this night-lamp
  Has leaked out all its oil. I think
  It's best to go home and resume my hunt
  Another day.' But now he pauses, suddenly
  Let's out a wail: 'Oh foolish mouth, calling
  Down a curse on your own head! Your lamp
  Has leaked out all its oil, has it?'
  Forwards or backwards now he dare not move.
  To search for leaves and make etutu
  On that spot? Or race home to the safety
  Of his hearth? Ten market-days have passed
  My friends, and still he's rooted there
  Rigid as the plinth of Orayan.

  The mouth of the courtesan barely
  Opened wide enough to take a ha'penny robo
  When she wailed: 'Not I.' All dressed she was
  To call upon my friend the Chief Tax Officer.
  But now she sends her go-between instead:
  'Tell him I'm ill: my period has come suddenly
  But not – I hope – my time.'

  Why is the pupil crying?
  His hapless head was made to taste
  The knuckles of my friend the Mallam:
  'If you were then reciting the Koran
  Would you have ears for idle noises
  Darkening the trees, you child of ill omen?'
  He shuts down school before its time
  Runs home and rings himself with amulets.

And take my good kinsman Ifawomi.
His hands were like a carver's, strong
And true. I saw them
Tremble like wet wings of a fowl.
One day he cast his time-smoothed opele
Across the divination board. And all because
The suppliant looked him in the eye and asked,
'Did you hear that whisper in the leaves?'
'Not I,' was his reply; 'perhaps I'm growing deaf –
Good-day.' And Ifa spoke no more that day
The priest locked fast his doors,
Sealed up his leaking roof – but wait!
This sudden care was not for Fawomi
But for Osanyin, a courier-bird of Ifa's
Heart of wisdom. I did not know a kite
Was hovering in the sky
And Ifa now a twittering chicken in
The brood of Fawomi the Mother Hen.

Ah, but I must not forget my evening
Courier from the abundant palm, whose groan
Became Not I, as he constipated down
A wayside bush. He wonders if Elegbara
Has tricked his buttocks to discharge
Against a sacred grove. Hear him
Mutter spells to ward off penalties
For an abomination he did not intend.
If any here
Stumbles on a gourd of wine, fermenting
Near the road, and nearby hears a stream
Of spells issuing from a crouching form.
Brother to a sigidi, bring home my wine,
Tell my tapper I have ejected
Fear from home and farm. Assure him,
All is well.

Praise-Singer   In your time we do not doubt the peace of
farmstead and home, the peace of road and hearth, we do not
doubt the peace of the forest.

Elesin
There was fear in the forest too.
Not-I was lately heard even in the lair
Of beasts. The hyena cackled loud. Not I,
The civet twitched his fiery tail and glared:
Not I. Not-I became the answering-name
Of the restless bird, that little one
Whom Death found nesting in the leaves
When whisper of his coming ran
Before him on the wind. Not-I
Has long abandoned home. This same dawn
I heard him twitter in the gods' abode.
Ah, companions of this living world
What a thing this is, that even those
We call immortal
Should fear to die.

Iyaloja
But you, husband of multitudes?

Elesin
I, when that Not-I bird perched
Upon my roof, bade him seek his nest again.
Safe, without care or fear. I unrolled
My welcome mat for him to see. Not-I
Flew happily away, you'll hear his voice
No more in this lifetime – You all know
What I am.

Praise-Singer
That rock which turns its open lodes
Into the path of lightning. A gay
Thoroughbred whose stride disdains
To falter though an adder reared
Suddenly in his path.

Elesin
My rein is loosened.
I am master of my fate. When the hour comes
Watch me dance along the narrowing path
Glazed by the soles of my great precursors.
My soul is eager. I shall not turn aside.

Women

You will not delay?

Elesin

Where the storm pleases, and when, it directs
The giants of the forest. When friendship summons
Is when the true comrade goes.

Women

Nothing will hold you back?

Elesin

Nothing. What! Has no one told you yet
I go to keep my friend and master company.
Who says the mouth does not believe in
'No, I have chewed all that before?' I say I have.
The world is not a constant honey-pot.
Where I found little I made do with little.
Where there was plenty I gorged myself.
My master's hands and mine have always
Dipped together and, home or sacred feast,
The bowl was beaten bronze, the meats
So succulent our teeth accused us of neglect.
We shared the choicest of the season's
Harvest of yams. How my friend would read
Desire in my eyes before I knew the cause –
However rare, however precious, it was mine.

Women

The town, the very land was yours.

Elesin

The world was mine. Our joint hands
Raised houseposts of trust that withstood
The siege of envy and the termites of time.
But the twilight hour brings bats and rodents –
Shall I yield them cause to foul the rafters?

Praise-Singer

Elesin Oba! Are you not that man who
Looked out of doors that stormy day
The god of luck limped by, drenched

To the very lice that held
His rags together? You took pity upon
His sores and wished him fortune.
Fortune was footloose this dawn, he replied,
Till you trapped him in a heartfelt wish
That now returns to you. Elesin Oba!
I say you are that man who
Chanced upon the calabash of honour.
You thought it was palm wine and
Drained its contents to the final drop.

Elesin
Life has an end. A life that will outlive
Fame and friendship begs another name.
What elder takes his tongue to his plate,
Licks it clean of every crumb? He will encounter
Silence when he calls on children to fulfil
The smallest errand! Life is honour.
It ends when honour ends.

Women
We know you for a man of honour.

Elesin Stop! Enough of that!

Women (*puzzled, they whisper among themselves, turning mostly to*
Iyaloja) What is it? Did we say something to give offence?
Have we slighted him in some way?

Elesin Enough of that sound I say. Let me hear no more in
that vein. I've heard enough.

Iyaloja We must have said something wrong. (*Comes forward
a little.*) Elesin Oba, we ask forgiveness before you speak.

Elesin I am bitterly offended.

Iyaloja Our unworthiness has betrayed us. All we can do is
ask your forgiveness. Correct us like a kind father.

Elesin This day of all days . . .

Iyaloja It does not bear thinking. If we offend you now we
have mortified the gods. We offend heaven itself. Father of us

all, tell us where we went astray. (*She kneels, the other* **Women**
follow.)

Elesin
Are you not ashamed? Even a tear-veiled
Eye preserves its function of sight.
Because my mind was raised to horizons
Even the boldest man lowers his gaze
In thinking of, must my body here
Be taken for a vagrant's?

Iyaloja   Horseman of the King, I am more baffled than
ever.

Praise-Singer   The strictest father unbends his brow when
the child is penitent, Elesin. When time is short, we do not
spend it prolonging the riddle. Their shoulders are bowed with
the weight of fear lest they have marred your day beyond
repair. Speak now in plain words and let us pursue the
ailment to the home of remedies.

Elesin
Words are cheap. 'We know you for
A man of honour.' Well tell me, is this how
A man of honour should be seen?
Are these not the same clothes in which
I came among you a full half-hour ago?

He roars with laughter and the **Women**, *relieved, rise and rush into*
stalls to fetch rich clothes.

Women   The gods are kind. A fault soon remedied is soon
forgiven. Elesin Oba, even as we match our words with deed,
let your heart forgive us completely.

Elesin
You who are breath and giver of my being
How shall I dare refuse you forgiveness
Even if the offence was real.

Iyaloja (*dancing round him. Sings*)
He forgives us. He forgives us.
What a fearful thing it is when

The voyager sets forth
But a curse remains behind.

Women
For a while we truly feared
Our hands had wrenched the world adrift
In emptiness.

Iyaloja
Richly, richly, robe him richly
The cloth of honour is alari
Sanyan is the band of friendship
Boa-skin makes slippers of esteem.

Women
For a while we truly feared
Our hands had wrenched the world adrift
In emptiness.

Praise-Singer
He who must, must voyage forth
The world will not roll backwards
It is he who must, with one
Great gesture overtake the world.

Women
For a while we truly feared
Our hands had wrenched the world
In emptiness.

Praise-Singer
The gourd you bear is not for shirking
The gourd is not for setting down
At the first crossroad or wayside grove
Only one river may know its contents.

Women
We shall all meet at the great market
We shall all meet at the great market
He who goes early takes the best bargains
But we shall meet, and resume our banter.

Elesin *stands resplendent in rich clothes, cap, shawl, etc. His sash is of* *a bright red alari cloth. The* **Women** *dance round him. Suddenly, his attention is caught by an object off-stage.*

Elesin
   The world I know is good.

Women
   We know you'll leave it so.

Elesin
   The world I know is the bounty
   Of hives after bees have swarmed.
   No goodness teems with such open hands
   Even in the dreams of deities.

Women
   And we know you'll leave it so.

Elesin
   I was born to keep it so. A hive
   Is never known to wander. An anthill
   Does not desert its roots. We cannot see
   The still great womb of the world –
   No man beholds his mother's womb –
   Yet who denies it's there? Coiled
   To the navel of the world is that
   Endless cord that links us all
   To the great origin. If I lose my way
   The trailing cord will bring me to the roots.

Women
   The world is in your hands.

The earlier distraction, a beautiful young girl, comes along the passage through which **Elesin** *first made his entry.*

Elesin
   I embrace it. And let me tell you, women –
   I like this farewell that the world designed,
   Unless my eyes deceive me, unless
   We are already parted, the world and I,
   And all that breeds desire is lodged

Among our tireless ancestors. Tell me friends,
Am I still earthed in that beloved market
Of my youth? Or could it be my will
Has outleapt the conscious act and I have come
Among the great departed?

Praise-Singer   Elesin Oba why do your eyes roll like a
bush-rat who sees his fate like his father's spirit, mirrored in
the eye of a snake? And all those questions! You're standing
on the same earth you've always stood upon. This voice you
hear is mine, Oluhun-iyo, not that of an acolyte in heaven.

Elesin
How can that be? In all my life
As Horseman of the King, the juiciest
Fruit on every tree was mine. I saw,
I touched, I wooed, rarely was the answer No.
The honour of my place, the veneration I
Received in the eye of man or woman
Prospered my suit and
Played havoc with my sleeping hours.
And they tell me my eyes were a hawk
In perpetual hunger. Split an iroko tree
In two, hide a woman's beauty in its heartwood
And seal it up again – Elesin, journeying by,
Would make his camp beside that tree
Of all the shades in the forest.

Praise-Singer   Who would deny your reputation, snake-on-
the-loose in dark passages of the market! Bed-bug who wages
war on the mat and receives the thanks of the vanquished!
When caught with his bride's own sister he protested – but I
was only prostrating myself to her as becomes a grateful in-
law. Hunter who carries his powder-horn on the hips and fires
crouching or standing! Warrior who never makes that excuse
of the whining coward – but how can I go to battle without
my trousers? – trouserless or shirtless it's all one to him. Oka-
rearing-from-a-camouflage-of-leaves, before he strikes the
victim is already prone! Once they told him, Howu, a stallion
does not feed on the grass beneath him: he replied, true, but
surely he can roll on it!

Women   Ba-a-a-ba O!

Praise-Singer   Ah, but listen yet. You know there is the leaf-nibbling grub and there is the cola-chewing beetle; the leaf-nibbling grub lives on the leaf, the cola-chewing beetle lives in the colanut. Don't we know what our man feeds on when we find him cocooned in a woman's wrapper?

Elesin
> Enough, enough, you all have cause
> To know me well. But, if you say this earth
> Is still the same as gave birth to those songs,
> Tell me who was that goddess through whose lips
> I saw the ivory pebbles of Oya's river-bed.
> Iyaloja, who is she? I saw her enter
> Your stall; all your daughters I know well.
> No, not even Ogun-of-the-farm toiling
> Dawn till dusk on his tuber patch
> Not even Ogun with the finest hoe he ever
> Forged at the anvil could have shaped
> That rise of buttocks, not though he had
> The richest earth between his fingers.
> Her wrapper was no disguise
> For thighs whose ripples shamed the river's
> Coils around the hills of Ilesi. Her eyes
> Were new-laid eggs glowing in the dark.
> Her skin . . .

Iyaloja   Elesin Oba . . .

Elesin   What! Where do you all say I am?

Iyaloja   Still among the living.

Elesin
> And that radiance which so suddenly
> Lit up this market I could boast
> I knew so well?

Iyaloja   Has one step already in her husband's home. She is betrothed.

Elesin (*irritated*)   Why do you tell me that?

Iyaloja *falls silent. The* **Women** *shuffle uneasily.*

Iyaloja Not because we dare give you offence Elesin. Today is your day and the whole world is yours. Still, even those who leave town to make a new dwelling elsewhere like to be remembered by what they leave behind.

Elesin
Who does not seek to be remembered?
Memory is Master of Death, the chink
In his armour of conceit. I shall leave
That which makes my going the sheerest
Dream of an afternoon. Should voyagers
Not travel light? Let the considerate traveller
Shed, of his excessive load, all
That may benefit the living.

Women *(relieved)* Ah Elesin Oba, we knew you for a man of honour.

Elesin Then honour me. I deserve a bed of honour to lie upon.

Iyaloja The best is yours. We know you for a man of honour. You are not one who eats and leaves nothing on his plate for children. Did you not say it yourself? Not one who blights the happiness of others for a moment's pleasure.

Elesin
Who speaks of pleasure? O women, listen!
Pleasure palls. Our acts should have meaning.
The sap of the plantain never dries.
You have seen the young shoot swelling
Even as the parent stalk begins to wither.
Women, let my going be likened to
The twilight hour of the plantain.

Women What does he mean Iyaloja? This language is the language of our elders, we do not fully grasp it.

Iyaloja I dare not understand you yet Elesin.

Elesin
All you who stand before the spirit that dares

The opening of the last door of passage,
Dare to rid my going of regrets! My wish
Transcends the blotting out of thought
In one mere moment's tremor of the senses.
Do me credit. And do me honour.
I am girded for the route beyond
Burdens of waste and longing.
Then let me travel light. Let
Seed that will not serve the stomach
On the way remain behind. Let it take root
In the earth of my choice, in this earth
I leave behind.

Iyaloja (*turns to* **Women**) The voice I hear is already touched by the waiting fingers of our departed. I dare not refuse.

Woman But Iyaloja . . .

Iyaloja The matter is no longer in our hands.

Woman But she is betrothed to your own son. Tell him.

Iyaloja My son's wish is mine. I did the asking for him, the loss can be remedied. But who will remedy the blight of closed hands on the day when all should be openness and light? Tell him, you say! You wish that I burden him with knowledge that will sour his wish and lay regrets on the last moments of his mind. You pray to him who is your intercessor to the world – don't set this world adrift in your own time; would you rather it was my hand whose sacrilege wrenched it loose?

Woman Not many men will brave the curse of a dispossessed husband.

Iyaloja Only the curses of the departed are to be feared. The claims of one whose foot is on the threshold of their abode surpasses even the claims of blood. It is impiety even to place hindrances in their ways.

Elesin
What do my mothers say? Shall I step

Burdened into the unknown?

Iyaloja   Not we, but the very earth says No. The sap in the
plantain does not dry. Let grain that will not feed the voyager
at his passage drop here and take root as he steps beyond this
earth and us. Oh you who fill the home from hearth to
threshold with the voices of children, you who now bestride
the hidden gulf and pause to draw the right foot across and
into the resting-home of the great forebears, it is good that
your loins be drained into the earth we know, that your last
strength be ploughed back into the womb that gave you
being.

Praise-Singer   Iyaloja, mother of multitudes in the teeming
market of the world, how your wisdom transfigures you!

Iyaloja (*smiling broadly, completely reconciled*)   Elesin, even at the
narrow end of the passage I know you will look back and sigh
a last regret for the flesh that flashed past your spirit in flight.
You always had a restless eye. Your choice has my blessing.
(*To the* **Women**.) Take the good news to our daughter and
make her ready. (*Some* **Women** *go off.*)

Elesin   Your eyes were clouded at first.

Iyaloja   Not for long. It is those who stand at the gateway
of the great change to whose cry we must pay heed. And
then, think of this – it makes the mind tremble. The fruit of
such a union is rare. It will be neither of this world nor of the
next. Nor of the one behind us. As if the timelessness of the
ancestor world and the unborn have joined spirits to wring an
issue of the elusive being of passage ... Elesin!

Elesin   I am here. What is it?

Iyaloja   Did you hear all I said just now?

Elesin   Yes.

Iyaloja   The living must eat and drink. When the moment
comes, don't turn the food to rodents' droppings in their
mouth. Don't let them taste the ashes of the world when they
step out at dawn to breathe the morning dew.

Elesin   This doubt is unworthy of you Iyaloja.

Iyaloja   Eating the awusa nut is not so difficult as drinking water afterwards.

Elesin
The waters of the bitter stream are honey to a man
Whose tongue has savoured all.

Iyaloja   No one knows when the ants desert their home; they leave the mound intact. The swallow is never seen to peck holes in its nest when it is time to move with the season. There are always throngs of humanity behind the leave-taker. The rain should not come through the roof for them, the wind must not blow through the walls at night.

Elesin   I refuse to take offence.

Iyaloja   You wish to travel light. Well, the earth is yours. But be sure the seed you leave in it attracts no curse.

Elesin   You really mistake my person Iyaloja.

Iyaloja   I said nothing. Now we must go prepare your bridal chamber. Then these same hands will lay your shrouds.

Elesin (*exasperated*)   Must you be so blunt? (*Recovers.*) Well, weave your shrouds, but let the fingers of my bride seal my eyelids with earth and wash my body.

Iyaloja   Prepare yourself Elesin.

She gets up to leave. At that moment the **Women** *return, leading the* **Bride**. **Elesin**'s *face glows with pleasure. He flicks the sleeves of his agbada with renewed confidence and steps forward to meet the group. As the girl kneels before* **Iyaloja**, *lights fade out on the scene.*

Scene Two

The verandah of the District Officer's bungalow. A tango is playing from an old hand-cranked gramophone and, glimpsed through the wide windows and doors which open onto the forestage verandah, are the shapes of **Simon Pilkings** *and his wife,* **Jane**, *tangoing in and out of* *shadows in the living-room. They are wearing what is immediately apparent as some form of fancy-dress. The dance goes on for some moments and then the figure of a 'Native Administration' policeman emerges and climbs up the steps onto the verandah. He peeps through and observes the dancing couple, reacting with what is obviously a long-standing bewilderment. He stiffens suddenly, his expression changes to one of disbelief and horror. In his excitement he upsets a flower-pot and attracts the attention of the couple. They stop dancing.*

Pilkings Is there anyone out there?

Jane I'll turn off the gramophone.

Pilkings (*approaching the verandah*) I'm sure I heard something fall over. (*The constable retreats slowly, open-mouthed as* **Pilkings** *approaches the verandah.*) Oh it's you Amusa. Why didn't you just knock instead of knocking things over?

Amusa (*stammers badly and points a shaky finger at his dress*) Mista Pirinkin . . . Mista Pirinkin . . .

Pilkings What is the matter with you?

Jane (*emerging*) Who is it dear? Oh, Amusa . . .

Pilkings Yes it's Amusa, and acting most strangely.

Amusa (*his attention now transferred to* **Jane Pilkings**) Mammadam . . . you too!

Pilkings What the hell is the matter with you man!

Jane Your costume darling. Our fancy-dress.

Pilkings Oh hell, I'd forgotten all about that. (*Lifts the face mask over his head showing his face. His wife follows suit.*)

Jane I think you've shocked his big pagan heart bless him.

Pilkings Nonsense, he's a Moslem. Come on Amusa, you don't believe in all that nonsense do you? I thought you were a good Moslem.

Amusa Mista Pirinkin, I beg you sir, what you think you do with that dress? It belong to dead cult, not for human being.

Pilkings Oh Amusa, what a let-down you are. I swear by

you at the club you know – thank God for Amusa, he doesn't believe in any mumbo-jumbo. And now look at you!

Amusa   Mista Pirinkin, I beg you, take it off. Is not good for man like you to touch that cloth.

Pilkings   Well, I've got it on. And what's more Jane and I have bet on it we're taking first prize at the ball. Now, if you can just pull yourself together and tell me what you wanted to see me about . . .

Amusa   Sir, I cannot talk this matter to you in that dress. I no fit.

Pilkings   What's that rubbish again?

Jane   He is dead earnest too Simon. I think you'll have to handle this delicately.

Pilkings   Delicately my. . . ! Look here Amusa, I think this little joke has gone far enough hm? Let's have some sense. You seem to forget that you are a police officer in the service of His Majesty's Government. I order you to report your business at once or face disciplinary action.

Amusa   Sir, it is a matter of death. How can man talk against death to person in uniform of death? Is like talking against government to person in uniform of police. Please sir, I go and come back.

Pilkings (*roars*)   Now!

Amusa *switches his gaze to the ceiling suddenly, remains mute.*

Jane   Oh Amusa, what is there to be scared of in the costume? You saw it confiscated last month from those egungun men who were creating trouble in town. You helped arrest the cult leaders yourself – if the juju didn't harm you at the time how could it possibly harm you now? And merely by looking at it?

Amusa (*without looking down*)   Madam, I arrest the ringleaders who make trouble but me I no touch egungun. That egungun inself, I no touch. And I no abuse 'am. I arrest ringleader but I treat egungun with respect.

Pilkings   It's hopeless. We'll merely end up missing the best part of the ball. When they get this way there is nothing you can do. It's simply hammering against a brick wall. Write your report or whatever it is on that pad Amusa and take yourself out of here. Come on Jane. We only upset his delicate sensibilities by remaining here.

*Amusa waits for them to leave, then writes in the notebook, somewhat laboriously. Drumming from the direction of the town wells up. **Amusa** listens, makes a movement as if he wants to recall **Pilkings** but changes his mind. Completes his note and goes. A few moments later **Pilkings** emerges, picks up the pad and reads.*

Pilkings   Jane!

Jane *(from the bedroom)*   Coming darling. Nearly ready.

Pilkings   Never mind being ready, just listen to this.

Jane   What is it?

Pilkings   Amusa's report. Listen. 'I have to report that it come to my information that one prominent chief, namely, the Elesin Oba, is to commit death tonight as a result of native custom. Because this is criminal offence I await further instruction at charge office. Sergeant Amusa.'

Jane comes out onto the verandah while he is reading.

Jane   Did I hear you say commit death?

Pilkings   Obviously he means murder.

Jane   You mean a ritual murder?

Pilkings   Must be. You think you've stamped it all out but it's always lurking under the surface somewhere.

Jane   Oh. Does it mean we are not getting to the ball at all?

Pilkings   No-o. I'll have the man arrested. Everyone remotely involved. In any case there may be nothing to it. Just rumours.

Jane   Really? I thought you found Amusa's rumours generally reliable.

Pilkings   That's true enough. But who knows what may have been giving him the scare lately. Look at his conduct tonight.

Jane (*laughing*)   You have to admit he had his own peculiar logic. (*Deepens her voice.*) How can man talk against death to person in uniform of death? (*Laughs.*) Anyway, you can't go into the police station dressed like that.

Pilkings   I'll send Joseph with instructions. Damn it, what a confounded nuisance!

Jane   But don't you think you should talk first to the man, Simon?

Pilkings   Do you want to go to the ball or not?

Jane   Darling, why are you getting rattled? I was only trying to be intelligent. It seems hardly fair just to lock up a man – and a chief at that – simply on the er . . . what is the legal word again? – uncorroborated word of a sergeant.

Pilkings   Well, that's easily decided. Joseph!

Joseph (*from within*)   Yes master.

Pilkings   You're quite right of course, I am getting rattled. Probably the effect of those bloody drums. Do you hear how they go on and on?

Jane   I wondered when you'd notice. Do you suppose it has something to do with this affair?

Pilkings   Who knows? They always find an excuse for making a noise . . . (*Thoughtfully.*) Even so . . .

Jane   Yes Simon?

Pilkings   It's different Jane. I don't think I've heard this particular – sound – before. Something unsettling about it.

Jane   I thought all bush drumming sounded the same.

Pilkings   Don't tease me now Jane. This may be serious.

Jane   I'm sorry. (*Gets up and throws her arms around his neck. Kisses him. The houseboy enters, retreats and knocks.*)

Pilkings (*wearily*)   Oh, come in Joseph! I don't know where you pick up all these elephantine notions of tact. Come over here.

Joseph   Sir?

Pilkings   Joseph, are you a Christian or not?

Joseph   Yessir.

Pilkings   Does seeing me in this outfit bother you?

Joseph   No sir, it has no power.

Pilkings   Thank God for some sanity at last. Now Joseph, answer me on the honour of a Christian – what is supposed to be going on in town tonight?

Joseph   Tonight sir? You mean the chief who is going to kill himself?

Pilkings   What?

Jane   What do you mean, kill himself?

Pilkings   You do mean he is going to kill somebody don't you?

Joseph   No master. He will not kill anybody and no one will kill him. He will simply die.

Jane   But why Joseph?

Joseph   It is native law and custom. The King die last month. Tonight is his burial. But before they can bury him, the Elesin must die so as to accompany him to heaven.

Pilkings   I seem to be fated to clash more often with that man than with any of the other chiefs.

Joseph   He is the King's Chief Horseman.

Pilkings (*in a resigned way*)   I know.

Jane   Simon, what's the matter?

Pilkings   It would have to be him!

Jane   Who is he?

Pilkings Don't you remember? He's that chief with whom I
had a scrap some three or four years ago. I helped his son get
to a medical school in England, remember? He fought tooth
and nail to prevent it.

Jane Oh now I remember. He was that very sensitive young
man. What was his name again?

Pilkings Olunde. Haven't replied to his last letter come to
think of it. The old pagan wanted him to stay and carry on
some family tradition or the other. Honestly I couldn't
understand the fuss he made. I literally had to help the boy
escape from close confinement and load him onto the next
boat. A most intelligent boy, really bright.

Jane I rather thought he was much too sensitive you know.
The kind of person you feel should be a poet munching rose
petals in Bloomsbury.

Pilkings Well, he's going to make a first-class doctor. His
mind is set on that. And as long as he wants my help he is
welcome to it.

Jane (*after a pause*) Simon.

Pilkings Yes?

Jane This boy, he was the eldest son wasn't he?

Pilkings I'm not sure. Who could tell with that old ram?

Jane Do you know, Joseph?

Joseph Oh yes madam. He was the eldest son. That's why
Elesin cursed master good and proper. The eldest son is not
supposed to travel away from the land.

Jane (*giggling*) Is that true Simon? Did he really curse you
good and proper?

Pilkings By all accounts I should be dead by now.

Joseph Oh no, master is white man. And good Christian.
Black man juju can't touch master.

Jane If he was his eldest, it means that he would be the

Elesin to the next king. It's a family thing isn't it Joseph?

Joseph   Yes madam. And if this Elesin had died before the King, his eldest son must take his place.

Jane   That would explain why the old chief was so mad you took the boy away.

Pilkings   Well it makes me all the more happy I did.

Jane   I wonder if he knew.

Pilkings   Who? Oh, you mean Olunde?

Jane   Yes. Was that why he was so determined to get away? I wouldn't stay if I knew I was trapped in such a horrible custom.

Pilkings (*thoughtfully*)   No, I don't think he knew. At least he gave no indication. But you couldn't really tell with him. He was rather close you know, quite unlike most of them. Didn't give much away, not even to me.

Jane   Aren't they all rather close, Simon?

Pilkings   These natives here? Good gracious. They'll open their mouths and yap with you about their family secrets before you can stop them. Only the other day . . .

Jane   But Simon, do they really give anything away? I mean, anything that really counts. This affair for instance, we didn't know they still practised that custom did we?

Pilkings   Ye-e-es, I suppose you're right there. Sly, devious bastards.

Joseph (*stiffly*)   Can I go now master? I have to clean the kitchen.

Pilkings   What? Oh, you can go. Forgot you were still there.

Joseph *goes.*

Jane   Simon, you really must watch your language. Bastard isn't just a simple swear-word in these parts, you know.

Pilkings   Look, just when did you become a social anthropologist, that's what I'd like to know.

Jane   I'm not claiming to know anything. I just happen to have overheard quarrels among the servants. That's how I know they consider it a smear.

Pilkings   I thought the extended family system took care of all that. Elastic family, no bastards.

Jane (*shrugs*)   Have it your own way.

Awkward silence. The drumming increases in volume. **Jane** *gets up suddenly, restless.*

That drumming Simon, do you think it might really be connected with this ritual? It's been going on all evening.

Pilkings   Let's ask our native guide. Joseph! Just a minute Joseph. (**Joseph** *re-enters.*) What's the drumming about?

Joseph   I don't know master.

Pilkings   What do you mean you don't know? It's only two years since your conversion. Don't tell me all that holy water nonsense also wiped out your tribal memory.

Joseph (*visibly shocked*)   Master!

Jane   Now you've done it.

Pilkings   What have I done now?

Jane   Never mind. Listen Joseph, just tell me this. Is that drumming connected with dying or anything of that nature?

Joseph   Madam, this is what I am trying to say: I am not sure. It sounds like the death of a great chief and then, it sounds like the wedding of a great chief. It really mix me up.

Pilkings   Oh get back to the kitchen. A fat lot of help you are.

Joseph   Yes master. (*Goes.*)

Jane   Simon . . .

Pilkings   All right, all right. I'm in no mood for preaching.

Jane It isn't my preaching you have to worry about, it's the preaching of the missionaries who preceded you here. When they make converts they really convert them. Calling holy water nonsense to our Joseph is really like insulting the Virgin Mary before a Roman Catholic. He's going to hand in his notice tomorrow you mark my word.

Pilkings Now you're being ridiculous.

Jane Am I? What are you willing to bet that tomorrow we are going to be without a steward-boy? Did you see his face?

Pilkings I am more concerned about whether or not we will be one native chief short by tomorrow. Christ! Just listen to those drums. (*He strides up and down, undecided.*)

Jane (*getting up*) I'll change and make up some supper.

Pilkings What's that?

Jane Simon, it's obvious we have to miss this ball.

Pilkings Nonsense. It's the first bit of real fun the European club has managed to organise for over a year, I'm damned if I'm going to miss it. And it is a rather special occasion. Doesn't happen every day.

Jane You know this business has to be stopped Simon. And you are the only man who can do it.

Pilkings I don't have to stop anything. If they want to throw themselves off the top of a cliff or poison themselves for the sake of some barbaric custom what is that to me? If it were ritual murder or something like that I'd be duty-bound to do something. I can't keep an eye on all the potential suicides in this province. And as for that man – believe me it's good riddance.

Jane (*laughs*) I know you better than that Simon. You are going to have to do something to stop it – after you've finished blustering.

Pilkings (*shouts after her*) And suppose after all it's only a wedding? I'd look a proper fool if I interrupted a chief on his honeymoon, wouldn't I? (*Resumes his angry stride, slows down.*) Ah well, who can tell what those chiefs actually do on their honeymoon anyway? (*He takes up the pad and scribbles rapidly on it.*) Joseph! Joseph! Joseph! (*Some moments later* **Joseph** *puts in a sulky appearance.*) Did you hear me call you? Why the hell didn't you answer?

Joseph   I didn't hear master.

Pilkings   You didn't hear me! How come you are here then?

Joseph (*stubbornly*)   I didn't hear master.

Pilkings (*controls himself with an effort*)   We'll talk about it in the morning. I want you to take this note directly to Sergeant Amusa. You'll find him at the charge office. Get on your bicycle and race there with it. I expect you back in twenty minutes exactly. Twenty minutes, is that clear?

Joseph   Yes master. (*Going.*)

Pilkings   Oh er ... Joseph.

Joseph   Yes master?

Pilkings (*between gritted teeth*)   Er ... forget what I said just now. The holy water is not nonsense. *I* was talking nonsense.

Joseph   Yes master. (*Goes.*)

Jane (*pokes her head round the door*)   Have you found him?

Pilkings   Found who?

Jane   Joseph. Weren't you shouting for him?

Pilkings   Oh yes, he turned up finally.

Jane   You sounded desperate. What was it all about?

Pilkings   Oh nothing. I just wanted to apologise to him. Assure him that the holy water isn't really nonsense.

Jane   Oh? And how did he take it?

Pilkings   Who the hell gives a damn! I had a sudden vision of our Very Reverend Macfarlane drafting another letter of complaint to the Resident about my unchristian language towards his parishioners.

Jane Oh I think he's given up on you by now.

Pilkings Don't be too sure. And anyway, I wanted to make sure Joseph didn't 'lose' my note on the way. He looked sufficiently full of the holy crusade to do some such thing.

Jane If you've finished exaggerating, come and have something to eat.

Pilkings No, put it all away. We can still get to the ball.

Jane Simon . . .

Pilkings Get your costume back on. Nothing to worry about. I've instructed Amusa to arrest the man and lock him up.

Jane But that station is hardly secure Simon. He'll soon get his friends to help him escape.

Pilkings A-ah, that's where I have out-thought you. I'm not having him put in the station cell. Amusa will bring him right here and lock him up in my study. And he'll stay with him till we get back. No one will dare come here to incite him to anything.

Jane How clever of you darling. I'll get ready.

Pilkings Hey.

Jane Yes darling.

Pilkings I have a surprise for you. I was going to keep it until we actually got to the ball.

Jane What is it?

Pilkings You know the Prince is on a tour of the colonies don't you? Well, he docked in the capital only this morning but he is already at the Residency. He is going to grace the ball with his presence later tonight.

Jane Simon! Not really.

Pilkings Yes he is. He's been invited to give away the

prizes and he has agreed. You must admit old Engleton is the best Club Secretary we ever had. Quick off the mark that lad.

Jane   But how thrilling.

Pilkings   The other provincials are going to be damned envious.

Jane   I wonder what he'll come as.

Pilkings   Oh I don't know. As a coat-of-arms perhaps. Anyway it won't be anything to touch this.

Jane   Well that's lucky. If we are to be presented I won't have to start looking for a pair of gloves. It's all sewn on.

Pilkings (*laughing*)   Quite right. Trust a woman to think of that. Come on, let's get going.

Jane (*rushing off*)   Won't be a second. (*Stops.*) Now I see why you've been so edgy all evening. I thought you weren't handling this affair with your usual brilliance – to begin with that is.

Pilkings (*his mood is much improved*)   Shut up woman and get your things on.

Jane   All right boss, coming.

Pilkings *suddenly begins to hum the tango to which they were dancing before. Starts to execute a few practice steps. Lights fade.*

Scene Three

A swelling, agitated hum of women's voices rises immediately in the background. The lights come on and we see the frontage of a converted cloth stall in the market. The floor leading up to the entrance is covered in rich velvets and woven cloth. The **Women** *come on stage, borne backwards by the determined progress of Sergeant* **Amusa** *and his two constables who already have their batons out and use them as a pressure against the* **Women**. *At the edge of the cloth-covered floor, however, the* **Women** *take a determined stand and block all further progress of the men. They begin to tease them mercilessly.*

Amusa   I am tell you women for last time to commot my road. I am here on official business.

Woman   Official business you white man's eunuch? Official business is taking place where you want to go and it's a business you wouldn't understand.

Woman   (*makes a quick tug at the constable's baton*)   That doesn't fool anyone you know. It's the one you carry under your government knickers that counts. (*She bends low as if to peep under the baggy shorts. The embarrassed constable quickly puts his knees together. The* **Women** *roar.*)

Woman   You mean there is nothing there at all?

Woman   Oh there was something. You know that handbell which the white man uses to summon his servants . . . ?

Amusa   (*he manages to preserve some dignity throughout*)   I hope you women know that interfering with officer in execution of his duty is criminal offence.

Woman   Interfere? He says we're interfering with him. You foolish man we're telling you there's nothing to interfere with.

Amusa   I am order you now to clear the road.

Woman   What road? The one your father built?

Woman   You are a policeman not so? Then you know what they call trespassing in court. Or – (*Pointing to the cloth-lined steps.*) – do you think that kind of road is built for every kind of feet.

Woman   Go back and tell the white man who sent you to come himself.

Amusa   If I go I will come back with reinforcement. And we will all return carrying weapons.

Woman   Oh, now I understand. Before they can put on those knickers the white man first cuts off their weapons.

Woman   What a cheek! You mean you come here to show power to women and you don't even have a weapon.

Amusa (*shouting above the laughter*) For the last time I warn you women to clear the road.

Woman To where?

Amusa To that hut. I know he dey dere.

Woman Who?

Amusa The chief who call himself Elesin Oba.

Woman You ignorant man. It is not he who calls himself Elesin Oba, it is his blood that says it. As it called out to his father before him and will to his son after him. And that is in spite of everything your white man can do.

Woman Is it not the same ocean that washes this land and the white man's land? Tell your white man he can hide our son away as long as he likes. When the time comes for him, the same ocean will bring him back.

Amusa The government say dat kin' ting must stop.

Woman Who will stop it? You? Tonight our husband and father will prove himself greater than the laws of strangers.

Amusa I tell you nobody go prove anyting tonight or anytime. Is ignorant and criminal to prove dat kin' prove.

Iyaloja (*entering from the hut. She is accompanied by a group of young Girls who have been attending the* **Bride**) What is it Amusa? Why do you come here to disturb the happiness of others.

Amusa Madame Iyaloja, I glad you come. You know me, I no like trouble but duty is duty. I am here to arrest Elesin for criminal intent. Tell these women to stop obstructing me in the performance of my duty.

Iyaloja And you? What gives you the right to obstruct our leader of men in the performance of his duty.

Amusa What kin' duty be dat one Iyaloja.

Iyaloja What kin' duty? What kin' duty does a man have to his new bride?

Amusa (*bewildered, looks at the* **Women** *and at the entrance to the* *hut*)　Iyaloja, is it wedding you call dis kin' ting?

Iyaloja　You have wives haven't you? Whatever the white man has done to you he hasn't stopped you having wives. And if he has, at least he is married. If you don't know what a marriage is, go and ask him to tell you.

Amusa　This no to wedding.

Iyaloja　And ask him at the same time what he would have done if anyone had come to disturb him on his wedding night.

Amusa　Iyaloja, I say dis no to wedding.

Iyaloja　You want to look inside the bridal chamber? You want to see for yourself how a man cuts the virgin knot?

Amusa　Madam . . .

Woman　Perhaps his wives are still waiting for him to learn.

Amusa　Iyaloja, make you tell dese women make den no insult me again. If I hear dat kin' insult once more . . .

Girl (*pushing her way through*)　You will do what?

Girl　He's out of his mind. It's our mothers you're talking to, do you know that? Not to any illiterate villager you can bully and terrorise. How dare you intrude here anyway?

Girl　What a cheek, what impertinence!

Girl　You've treated them too gently. Now let them see what it is to tamper with the mothers of this market.

Girl　Your betters dare not enter the market when the women say no!

Girl　Haven't you learnt that yet, you jester in khaki and starch?

Iyaloja　Daughters . . .

Girl　No no Iyaloja, leave us to deal with him. He no longer knows his mother, we'll teach him.

With a sudden movement they snatch the batons of the two constables.

They begin to hem them in.

Girl   What next? We have your batons? What next? What are you going to do?

With equally swift movements they knock off their hats.

Girl   Move if you dare. We have your hats, what will you do about it? Didn't the white man teach you to take off your hats before women?

Iyaloja   It's a wedding night. It's a night of joy for us. Peace . . .

Girl   Not for him. Who asked him here?

Girl   Does he dare go to the Residency without an invitation?

Girl   Not even where the servants eat the left-overs.

Girls (*in turn. In an 'English' accent*)   Well well it's Mister Amusa. Were you invited? (*Play-acting to one another. The older* **Women** *encourage them with their titters.*)
—Your invitation card please?
—Who are you? Have we been introduced?
—And who did you say you were?
—Sorry, I didn't quite catch your name.
—May I take your hat?
—If you insist. May I take yours? (*Exchanging the policemen's hats.*)
—How very kind of you.
—Not at all. Won't you sit down?
—After you.
—Oh no.
—I insist.
—You're most gracious.
—And how do you find the place?
—The natives are all right.
—Friendly?
—Tractable.
—Not a teeny-weeny bit restless?
—Well, a teeny-weeny bit restless.

—One might even say, difficult?
—Indeed one might be tempted to say, difficult.
—But you do manage to cope?
—Yes indeed I do. I have a rather faithful ox called Amusa.
—He's loyal?
—Absolutely.
—Lay down his life for you what?
—Without a moment's thought.
—Had one like that once. Trust him with my life.
—Mostly of course they are liars.
—Never known a native to tell the truth.
—Does it get rather close around here?
—It's mild for this time of the year.
—But the rains may still come.
—They are late this year aren't they?
—They are keeping African time.
—Ha ha ha ha.
—Ha ha ha ha.
—The humidity is what gets me.
—It used to be whisky.
—Ha ha ha ha.
—Ha ha ha ha.
—What's your handicap old chap?
—Is there racing by golly?
—Splendid golf course, you'll like it.
—I'm beginning to like it already.
—And a European club, exclusive.
—You've kept the flag flying.
—We do our best for the old country.
—It's a pleasure to serve.
—Another whisky old chap?
—You are indeed too too kind.
—Not at all sir. Where is that boy? (*With a sudden bellow.*)
Sergeant!

Amusa (*snaps to attention*)   Yessir!

The **Women** *collapse with laughter.*

Girl   Take your men out of here.

Amusa (*realising the trick, he rages from loss of face*) I'm give you warning . . .

Girl All right then. Off with his knickers! (*They surge slowly forward.*)

Iyaloja Daughters, please.

Amusa (*squaring himself for defence*) The first woman wey touch me.

Iyaloja My children, I beg of you . . .

Girl Then tell him to leave this market. This is the home of our mothers. We don't want the eater of white left-overs at the feast their hands have prepared.

Iyaloja You heard them Amusa. You had better go.

Girl Now!

Amusa (*commencing his retreat*) We dey go now, but make you no say we no warn you.

Girl Now!

Girl Before we read the riot act – you should know all about that.

Amusa Make we go. (*They depart, more precipitately.*)

The **Women** *strike their palms across in the gesture of wonder.*

Women Do they teach you all that at school?

Woman And to think I nearly kept Apinke away from the place.

Woman Did you hear them? Did you see how they mimicked the white man?

Woman The voices exactly. Hey, there are wonders in this world!

Iyaloja Well, our elders have said it: Dada may be weak, but he has a younger sibling who is truly fearless.

Woman The next time the white man shows his face in this market I will set Wuraola on his tail.

A **Woman** *bursts into song and dance of euphoria* – *'Tani l'awa o l'ogbeja? Kayi! A l'ogbeja. Omo Kekere l'ogbeja.'** The rest of the* **Women** *join in, some placing the* **Girls** *on their back like infants, others dancing round them. The dance becomes general, mounting in excitement.* **Elesin** *appears, in wrapper only. In his hands a white velvet cloth folded loosely as if it held some delicate object. He cries out.*

Elesin   Oh you mothers of beautiful brides! (*The dancing stops. They turn and see him, and the object in his hands.* **Iyaloja** *approaches and gently takes the cloth from him.*) Take it. It is no mere virgin stain, but the union of life and the seeds of passage. My vital flow, the last from this flesh is intermingled with the promise of future life. All is prepared. Listen! (*A steady drumbeat from the distance.*) Yes. It is nearly time. The King's dog has been killed. The King's favourite horse is about to follow his master. My brother chiefs know their task and perform it well. (*He listens again.*)

The **Bride** *emerges, stands shyly by the door. He turns to her.*

Elesin   Our marriage is not yet wholly fulfilled. When earth and passage wed, the consummation is complete only when there are grains of earth on the eyelids of passage. Stay by me till then. My faithful drummers, do me your last service. This is where I have chosen to do my leave-taking, in this heart of life, this hive which contains the swarm of the world in its small compass. This is where I have known love and laughter away from the palace. Even the richest food cloys when eaten days on end; in the market, nothing ever cloys. Listen. (*They listen to the drums.*) They have begun to seek out the heart of the King's favourite horse. Soon it will ride in its bolt of raffia with the dog at its feet. Together they will ride on the shoulders of the King's grooms through the pulse centres of the town. They know it is here I shall await them. I have told them (*His eyes appear to cloud. He passes his hand over them as if to clear his sight. He gives a faint smile.*) It promises well; just then I felt my spirit's eagerness. The kite makes for wide spaces and

---

* 'Who says we haven't a defender? Silence! We have our defenders. Little children are our champions.'

the wind creeps up behind its tail; can the kite say less than –
thank you, the quicker the better? But wait a while my spirit.
Wait. Wait for the coming of the courier of the King. Do you
know, friends, the horse is born to this one destiny, to bear
the burden that is man upon its back. Except for this night,
this night alone when the spotless stallion will ride in triumph
on the back of man. In the time of my father I witnessed the
strange sight. Perhaps tonight also I shall see it for the last
time. If they arrive before the drums beat for me, I shall tell
them to let the Alafin know I follow swiftly. If they come after
the drums have sounded, why then, all is well for I have gone
ahead. Our spirits shall fall in step along the great passage.
(*He listens to the drums. He seems again to be falling into a state of
semi-hypnosis; his eyes scan the sky but it is in a kind of daze. His
voice is a little breathless.*) The moon has fed, a glow from its full
stomach fills the sky and air, but I cannot tell where is that
gateway through which I must pass. My faithful friends, let
our feet touch together this last time, lead me into the other
market with sounds that cover my skin with down yet make
my limbs strike earth like a thoroughbred. Dear mothers, let
me dance into the passage even as I have lived beneath your
roofs.

*He comes down progressively among them. They make way for him, the
drummers playing. His dance is one of solemn, regal motions, each gesture
of the body is made with a solemn finality. The* **Women** *join him,
their steps a somewhat more fluid version of his. Beneath the* **Praise-
Singer**'s *exhortations the* **Women** *dirge 'Ale le le, awo mi lo'.*

Praise-Singer
Elesin Alafin, can you hear my voice?

Elesin
Faintly, my friend, faintly.

Praise-Singer
Elesin Alafin, can you hear my call?

Elesin
Faintly my King, faintly.

Praise-Singer

Is your memory sound Elesin?
Shall my voice be a blade of grass and
Tickle the armpit of the past?

Elesin

My memory needs no prodding but
What do you wish to say to me?

Praise-Singer

Only what has been spoken. Only what concerns
The dying wish of the father of all.

Elesin

It is buried like seed-yam in my mind.
This is the season of quick rains, the harvest
Is this moment due for gathering.

Praise-Singer

If you cannot come, I said, swear
You'll tell my favourite horse. I shall
Ride on through the gates alone.

Elesin

Elesin's message will be read
Only when his loyal heart no longer beats.

Praise-Singer

If you cannot come Elesin, tell my dog.
I cannot stay the keeper too long
At the gate.

Elesin

A dog does not outrun the hand
That feeds it meat. A horse that throws its rider
Slows down to a stop. Elesin Alafin
Trusts no beasts with messages between
A king and his companion.

Praise-Singer

If you get lost my dog will track
The hidden path to me.

Elesin

The seven-way crossroads confuses

Only the stranger. The Horseman of the King
Was born in the recesses of the house.

Praise-Singer
I know the wickedness of men. If there is
Weight on the loose end of your sash, such weight
As no mere man can shift; if your sash is earthed
By evil minds who mean to part us at the last . . .

Elesin
My sash is of the deep purple alari;
It is no tethering-rope. The elephant
Trails no tethering-rope; that king
Is not yet crowned who will peg an elephant –
Not even you my friend and King.

Praise-Singer
And yet this fear will not depart from me,
The darkness of this new abode is deep –
Will your human eyes suffice?

Elesin
In a night which falls before our eyes
However deep, we do not miss our way.

Praise-Singer
Shall I now not acknowledge I have stood
Where wonders met their end? The elephant deserves
Better than that we say 'I have caught
A glimpse of something'. If we see the tamer
Of the forest let us say plainly, we have seen
An elephant.

Elesin (*his voice is drowsy*)
I have freed myself of earth and now
It's getting dark. Strange voices guide my feet.

Praise-Singer
The river is never so high that the eyes
Of a fish are covered. The night is not so dark
That the albino fails to find his way. A child
Returning homewards craves no leading by the hand.

Gracefully does the mask regain his grove at the end of the
day . . .
Gracefully. Gracefully does the mask dance
Homeward at the end of the day, gracefully . . .

Elesin's trance appears to be deepening, his steps heavier.

Iyaloja
It is the death of war that kills the valiant,
Death of water is how the swimmer goes.
It is the death of markets that kills the trader
And death of indecision takes the idle away.
The trade of the cutlass blunts its edge
And the beautiful die the death of beauty.
It takes an Elesin to die the death of death . . .
Only Elesin . . . dies the unknowable death of death . . .
Gracefully, gracefully does the horseman regain
The stables at the end of day, gracefully . . .

Praise-Singer   How shall I tell what my eyes have seen?
The Horseman gallops on before the courier, how shall I tell
what my eyes have seen? He says a dog may be confused by
new scents of beings he never dreamt of, so he must precede
the dog to heaven. He says a horse may stumble on strange
boulders and be lamed, so he races on before the horse to
heaven. It is best, he says, to trust no messenger who may
falter at the outer gate; oh how shall I tell what my ears have
heard? But do you hear me still Elesin, do you hear your
faithful one?

*Elesin in his motions appears to feel for a direction of sound, subtly,
but he only sinks deeper into his trance-dance.*

Praise-Singer   Elesin Alafin, I no longer sense your flesh.
The drums are changing now but you have gone far ahead of
the world. It is not yet noon in heaven; let those who claim it
is begin their own journey home. So why must you rush like
an impatient bride: why do you race to desert your Olohun-
iyo?

*Elesin is now sunk fully deep in his trance, there is no longer sign of
any awareness of his surroundings.*

Praise-Singer   Does the deep voice of gbedu cover you

then, like the passage of royal elephants? Those drums that
brook no rivals, have they blocked the passage to your ears
that my voice passes into wind, a mere leaf floating in the
night? Is your flesh lightened Elesin, is that lump of earth I
slid between your slippers to keep you longer slowly sifting
from your feet? Are the drums on the other side now tuning
skin to skin with ours in osugbo? Are there sounds there I
cannot hear, do footsteps surround you which pound the earth
like gbedu, roll like thunder round the dome of the world? Is
the darkness gathering in your head Elesin? Is there now a
streak of light at the end of the passage, a light I dare not
look upon? Does it reveal whose voices we often heard, whose
touches we often felt, whose wisdoms come suddenly into the
mind when the wisest have shaken their heads and murmured,
It cannot be done? Elesin Alafin, don't think I do not know
why your lips are heavy, why your limbs are drowsy as palm
oil in the cold of harmattan. I would call you back but when
the elephant heads for the jungle, the tail is too small a
handhold for the hunter that would pull him back. The sun
that heads for the sea no longer heeds the prayers of the
farmer. When the river begins to taste the salt of the ocean,
we no longer know what deity to call on, the river-god or
Olokun. No arrow flies back to the string, the child does not
return through the same passage that gave it birth. Elesin
Oba, can you hear me at all? Your eyelids are glazed like a
courtesan's, is it that you see the dark groom and master of
life? And will you see my father? Will you tell him that I
stayed with you to the last? Will my voice ring in your ears
awhile, will you remember Olohun-iyo even if the music on
the other side surpasses his mortal craft? But will they know
you over there? Have they eyes to gauge your worth, have
they the heart to love you, will they know what thoroughbred
prances towards them in caparisons of honour? If they do not
Elesin, if any there cuts your yam with a small knife, or pours
you wine in a small calabash, turn back and return to
welcoming hands. If the world were not greater than the
wishes of Olohun-iyo, I would not let you go . . .

He appears to break down. **Elesin** *dances on, completely in a trance.*
The dirge wells up louder and stronger. **Elesin**'s *dance does not lose its*

elasticity but his gestures become, if possible, even more weighty. Lights fade slowly on the scene.

Scene Four

A masque. The front side of the stage is part of a wide corridor around the great hall of the Residency extending beyond vision into the rear and wings. It is redolent of the tawdry decadence of a far-flung but key imperial frontier. The couples in a variety of fancy-dress are ranged around the walls, gazing in the same direction. The guest-of-honour is about to make an appearance. A portion of the local police brass band with its white conductor is just visible. At last, the entrance of Royalty. The band plays 'Rule Britannia', badly, beginning long before he is visible. The couples bow and curtsey as he passes by them. Both he and his companions are dressed in seventeenth-century European costume. Following behind are the Resident and his partner similarly attired. As they gain the end of the hall where the orchestra dais begins the music comes to an end. The Prince bows to the guests. The band strikes up a Viennese waltz and the Prince formally opens the floor. Several bars later the Resident and his companion follow suit. Others follow in appropriate pecking order. The orchestra's waltz rendition is not of the highest musical standard.

Some time later the Prince dances again into view and is settled into a corner by the Resident who then proceeds to select couples as they dance past for introduction, sometimes threading his way through the dancers to tap the lucky couple on the shoulder. Desperate efforts from many to ensure that they are recognised in spite of, perhaps, their costume. The ritual of introductions soon takes in Pilkings and his wife. The Prince is quite fascinated by their costume and they demonstrate the adaptations they have made to it, pulling down the mask to demonstrate how the egungun normally appears, then showing the various press-button controls they have innovated for the face flaps, the sleeves, etc. They demonstrate the dance steps and the guttural sounds made by the egungun, harass other dancers in the hall, Mrs Pilkings playing the 'restrainer' to Pilkings' manic darts. Everyone is highly entertained, the Royal Party especially who lead the applause.

At this point a liveried footman comes in with a note on a salver and is intercepted almost absent-mindedly by the **Resident** *who takes the note and reads it. After polite coughs he succeeds in excusing the* **Pilkings** *from the* **Prince** *and takes them aside. The* **Prince** *considerately offers the* **Resident**'s *wife his hand and dancing is resumed.*

On their way out the **Resident** *gives an order to his* **Aide-de-Camp**. *They come into the side corridor where the* **Resident** *hands the note to* **Pilkings**.

Resident As you see it says 'emergency' on the outside. I took the liberty of opening it because His Highness was obviously enjoying the entertainment. I didn't want to interrupt unless really necessary.

Pilkings Yes, yes of course, sir.

Resident Is it really as bad as it says? What's it all about?

Pilkings Some strange custom they have, sir. It seems because the King is dead some important chief has to commit suicide.

Resident The King? Isn't it the same one who died nearly a month ago?

Pilkings Yes, sir.

Resident Haven't they buried him yet?

Pilkings They take their time about these things, sir. The pre-burial ceremonies last nearly thirty days. It seems tonight is the final night.

Resident But what has it got to do with the market women? Why are they rioting? We've waived that troublesome tax haven't we?

Pilkings We don't quite know that they are exactly rioting yet, sir. Sergeant Amusa is sometimes prone to exaggerations.

Resident He sounds desperate enough. That comes out even in his rather quaint grammar. Where is the man anyway? I asked my aide-de-camp to bring him here.

Pilkings They are probably looking in the wrong verandah. I'll fetch him myself.

Resident No no you stay here. Let your wife go and look for them. Do you mind my dear . . . ?

Jane Certainly not, your Excellency. (*Goes.*)

Resident You should have kept me informed, Pilkings. You realise how disastrous it would have been if things had erupted while His Highness was here.

Pilkings I wasn't aware of the whole business until tonight, sir.

Resident Nose to the ground Pilkings, nose to the ground. If we all let these little things slip past us where would the empire be eh? Tell me that. Where would we all be?

Pilkings (*low voice*) Sleeping peacefully at home I bet.

Resident What did you say, Pilkings?

Pilkings It won't happen again, sir.

Resident It mustn't, Pilkings. It mustn't. Where is that damned sergeant? I ought to get back to His Highness as quickly as possible and offer him some plausible explanation for my rather abrupt conduct. Can you think of one, Pilkings?

Pilkings You could tell him the truth, sir.

Resident I could? No no no Pilkings, that would never do. What! Go and tell him there is a riot just two miles away from him? This is supposed to be a secure colony of His Majesty, Pilkings.

Pilkings Yes, sir.

Resident Ah, there they are. No, these are not our native police. Are these the ring-leaders of the riot?

Pilkings Sir, these are my police officers.

Resident Oh, I beg your pardon officers. You do look a little . . . I say, isn't there something missing in their uniform? I think they used to have some rather colourful sashes. If I remember rightly I recommended them myself in my young days in the service. A bit of colour always appeals to the natives, yes, I remember putting that in my report. Well well well, where are we? Make your report man.

Pilkings (*moves close to* **Amusa**, *between his teeth*)   And let's have no more superstitious nonsense from you Amusa or I'll throw you in the guardroom for a month and feed you pork!

Resident   What's that? What has pork to do with it?

Pilkings   Sir, I was just warning him to be brief. I'm sure you are most anxious to hear his report.

Resident   Yes yes yes of course. Come on man, speak up. Hey, didn't we give them some colourful fez hats with all those wavy things, yes, pink tassels . . .

Pilkings   Sir, I think if he was permitted to make his report we might find that he lost his hat in the riot.

Resident   Ah yes indeed. I'd better tell His Highness that. Lost his hat in the riot, ha ha. He'll probably say well, as long as he didn't lose his head. (*Chuckles to himself.*) Don't forget to send me a report first thing in the morning young Pilkings.

Pilkings   No, sir.

Resident   And whatever you do, don't let things get out of hand. Keep a cool head and – nose to the ground Pilkings. (*Wanders off in the general direction of the hall.*)

Pilkings   Yes, sir.

Aide-de-Camp   Would you be needing me, sir?

Pilkings   No thanks, Bob. I think His Excellency's need of you is greater than ours.

Aide-de-Camp   We have a detachment of soldiers from the capital, sir. They accompanied His Highness up here.

Pilkings   I doubt if it will come to that but, thanks, I'll bear it in mind. Oh, could you send an orderly with my cloak.

Aide-de-Camp   Very good, sir. (*Goes.*)

Pilkings   Now, sergeant.

Amusa Sir ... (*Makes an effort, stops dead. Eyes to the ceiling.*)

Pilkings Oh, not again.

Amusa I cannot against death to dead cult. This dress get power of dead.

Pilkings All right, let's go. You are relieved of all further duty Amusa. Report to me first thing in the morning.

Jane Shall I come, Simon?

Pilkings No, there's no need for that. If I can get back later I will. Otherwise get Bob to bring you home.

Jane Be careful Simon ... I mean, be clever.

Pilkings Sure I will. You two, come with me. (*As he turns to go, the clock in the Residency begins to chime.* **Pilkings** *looks at his watch then turns, horror-stricken, to stare at his wife. The same thought clearly occurs to her. He swallows hard. An orderly brings his cloak.*) It's midnight. I had no idea it was that late.

Jane But surely ... they don't count the hours the way we do. The moon, or something ...

Pilkings I am ... not so sure.

He turns and breaks into a sudden run. The two constables follow, also at a run. **Amusa**, *who has kept his eyes on the ceiling throughout, waits until the last of the footsteps has faded out of hearing. He salutes suddenly, but without once looking in the direction of the woman.*

Amusa Goodnight, madam.

Jane Oh. (*She hesitates.*) Amusa ... (*He goes off without seeming to have heard.*) Poor Simon ...

A figure emerges from the shadows, a young black man dressed in a sober western suit. He peeps into the hall, trying to make out the figures of the dancers.

Jane Who is that?

Olunde (*emerges into the light*) I didn't mean to startle you madam. I am looking for the District Officer.

Jane Wait a minute . . . don't I know you? Yes, you are
Olunde, the young man who . . .

Olunde Mrs Pilkings! How fortunate. I came here to look
for your husband.

Jane Olunde! Let's look at you. What a fine young man
you've become. Grand but solemn. Good God, when did you
return? Simon never said a word. But you do look well
Olunde. Really!

Olunde You are . . . well, you look quite well yourself Mrs
Pilkings. From what little I can see of you.

Jane Oh, this. It's caused quite a stir I assure you, and not
all of it very pleasant. You are not shocked I hope?

Olunde Why should I be? But don't you find it rather hot
in there? Your skin must find it difficult to breathe.

Jane Well, it is a little hot I must confess, but it's all in a
good cause.

Olunde What cause Mrs Pilkings?

Jane All this. The ball. And His Highness being here in
person and all that.

Olunde (*mildly*) And that is the good cause for which you
desecrate an ancestral mask?

Jane Oh, so you are shocked after all. How disappointing.

Olunde No I am not shocked, Mrs Pilkings. You forget that
I have now spent four years among your people. I discovered
that you have no respect for what you do not understand.

Jane Oh. So you've returned with a chip on your shoulder.
That's a pity Olunde. I am sorry.

An uncomfortable silence follows.

I take it then that you did not find you stay in England
altogether edifying.

Olunde I don't say that. I found your people quite
admirable in many ways, their conduct and courage in this

war for instance.

Jane Ah yes, the war. Here of course it is all rather remote.
From time to time we have a black-out drill just to remind us
that there is a war on. And the rare convoy passes through on
its way somewhere or on manoeuvres. Mind you there is the
occasional bit of excitement like that ship that was blown up
in the harbour.

Olunde Here? Do you mean through enemy action?

Jane Oh no, the war hasn't come that close. The captain
did it himself. I don't quite understand it really. Simon tried
to explain. The ship had to be blown up because it had
become dangerous to other ships, even to the city itself.
Hundreds of the coastal population would have died.

Olunde Maybe it was loaded with ammunition and had
caught fire. Or some of those lethal gases they've been
experimenting on.

Jane Something like that. The captain blew himself up with
it. Deliberately. Simon said someone had to remain on board
to light the fuse.

Olunde It must have been a very short fuse.

Jane (*shrugs*) I don't know much about it. Only that there
was no other way to save lives. No time to devise anything
else. The captain took the decision and carried it out.

Olunde Yes . . . I quite believe it. I met men like that in
England.

Jane Oh just look at me! Fancy welcoming you back with
such morbid news. Stale too. It was at least six months ago.

Olunde I don't find it morbid at all. I find it rather
inspiring. It is an affirmative commentary on life.

Jane What is?

Olunde That captain's self-sacrifice.

Jane Nonsense. Life should never be thrown deliberately
away.

Olunde   And the innocent people around the harbour?

Jane   Oh, how does one know? The whole thing was probably exaggerated anyway.

Olunde   That was a risk the captain couldn't take. But please Mrs Pilkings, do you think you could find your husband for me? I have to talk to him.

Jane   Simon? (*As she recollects for the first time the full significance of* **Olunde***'s presence.*) Simon is . . . there is a little problem in town. He was sent for. But . . . when did you arrive? Does Simon know you're here?

Olunde (*suddenly earnest*)   I need your help Mrs Pilkings. I've always found you somewhat more understanding than your husband. Please find him for me and when you do, you must help me talk to him.

Jane   I'm afraid I don't quite . . . follow you. Have you seen my husband already?

Olunde   I went to your house. Your houseboy told me you were here. (*He smiles.*) He even told me how I would recognise you and Mr Pilkings.

Jane   Then you must know what my husband is trying to do for you.

Olunde   For me?

Jane   For you. For your people. And to think he didn't even know you were coming back! But how do you happen to be here? Only this evening we were talking about you. We thought you were still four thousand miles away.

Olunde   I was sent a cable.

Jane   A cable? Who did? Simon? The business of your father didn't begin till tonight.

Olunde   A relation sent it weeks ago, and it said nothing about my father. All it said was, Our King is dead. But I knew I had to return home at once so as to bury my father. I understood that.

Jane Well, thank God you don't have to go through that agony. Simon is going to stop it.

Olunde That's why I want to see him. He's wasting his time. And since he has been so helpful to me I don't want him to incur the enmity of our people. Especially over nothing.

Jane (*sits down open-mouthed*) You . . . you Olunde!

Olunde Mrs Pilkings, I came home to bury my father. As soon as I heard the news I booked my passage home. In fact we were fortunate. We travelled in the same convoy as your Prince, so we had excellent protection.

Jane But you don't think your father is also entitled to whatever protection is available to him?

Olunde How can I make you understand? He *has* protection. No one can undertake what he does tonight without the deepest protection the mind can conceive. What can you offer him in place of his peace of mind, in place of the honour and veneration of his own people? What would you think of your Prince if he refused to accept the risk of losing his life on this voyage? This . . . showing-the-flag tour of colonial possessions.

Jane I see. So it isn't just medicine you studied in England.

Olunde Yet another error into which your people fall. You believe that everything which appears to make sense was learnt from you.

Jane Not so fast Olunde. You have learnt to argue I can tell that, but I never said you made sense. However clearly you try to put it, it is still a barbaric custom. It is even worse – it's feudal! The King dies and a chieftain must be buried with him. How feudalistic can you get!

Olunde (*waves his hand towards the background. The* **Prince** *is dancing past again – to a different step – and all the guests are bowing and curtseying as he passes*) And this? Even in the midst of a devastating war, look at that. What name would you give to that?

Jane   Therapy, British style. The preservation of sanity in the midst of chaos.

Olunde   Others would call it decadence. However, it doesn't really interest me. You white races know how to survive; I've seen proof of that. By all logical and natural laws this war should end with all the white races wiping out one another, wiping out their so-called civilisation for all time and reverting to a state of primitivism the like of which has so far only existed in your imagination when you thought of us. I thought all that at the beginning. Then I slowly realised that your greatest art is the art of survival. But at least have the humility to let others survive in their own way.

Jane   Through ritual suicide?

Olunde   Is that worse than mass suicide? Mrs Pilkings, what do you call what those young men are sent to do by their generals in this war? Of course you have also mastered the art of calling things by names which don't remotely describe them.

Jane   You talk! You people with your long-winded, roundabout way of making conversation.

Olunde   Mrs Pilkings, whatever we do, we never suggest that a thing is the opposite of what it really is. In your newsreels I heard defeats, thorough, murderous defeats described as strategic victories. No wait, it wasn't just on your newsreels. Don't forget I was attached to hospitals all the time. Hordes of your wounded passed through those wards. I spoke to them. I spent long evenings by their bedsides while they spoke terrible truths of the realities of that war. I know now how history is made.

Jane   But surely, in a war of this nature, for the morale of the nation you must expect . . .

Olunde   That a disaster beyond human reckoning be spoken of as a triumph? No. I mean, is there no mourning in the home of the bereaved that such blasphemy is permitted?

Jane   (*after a moment's pause*)   Perhaps I can understand you now. The time we picked for you was not really one for seeing us at our best.

Olunde Don't think it was just the war. Before that even started I had plenty of time to study your people. I saw nothing, finally, that gave you the right to pass judgement on other peoples and their ways. Nothing at all.

Jane *(hesitantly)* Was it the . . . colour thing? I know there is some discrimination.

Olunde Don't make it so simple, Mrs Pilkings. You make it sound as if when I left, I took nothing at all with me.

Jane Yes . . . and to tell the truth, only this evening, Simon and I agreed that we never really knew what you left with.

Olunde Neither did I. But I found out over there. I am grateful to your country for that. And I will never give it up.

Jane Olunde, please . . . promise me something. Whatever you do, don't throw away what you have started to do. You want to be a doctor. My husband and I believe you will make an excellent one, sympathetic and competent. Don't let anything make you throw away your training.

Olunde *(genuinely surprised)* Of course not. What a strange idea. I intend to return and complete my training. Once the burial of my father is over.

Jane Oh, please. . . !

Olunde Listen! Come outside. You can't hear anything against that music.

Jane What is it?

Olunde The drums. Can you hear the drums? Listen.

The drums come over, still distant but more distinct. There is a change of rhythm, it rises to a crescendo and then, suddenly, it is cut off. After a silence, a new beat begins, slow and resonant.

Olunde There it's all over.

Jane You mean he's . . .

Olunde   Yes, Mrs Pilkings, my father is dead. His will-power has always been enormous; I know he is dead.

Jane (*screams*)   How can you be so callous! So unfeeling! You announce your father's own death like a surgeon looking down on some strange . . . stranger's body! You're just a savage like all the rest.

Aide-de-Camp (*rushing out*)   Mrs Pilkings. Mrs Pilkings. (*She breaks down, sobbing.*) Are you all right, Mrs Pilkings?

Olunde   She'll be all right. (*Turns to go.*)

Aide-de-Camp   Who are you? And who the hell asked your opinion?

Olunde   You're quite right, nobody. (*Going.*)

Aide-de-Camp   What the hell! Did you hear me ask you who you were?

Olunde   I have business to attend to.

Aide-de-Camp   I'll give you business in a moment you impudent nigger. Answer my question!

Olunde   I have a funeral to arrange. Excuse me. (*Going.*)

Aide-de-Camp   I said stop! Orderly!

Jane   No, no, don't do that. I'm all right. And for heaven's sake don't act so foolishly. He's a family friend.

Aide-de-Camp   Well he'd better learn to answer civil questions when he's asked them. These natives put a suit on and they get high opinions of themselves.

Olunde   Can I go now?

Jane   No no don't go. I must talk to you. I'm sorry about what I said.

Olunde   It's nothing, Mrs Pilkings. And I'm really anxious to go. I couldn't see my father before, it's forbidden for me, his heir and successor, to set eyes on him from the moment of the King's death. But now . . . I would like to touch his body while it is still warm.

Jane   You will. I promise I shan't keep you long. Only, I couldn't possibly let you go like that. Bob, please excuse us.

Aide-de-Camp   If you're sure . . .

Jane   Of course I'm sure. Something happened to upset me just then, but I'm all right now. Really.

The **Aide-de-Camp** *goes, somewhat reluctantly.*

Olunde   I mustn't stay long.

Jane   Please, I promise not to keep you. It's just that . . . oh you saw yourself what happens to one in this place. The Resident's man thought he was being helpful, that's the way we all react. But I can't go in among that crowd just now and if I stay by myself somebody will come looking for me. Please, just say something for a few moments and then you can go. Just so I can recover myself.

Olunde   What do you want me to say?

Jane   Your calm acceptance for instance, can you explain that? It was so unnatural. I don't understand that at all. I feel a need to understand all I can.

Olunde   But you explained it yourself. My medical training perhaps. I have seen death too often. And the soldiers who returned from the front, they died on our hands all the time.

Jane   No. It has to be more than that. I feel it has to do with the many things we don't really grasp about your people. At least you can explain.

Olunde   All these things are part of it. And anyway, my father has been dead in my mind for nearly a month. Ever since I learnt of the King's death. I've lived with my bereavement so long now that I cannot think of him alive. On that journey on the boat, I kept my mind on my duties as the one who must perform the rites over his body. I went through it all again and again in my mind as he himself had taught me. I didn't want to do anything wrong, something which might jeopardise the welfare of my people.

Jane   But he had disowned you. When you left he swore

publicly you were no longer his son.

Olunde   I told you, he was a man of tremendous will. Sometimes that's another way of saying stubborn. But among our people, you don't disown a child just like that. Even if I had died before him I would still be buried like his eldest son. But it's time for me to go.

Jane   Thank you. I feel calmer. Don't let me keep you from your duties.

Olunde   Goodnight, Mrs Pilkings.

Jane   Welcome home.

She holds out her hand. As he takes it footsteps are heard approaching the drive. A short while later a woman's sobbing is also heard.

Pilkings (*off*)   Keep them here till I get back. (*He strides into view, reacts at the sight of* **Olunde** *but turns to his wife.*) Thank goodness you're still here.

Jane   Simon, what happened?

Pilkings   Later Jane, please. Is Bob still here?

Jane   Yes, I think so. I'm sure he must be.

Pilkings   Try and get him out here as quickly as you can. Tell him it's urgent.

Jane   Of course. Oh Simon, you remember . . .

Pilkings   Yes yes. I can see who it is. Get Bob out here. (*She runs off.*) At first I thought I was seeing a ghost.

Olunde   Mr Pilkings, I appreciate what you tried to do. I want you to believe that. I can tell you it would have been a terrible calamity if you'd succeeded.

Pilkings (*opens his mouth several times, shuts it*)   You . . . said what?

Olunde   A calamity for us, the entire people.

Pilkings (*sighs*)   I see. Hm.

Olunde   And now I must go. I must see him before he

turns cold.

Pilkings Oh ah . . . em . . . but this is a shock to see you. I mean er thinking all this while you were in England and thanking God for that.

Olunde I came on the mail boat. We travelled in the Prince's convoy.

Pilkings Ah yes, a-ah, hm . . . er well . . .

Olunde Goodnight. I can see you are shocked by the whole business. But you must know by now there are things you cannot understand – or help.

Pilkings Yes. Just a minute. There are armed policemen that way and they have instructions to let no one pass. I suggest you wait a little. I'll er . . . give you an escort.

Olunde That's very kind of you. But do you think it could be quickly arranged.

Pilkings Of course. In fact, yes, what I'll do is send Bob over with some men to the er . . . place. You can go with them. Here he comes now. Excuse me a minute.

Aide-de-Camp Anything wrong sir?

Pilkings (*takes him to one side*) Listen Bob, that cellar in the disused annexe of the Residency, you know, where the slaves were stored before being taken down to the coast . . .

Aide-de-Camp Oh yes, we use it as a storeroom for broken furniture.

Pilkings But it's still got the bars on it?

Aide-de-Camp Oh yes, they are quite intact.

Pilkings Get the keys please. I'll explain later. And I want a strong guard over the Residency tonight.

Aide-de-Camp We have that already. The detachment from the coast . . .

Pilkings No, I don't want them at the gates of the Residency. I want you to deploy them at the bottom of the hill, a long way from the main hall so they can deal with any situation long before the sound carries to the house.

Aide-de-Camp   Yes of course.

Pilkings   I don't want His Highness alarmed.

Aide-de-Camp   You think the riot will spread here?

Pilkings   It's unlikely but I don't want to take a chance. I made them believe I was going to lock the man up in my house, which was what I had planned to do in the first place. They are probably assailing it by now. I took a roundabout route here so I don't think there is any danger at all. At least not before dawn. Nobody is to leave the premises of course – the native employees I mean. They'll soon smell something is up and they can't keep their mouths shut.

Aide-de-Camp   I'll give instructions at once.

Pilkings   I'll take the prisoner down myself. Two policemen will stay with him throughout the night. Inside the cell.

Aide-de-Camp   Right sir. (*Salutes and goes off at the double.*)

Pilkings   Jane. Bob is coming back in a moment with a detachment. Until he gets back please stay with Olunde. (*He makes an extra warning gesture with his eyes.*)

Olunde   Please, Mr Pilkings . . .

Pilkings   I hate to be stuffy old son, but we have a crisis on our hands. It has to do with your father's affair if you must know. And it happens also at a time when we have His Highness here. I am responsible for security so you'll simply have to do as I say. I hope that's understood. (*Marches off quickly, in the direction from which he made his first appearance.*)

Olunde   What's going on? All this can't be just because he failed to stop my father killing himself.

Jane   I honestly don't know. Could it have sparked off a riot?

Olunde   No. If he'd succeeded that would be more likely to start the riot. Perhaps there were other factors involved. Was there a chieftaincy dispute?

Jane   None that I know of.

Elesin (*an animal bellow from off*)   Leave me alone! Is it not enough that you have covered me in shame! White man, take your hand from my body!

Olunde *stands frozen to the spot.* **Jane,** *understanding at last, tries to move him.*

Jane   Let's go in. It's getting chilly out here.

Pilkings (*off*)   Carry him.

Elesin   Give me back the name you have taken away from me you ghost from the land of the nameless!

Pilkings   Carry him! I can't have a disturbance here. Quickly! stuff up his mouth.

Jane   Oh God! Let's go in. Please Olunde.

Olunde *does not move.*

Elesin   Take your albino's hand from me you . . .

Sounds of a struggle. His voice chokes as he is gagged.

Olunde (*quietly*)   That was my father's voice.

Jane   Oh you poor orphan, what have you come home to?

There is a sudden explosion of rage from off-stage and powerful steps come running up the drive.

Pilkings   You bloody fools, after him!

Immediately **Elesin,** *in handcuffs, comes pounding in the direction of* **Jane** *and* **Olunde,** *followed some moments afterwards by* **Pilkings** *and the constables.* **Elesin,** *confronted by the seeming statue of his son, stops dead.* **Olunde** *stares above his head into the distance. The constables try to grab him.* **Jane** *screams at them.*

Jane   Leave him alone! Simon, tell them to leave him alone.

Pilkings   All right, stand aside you. (*Shrugs.*) Maybe just as well. It might help to calm him down.

For several moments they hold the same position. **Elesin** *moves a step forward, almost as if he's still in doubt.*

Elesin   Olunde? (*He moves his head, inspecting him from side to side.*) Olunde! (*He collapses slowly at* **Olunde**'s *feet.*) Oh son, don't let the sight of your father turn you blind!

Olunde (*he moves for the first time since he heard his voice, brings his head slowly down to look on him*)   I have no father, eater of leftovers.

He walks slowly down the way his father had run. Light fades out on **Elesin**, *sobbing into the ground.*

Scene Five

A wide iron-barred gate stretches almost the whole width of the cell in which **Elesin** *is imprisoned. His wrists are encased in thick iron bracelets, chained together; he stands against the bars, looking out. Seated on the ground to one side on the outside is his recent* **Bride**, *her eyes bent perpetually to the ground. Figures of the two guards can be seen deeper inside the cell, alert to every movement* **Elesin** *makes.* **Pilkings**, *now in a police officer's uniform, enters noiselessly, observes him a while. Then he coughs ostentatiously and approaches. Leans against the bars near a corner, his back to* **Elesin**. *He is obviously trying to fall in mood with him. Some moments' silence.*

Pilkings   You seem fascinated by the moon.

Elesin (*after a pause*)   Yes, ghostly one. Your twin-brother up there engages my thoughts.

Pilkings   It is a beautiful night.

Elesin   Is that so?

Pilkings   The light on the leaves, the peace of the night . . .

Elesin   The night is not at peace, District Officer.

Pilkings   No? I would have said it was. You know, quiet . . .

Elesin   And does quiet mean peace for you?

Pilkings   Well, nearly the same thing. Naturally there is a subtle difference . . .

Elesin   The night is not at peace, ghostly one. The world is not at peace. You have shattered the peace of the world for ever. There is no sleep in the world tonight.

Pilkings   It is still a good bargain if the world should lose one night's sleep as the price of saving a man's life.

Elesin   You did not save my life, District Officer. You destroyed it.

Pilkings   Now come on . . .

Elesin   And not merely my life but the lives of many. The end of the night's work is not over. Neither this year nor the next will see it. If I wished you well, I would pray that you do not stay long enough on our land to see the disaster you have brought upon us.

Pilkings   Well, I did my duty as I saw it. I have no regrets.

Elesin   No. The regrets of life always come later.

Some moments' pause.

You are waiting for dawn, white man. I hear you saying to yourself: only so many hours until dawn and then the danger is over. All I must do is to keep him alive tonight. You don't quite understand it all but you know that tonight is when what ought to be must be brought about. I shall ease your mind even more, ghostly one. It is not an entire night but a moment of the night, and that moment is past. The moon was my messenger and guide. When it reached a certain gateway in the sky, it touched that moment for which my whole life has been spent in blessings. Even I do not know the gateway. I have stood here and scanned the sky for a glimpse of that door but, I cannot see it. Human eyes are useless for a search of this nature. But in the house of osugbo, those who keep watch through the spirit recognised the moment, they sent word to me through the voice of our sacred drums to prepare myself. I heard them and I shed all thoughts of earth. I began to follow the moon to the abode of the gods . . .

servant of the white king, that was when you entered my chosen place of departure on feet of desecration.

Pilkings I'm sorry, but we all see our duty differently.

Elesin I no longer blame you. You stole from me my first-born, sent him to your country so you could turn him into something in your own image. Did you plan it all beforehand? There are moments when it seems part of a larger plan. He who must follow my footsteps is taken from me, sent across the ocean. Then, in my turn, I am stopped from fulfilling my destiny. Did you think it all out before, this plan to push our world from its course and sever the cord that links us to the great origin?

Pilkings You don't really believe that. Anyway, if that was my intention with your son, I appear to have failed.

Elesin You did not fail in the main, ghostly one. We know the roof covers the rafters, the cloth covers blemishes; who would have known that the white skin covered our future, preventing us from seeing the death our enemies had prepared for us. The world is set adrift and its inhabitants are lost. Around them, there is nothing but emptiness.

Pilkings Your son does not take so gloomy a view.

Elesin Are you dreaming now, white man? Were you not present at the reunion of shame? Did you not see when the world reversed itself and the father fell before his son, asking forgiveness?

Pilkings That was in the heat of the moment. I spoke to him and ... if you want to know, he wishes he could cut out his tongue for uttering the words he did.

Elesin No. What he said must never be unsaid. The contempt of my own son rescued something of my shame at your hands. You have stopped me in my duty but I know now that I did give birth to a son. Once I mistrusted him for seeking the companionship of those my spirit knew as enemies of our race. Now I understand. One should seek to obtain the secrets of his enemies. He will avenge my shame, white one.

His spirit will destroy you and yours.

Pilkings That kind of talk is hardly called for. If you don't want my consolation . . .

Elesin No white man, I do not want your consolation.

Pilkings As you wish. Your son, anyway, sends his consolation. He asks your forgiveness. When I asked him not to despise you his reply was: I cannot judge him, and if I cannot judge him, I cannot despise him. He wants to come to you and say goodbye and to receive your blessing.

Elesin Goodbye? Is he returning to your land?

Pilkings Don't you think that's the most sensible thing for him to do? I advised him to leave at once, before dawn, and he agrees that is the right course of action.

Elesin Yes, it is best. And even if I did not think so, I have lost the father's place of honour. My voice is broken.

Pilkings Your son honours you. If he didn't he would not ask your blessing.

Elesin No. Even a thoroughbred is not without pity for the turf he strikes with his hoof. When is he coming?

Pilkings As soon as the town is a little quieter. I advised it.

Elesin Yes, white man, I am sure you advised it. You advise all our lives although on the authority of what gods, I do not know.

Pilkings (*opens his mouth to reply, then appears to change his mind. Turns to go. Hesitates and stops again*) Before I leave you, may I ask just one thing of you?

Elesin I am listening.

Pilkings I wish to ask you to search the quiet of your heart and tell me – do you not find great contradictions in the wisdom of your own race?

Elesin Make yourself clear, white one.

Pilkings I have lived among you long enough to learn a

saying or two. One came to my mind tonight when I stepped into the market and saw what was going on. You were surrounded by those who egged you on with songs and praises. I thought, are these not the same people who say: the elder grimly approaches heaven and you ask him to bear your greetings yonder; do you really think he makes the journey willingly? After that, I did not hesitate.

A pause. **Elesin** *sighs. Before he can speak a sound of running feet is heard.*

Jane (*off*)   Simon! Simon!

Pilkings   What on earth. . . ! (*Runs off.*)

Elesin *turns to his new wife, gazes on her for some moments.*

Elesin   My young bride, did you hear the ghostly one? You sit and sob in your silent heart but say nothing to all this. First I blamed the white man, then I blamed my gods for deserting me. Now I feel I want to blame you for the mystery of the sapping of my will. But blame is a strange peace offering for a man to bring a world he has deeply wronged, and to its innocent dwellers. Oh little mother, I have taken countless women in my life but you were more than a desire of the flesh. I needed you as the abyss across which my body must be drawn, I filled it with earth and dropped my seed in it at the moment of preparedness for my crossing. You were the final gift of the living to their emissary to the land of the ancestors, and perhaps your warmth and youth brought new insights of this world to me and turned my feet leaden on this side of the abyss. For I confess to you, daughter, my weakness came not merely from the abomination of the white man who came violently into my fading presence, there was also a weight of longing on my earth-held limbs. I would have shaken it off, already my foot had begun to lift but then, the white ghost entered and all was defiled.

Approaching voices of **Pilkings** *and his wife.*

Jane   Oh Simon, you will let her in won't you?

Pilkings   I really wish you'd stop interfering.

They come into view. **Jane** *is in a dressing-gown.* **Pilkings** *is holding a note to which he refers from time to time.*

Jane Good gracious, I didn't initiate this. I was sleeping quietly, or trying to anyway, when the servant brought it. It's not my fault if one can't sleep undisturbed even in the Residency.

Pilkings He'd have done the same thing if we were sleeping at home so don't sidetrack the issue. He knows he can get round you or he wouldn't send you the petition in the first place.

Jane Be fair Simon. After all he was thinking of your own interests. He is grateful you know, you seem to forget that. He feels he owes you something.

Pilkings I just wish they'd leave this man alone tonight, that's all.

Jane Trust him Simon. He's pledged his word it will all go peacefully.

Pilkings Yes, and that's the other thing. I don't like being threatened.

Jane Threatened? (*Takes the note.*) I didn't spot any threat.

Pilkings It's there. Veiled, but it's there. The only way to prevent serious rioting tomorrow – what a cheek!

Jane I don't think he's threatening you Simon.

Pilkings He's picked up the idiom all right. Wouldn't surprise me if he's been mixing with commies or anarchists over there. The phrasing sounds too good to be true. Damn! If only the Prince hadn't picked this time for his visit.

Jane Well, even so Simon, what have you got to lose? You don't want a riot on your hands, not with the Prince here.

Pilkings (*going up to* **Elesin**) Let's see what he has to say. Chief Elesin, there is yet another person who wants to see you. As she is not a next-of-kin I don't really feel obliged to

let her in. But your son sent a note with her, so it's up to
you.

Elesin I know who that must be. So she found out your
hiding-place. Well, it was not difficult. My stench of shame is
so strong, it requires no hunter's dog to follow it.

Pilkings If you don't want to see her, just say so and I'll
send her packing.

Elesin Why should I not want to see her? Let her come. I
have no more holes in my rag of shame. All is laid bare.

Pilkings I'll bring her in. (*Goes off.*)

Jane (*hesitates, then goes to* **Elesin**) Please, try and understand.
Everything my husband did was for the best.

Elesin (*he gives her a long strange stare, as if he is trying to
understand who she is*) You are the wife of the District Officer?

Jane Yes. My name is Jane.

Elesin That is my wife sitting down there. You notice how
still and silent she sits? My business is with your husband.

Pilkings *returns with* **Iyaloja**.

Pilkings Here she is. Now first I want your word of honour
that you will try nothing foolish.

Elesin Honour? White one, did you say you wanted my
word of honour?

Pilkings I know you to be an honourable man. Give me
your word of honour you will receive nothing from her.

Elesin But I am sure you have searched her clothing as you
would never dare touch your own mother. And there are
these two lizards of yours who roll their eyes even when I
scratch.

Pilkings And I shall be sitting on that tree trunk watching
even how you blink. Just the same I want your word that you
will not let her pass anything to you.

Elesin You have my honour already. It is locked up in that
desk in which you will put away your report of this night's

events. Even the honour of my people you have taken already; it is tied together with those papers of treachery which make you masters in this land.

Pilkings All right. I am trying to make things easy but if you must bring in politics we'll have to do it the hard way. Madam, I want you to remain along this line and move no nearer to the cell door. Guards! (*They spring to attention.*) If she moves beyond this point, blow your whistle. Come on Jane. (*They go off.*)

Iyaloja How boldly the lizard struts before the pigeon when it was the eagle itself he promised us he would confront.

Elesin I don't ask you to take pity on me Iyaloja. You have a message for me or you would not have come. Even if it is the curses of the world, I shall listen.

Iyaloja You made so bold with the servant of the white king who took your side against death. I must tell your brother chiefs when I return how bravely you waged war against him. Especially with words.

Elesin I more than deserve your scorn.

Iyaloja (*with sudden anger*) I warned you, if you must leave a seed behind, be sure it is not tainted with the curses of the world. Who are you to open a new life when you dared not open the door to a new existence? I say who are you to make so bold? (*The Bride sobs and Iyaloja notices her. Her contempt noticeably increases as she turns back to Elesin.*) Oh you self-vaunted stem of the plantain, how hollow it all proves. The pith is gone in the parent stem, so how will it prove with the new shoot? How will it go with that earth that bears it? Who are you to bring this abomination on us!

Elesin My powers deserted me. My charms, my spells, even my voice lacked strength when I made to summon the powers that would lead me over the last measure of earth into the land of the fleshless. You saw it, Iyaloja. You saw me struggle to retrieve my will from the power of the stranger whose shadow fell across the doorway and left me floundering and blundering in a maze I had never before encountered. My senses were numbed when the touch of cold iron came upon my wrists. I could do nothing to save myself.

Iyaloja   You have betrayed us. We fed you sweetmeats such as we hoped awaited you on the other side. But you said No, I must·eat the world's left-overs. We said you were the hunter who brought the quarry down; to you belonged the vital portions of the game. No, you said, I am the hunter's dog and I shall eat the entrails of the game and the faeces of the hunter. We said you were the hunter returning home in triumph, a slain buffalo pressing down on his neck; you said Wait, I first must turn up this cricket hole with my toes. We said yours was the doorway at which we first spy the tapper when he comes down from the tree, yours was the blessing of the twilight wine, the purl that brings night spirits out of doors to steal their portion before the light of day. We said yours was the body of wine whose burden shakes the tapper like a sudden gust on his perch. You said, No, I am content to lick the dregs from each calabash when the drinkers are done. We said, the dew on earth's surface was for you to wash your feet along the slopes of honour. You said No, I shall step in the vomit of cats and the droppings of mice; I shall fight them for the left-overs of the world.

Elesin   Enough Iyaloja, enough.

Iyaloja   We called you leader and oh, how you led us on. What we have no intention of eating should not be held to the nose.

Elesin   Enough, enough. My shame is heavy enough.

Iyaloja   Wait. I came with a burden.

Elesin   You have more than discharged it.

Iyaloja   I wish I could pity you.

Elesin   I need neither your pity nor the pity of the world. I need understanding. Even I need to understand. You were present at my defeat. You were part of the beginnings. You brought about the renewal of my tie to earth, you helped in the binding of the cord.

Iyaloja   I gave you warning. The river which fills up before our eyes does not sweep us away in its flood.

Elesin   What were warnings beside the moist contact of living earth between my fingers? What were warnings beside the renewal of famished embers lodged eternally in the heart of man. But even that, even if it overwhelmed one with a thousandfold temptations to linger a little while, a man could overcome it. It is when the alien hand pollutes the source of will, when a stranger force of violence shatters the mind's calm resolution, this is when a man is made to commit the awful treachery of relief, commit in his thought the unspeakable blasphemy of seeing the hand of the gods in this alien rupture of his world. I know it was this thought that killed me, sapped my powers and turned me into an infant in the hands of unnamable strangers. I made to utter my spells anew but my tongue merely rattled in my mouth. I fingered hidden charms and the contact was damp; there was no spark left to sever the life-strings that should stretch from every finger-tip. My will was squelched in the spittle of an alien race, and all because I had committed this blasphemy of thought – that there might be the hand of the gods in a stranger's intervention.

Iyaloja   Explain it how you will, I hope it brings you peace of mind. The bush-rat fled his rightful cause, reached the market and set up a lamentation. 'Please save me!' – are these fitting words to hear from an ancestral mask? 'There's a wild beast at my heels' is not becoming language from a hunter.

Elesin   May the world forgive me.

Iyaloja   I came with a burden I said. It approaches the gates which are so well guarded by those jackals whose spittle will from this day be on your food and drink. But first, tell me, you who were once Elesin Oba, tell me, you who know so well the cycle of the plantain: is it the parent shoot which withers to give sap to the younger or, does your wisdom see it running the other way?

Elesin   I don't see your meaning Iyaloja?

Iyaloja Did I ask you for a meaning? I asked a question. Whose trunk withers to give sap to the other? The parent shoot or the younger?

Elesin The parent.

Iyaloja Ah. So you do know that. There are sights in this world which say different Elesin. There are some who choose to reverse the cycle of our being. Oh, you emptied bark that the world once saluted for a pith-laden being, shall I tell you what the gods have claimed of you?

In her agitation she steps beyond the line indicated by **Pilkings** *and the air is rent by piercing whistles. The two guards also leap forward and place safeguarding hands on* **Elesin**. **Iyaloja** *stops, astonished.* **Pilkings** *comes racing in, followed by* **Jane**.

Pilkings What is it? Did they try something?

Guard She stepped beyond the line.

Elesin (*in a broken voice*) Let her alone. She meant no harm.

Iyaloja Oh Elesin, see what you've become. Once you had no need to open your mouth in explanation because evil-smelling goats, itchy of hand and foot, had lost their senses. And it was a brave man indeed who dared lay hands on you because Iyaloja stepped from one side of the earth onto another. Now look at the spectacle of your life. I grieve for you.

Pilkings I think you'd better leave. I doubt you have done him much good by coming here. I shall make sure you are not allowed to see him again. In any case we are moving him to a different place before dawn, so don't bother to come back.

Iyaloja We foresaw that. Hence the burden I trudged here to lay beside your gates.

Pilkings What was that you said?

Iyaloja Didn't our son explain? Ask that one. He knows what it is. At least we hope the man we once knew as Elesin remembers the lesser oaths he need not break.

Pilkings   Do you know what she is talking about?

Elesin   Go to the gates, ghostly one. Whatever you find there, bring it to me.

Iyaloja   Not yet. It drags behind me on the slow, weary feet of women. Slow as it is Elesin, it has long overtaken you. It rides ahead of your laggard will.

Pilkings   What is she saying now? Christ! Must your people forever speak in riddles?

Elesin   It will come white man, it will come. Tell your men at the gates to let it through.

Pilkings (*dubiously*)   I'll have to see what it is.

Iyaloja   You will. (*Passionately.*) But this is one oath he cannot shirk. White one, you have a king here, a visitor from your land. We know of his presence here. Tell me, were he to die would you leave his spirit roaming restlessly on the surface of earth? Would you bury him here among those you consider less than human? In your land have you no ceremonies of the dead?

Pilkings   Yes. But we don't make our chiefs commit suicide to keep him company.

Iyaloja   Child, I have not come to help your understanding. (*Points to* **Elesin**.) This is the man whose weakened understanding holds us in bondage to you. But ask him if you wish. He knows the meaning of a king's passage; he was not born yesterday. He knows the peril to the race when our dead father, who goes as intermediary, waits and waits and knows he is betrayed. He knows when the narrow gate was opened and he knows it will not stay for laggards who drag their feet in dung and vomit, whose lips are reeking of the left-overs of lesser men. He knows he has condemned our King to wander in the void of evil with beings who are enemies of life.

Pilkings   Yes er . . . but look here . . .

Iyaloja   What we ask is little enough. Let him release our King so he can ride on homewards alone. The messenger is on his way on the backs of women. Let him send word through the heart that is folded up within the bolt. It is the least of all his oaths, it is the easiest fulfilled.

The **Aide-de-Camp** *runs in.*

Pilkings Bob?

Aide-de-Camp Sir, there's a group of women chanting up the hill.

Pilkings (*rounding on* **Iyaloja**) If you people want trouble . . .

Jane Simon, I think that's what Olunde referred to in his letter.

Pilkings He knows damned well I can't have a crowd here! Damn it, I explained the delicacy of my position to him. I think it's about time I got him out of town. Bob, send a car and two or three soldiers to bring him in. I think the sooner he takes his leave of his father and gets out the better.

Iyaloja Save your labour white one. If it is the father of your prisoner you want, Olunde, he who until this night we knew as Elesin's son, he comes soon himself to take his leave. He has sent the women ahead, so let them in.

Pilkings *remains undecided.*

Aide-de-Camp What do we do about the invasion? We can still stop them far from here.

Pilkings What do they look like?

Aide-de-Camp They're not many. And they seem quite peaceful.

Pilkings No men?

Aide-de-Camp Mm, two or three at the most.

Jane Honestly, Simon, I'd trust Olunde. I don't think he'll deceive you about their intentions.

Pilkings He'd better not. All right then, let them in Bob. Warn them to control themselves. Then hurry Olunde here. Make sure he brings his baggage because I'm not returning him into town.

Aide-de-Camp   Very good, sir. (*Goes.*)

Pilkings (*to* **Iyaloja**)   I hope you understand that if anything goes wrong it will be on your head. My men have orders to shoot at the first sign of trouble.

Iyaloja   To prevent one death you will actually make other deaths? Ah, great is the wisdom of the white race. But have no fear. Your Prince will sleep peacefully. So at long last will ours. We will disturb you no further, servant of the white King. Just let Elesin fulfil his oath and we will retire home and pay homage to our King.

Jane   I believe her Simon, don't you?

Pilkings   Maybe.

Elesin   Have no fear ghostly one. I have a message to send my King and then you have nothing more to fear.

Iyaloja   Olunde would have done it. The chiefs asked him to speak the words but he said no, not while you lived.

Elesin   Even from the depths to which my spirit has sunk, I find some joy that this little has been left to me.

The **Women** *enter, intoning the dirge 'Ale le le' and swaying from side to side. On their shoulders is borne a longish object roughly like a cylindrical bolt, covered in cloth. They set it down on the spot where* **Iyaloja** *had stood earlier, and form a semi-circle round it. The* **Praise-Singer** *and drummer stand on the inside of the semi-circle but the drum is not used at all. The drummer intones under the* **Praise-Singer**'s *invocations.*

Pilkings (*as they enter*)   What is *that*?

Iyaloja   The burden you have made white one, but we bring it in peace.

Pilkings   I said *what* is it?

Elesin   White man, you must let me out. I have a duty to perform.

Pilkings I most certainly will not.

Elesin There lies the courier of my King. Let me out so I can perform what is demanded of me.

Pilkings You'll do what you need to do from inside there or not at all. I've gone as far as I intend to with this business.

Elesin The worshipper who lights a candle in your church to bear a message to his god bows his head and speaks in a whisper to the flame. Have I not seen it ghostly one? His voice does not ring out to the world. Mine are no words for anyone's ears. They are not words even for the bearers of this load. They are words I must speak secretly, even as my father whispered them in my ears and I in the ears of my first-born. I cannot shout them to the wind and the open night-sky.

Jane Simon . . .

Pilkings Don't interfere. Please!

Iyaloja They have slain the favourite horse of the King and slain his dog. They have borne them from pulse to pulse centre of the land receiving prayers for their King. But the rider has chosen to stay behind. Is it too much to ask that he speak his heart to heart of the waiting courier? (**Pilkings** *turns his back on her.*) So be it, Elesin Oba, you see how even the mere leavings are denied you. (*She gestures to the* **Praise-Singer**.)

Praise-Singer Elesin Oba! I call you by that name only this last time. Remember when I said, if you cannot come, tell my horse. (*Pause.*) What? I cannot hear you? I said, if you cannot come, whisper in the ears of my horse. Is your tongue severed from the roots? Elesin? I can hear no response. I said, if there are boulders you cannot climb, mount my horse's back, this spotless black stallion, he'll bring you over them. (*Pauses.*) Elesin Oba, once you had a tongue that darted like a drummer's stick. I said, if you get lost my dog will track a path to me. My memory fails me but I think you replied: My feet have found the path, Alafin.

The dirge rises and falls.

I said at the last, if evil hands hold you back, just tell my horse there is weight on the hem of your smock. I dare not wait too long.

The dirge rises and falls.

There lies the swiftest ever messenger of a king, so set me free with the errand of your heart. There lie the head and heart of the favourite of the gods, whisper in his ears. Oh my companion, if you had followed when you should, we would not say that the horse preceded its rider. If you had followed when it was time, we would not say the dog has raced beyond and left his master behind. If you had raised your will to cut the thread of life at the summons of the drums, we would not say your mere shadow fell across the gateway and took its owner's place at the banquet. But the hunter, laden with slain buffalo, stayed to root in the cricket's hole with his toes. What now is left? If there is a dearth of bats, the pigeon must serve us for the offering. Speak the words over your shadow which must now serve in your place.

Elesin I cannot approach. Take off the cloth. I shall speak my message from heart to heart of silence.

Iyaloja (*moves forward and removes the covering*) Your courier Elesin, cast your eyes on the favoured companion of the King.

Rolled up in the mat, his head and feet showing at either end, is the body of **Olunde**.

There lies the honour of your household and of our race. Because he could not bear to let honour fly out of doors, he stopped it with his life. The son has proved the father, Elesin, and there is nothing left in your mouth to gnash but infant gums.

Praise-Singer Elesin, we placed the reins of the world in your hands yet you watched it plunge over the edge of the bitter precipice. You sat with folded arms while evil strangers tilted the world from its course and crashed it beyond the edge of emptiness – you muttered, there is little that one man can do, you left us floundering in a blind future. Your heir has taken the burden on himself. What the end will be, we

are not gods to tell. But this young shoot has poured its sap
into the parent stalk, and we know this is not the way of life.
Our world is tumbling in the void of strangers, Elesin.

Elesin *has stood rock-still, his knuckles taut on the bars, his eyes glued
to the body of his son. The stillness seizes and paralyses everyone,
including* **Pilkings** *who has turned to look. Suddenly* **Elesin** *flings one
arm round his neck, once, and with the loop of the chain, strangles
himself in a swift, decisive pull. The guards rush forward to stop him
but they are only in time to let his body down.* **Pilkings** *has leapt to
the door at the same time and struggles with the lock. He rushes within,
fumbles with the handcuffs and unlocks them, raises the body to a sitting
position while he tries to give resuscitation. The* **Women** *continue their
dirge, unmoved by the sudden event.*

Iyaloja Why do you strain yourself? Why do you labour at
tasks for which no one, not even the man lying there, would
give you thanks? He is gone at last into the passage but oh,
how late it all is. His son will feast on the meat and throw
him bones. The passage is clogged with droppings from the
King's stallion; he will arrive all stained in dung.

Pilkings (*in a tired voice*) Was this what you wanted?

Iyaloja No child, it is what you brought to be, you who
play with strangers' lives, who even usurp the vestments of our
dead, yet believe that the stain of death will not cling to you.
The gods demanded only the old expired plantain but you cut
down the sap-laden shoot to feed your pride. There is your
board, filled to overflowing. Feast on it. (*She screams at him
suddenly, seeing that* **Pilkings** *is about to close* **Elesin**'s *staring eyes.*)
Let him alone! However sunk he was in debt he is no
pauper's carrion abandoned on the road. Since when have
strangers donned clothes of indigo before the bereaved cries
out his loss?

She turns to the **Bride** *who has remained motionless throughout.*

Child.

The girl takes up a little earth, walks calmly into the cell and closes
Elesin's *eyes. She then pours some earth over each eyelid and comes out
again.*

Iyaloja   Now forget the dead, forget even the living. Turn your mind only to the unborn.

She goes off, accompanied by the **Bride***. The dirge rises in volume and the* **Women** *continue their sway. Lights fade to a blackout.*

Glossary

alari a rich, woven cloth, brightly coloured

egungun ancestral masquerade

etutu placatory rites or medicine

gbedu a deep-timbred royal drum

opele string of beads used in Ifa divination

osugbo secret 'executive' cult of the Yoruba; its meeting place

robo a delicacy made from crushed melon seeds, fried in tiny balls

sanyan a richly valued woven cloth

sigidi a squat, carved figure, endowed with the powers of an incubus

CPSIA information can be obtained at www.ICGtesting.com
Printed in the USA
LVOW102227240912

300169LV00006B/12/P